SOLDIERING

AGAINST

SUBVERSION

SOLDIERING

AGAINST

SUBVERSION

THE IRISH DEFENCE FORCES AND INTERNAL
SECURITY DURING THE TROUBLES 1969–1998

DAN HARVEY

MERRION
PRESS

Lieutenant Colonel Dan Harvey, now retired, served on operations at home and abroad for forty years, including tours of duty in the Middle East, Africa, the Balkans and South Caucasus, with the UN, EU, NATO PfP and OSCE. He is the author of *Into Action: Irish Peacekeepers Under Fire, 1960–2014* (2017), *A Bloody Day: The Irish at Waterloo* and *A Bloody Night: The Irish at Rorke's Drift* (both reissued 2017), and *Soldiers of the Short Grass: A History of the Curragh Camp* (2016).

Dedicated to Commandant Peter Young,
Military Archives, RIP. A friend and mentor.

First published in 2018 by
Merrion Press
An imprint of Irish Academic Press
10 George's Street
Newbridge
Co. Kildare
Ireland
www.merrionpress.ie

© Dan Harvey, 2018

9781785371851 (Paper)
9781785371868 (Kindle)
9781785371875 (Epub)
9781785371882 (PDF)

British Library Cataloguing in Publication Data
An entry can be found on request

Library of Congress Cataloging in Publication Data
An entry can be found on request

Interior design by www.jminfotechindia.com
Typeset in Minion Pro 11.5/14 pt

Cover design by www.phoenix-graphicdesign.com

Cover front: Irish Defence Forces Troops from the 4th Infantry Battalion, Collins
Barracks, Cork, on rotation to the border area deploy from a Panard Armoured
Personnel Carrier (APC) whilst on Border Duty during Operation Mallard.
Photograph courtesy of Captain Tony Doonan (retired).

Cover back: An Irish Army soldier, courtesy of Military Archives, Dublin.

Contents

Abbreviations

AC	(IRA) Army Council
APC	Armoured Personnel Carrier
ARW	Army Ranger Wing
ASU	Active Service Units
ATCP	Aid to the Civil Power
AVRE	Armoured Vehicle Royal Engineers
CIÉ	Córas Iompair Éireann (the Irish State-owned bus company)
CIS	Communications and Information Service Corps
COD	Current Operational Directive
CP	Checkpoint
ECIF	Eastern Command Infantry Force
EOD	Explosive Ordnance Disposal
ESB	Electricity Supply Board
FCÁ	Fórsa Cosanta Áitiúil (the Army Reserve)
FEBA	Forward Edge of the Battle Area
FFR	Fitted for Radio
G2	Directorate of Military Intelligence
GAC	(IRA) General Army Convention
GHQ	General Headquarters
HME	Homemade Explosive
HMS	Her Majesty's Ship
HMSU	Headquarters Mobile Support Unit
HQ	Headquarters
IED	Improvised Explosive Device
INLA	Irish National Liberation Army

IRA	Irish Republican Army
IRB	Irish Republican Brotherhood
IRSP	Irish Republican Socialist Party
LÉ	Long Éireannach (the designation given to ships in the Irish Naval Service)
MV	Merchant Vessel
NATO	North Atlantic Treaty Organisation
NCO	Non-Commissioned Officer
OP	Observation Post
PIRA	Provisional IRA
RTÉ	Radio Teilifís Éireann
RUC	Royal Ulster Constabulary
SAS	Special Air Service
SCC	Special Criminal Court
SDLP	Social Democratic and Labour Party
UDA	Ulster Defence Association
UDR	Ulster Defence Regiment
UNIFIL	United Nations Interim Force in Lebanon
UVF	Ulster Volunteer Force
XMG	Irish and British military code for Crossmaglen

Foreword

*S*oldiering against Subversion is the latest historical volume from the pen of Lt. Col. Dan Harvey. It makes an important contribution to our knowledge of a deeply contested period in Irish history. Written from the perspective of a serving Irish army officer, whose distinguished career spanned the 'Troubles' in Northern Ireland and beyond, the book's narrative strength is rooted in the combination of skills of an author who is both an historian and an expert in the study of international peace-keeping (and also a distinguished practitioner), guerrilla warfare and counter-insurgency.

Having reviewed the bloody events on the island of Ireland from the late 1960s, he concludes judiciously: 'However, the Aid to the Civil Power policy employed by the Government was very wise in the long run and the merits of a police-led counter-subversive campaign were vindicated. Its practice, applied purposefully on the ground by the Defence Forces, proved a highly relevant and appropriate approach to a very difficult security and political situation. This book lucidly chronicles – from the perspective of an officer with boots on the ground – how that policy, so succinctly expressed above, was formed and implemented during 'the Troubles' and how well it served to preserve democracy on this island. There was nothing inevitable about the choice of such a policy. It emerged, in inchoate form, in the late 1960s when the more hot-headed in government advocated paths mercifully not taken. The Irish army performed its professional task in the most difficult and testing of circumstances. This book may help the many realise the debt owed to the few who soldiered against subversion since the foundation of the state and, in particular, during thirty years of a futile, bloody and absolutely needless war.

It is sobering to reflect on the fact that Irish students in third level in the latter years of the second decade of the twentieth century were either infants or not yet born when the Belfast Agreement was signed on 10 April 1998. That generation, reading this volume, have no personal experience of living on an island when, in the 1970s, the press and television headlined the daily round of car-bomb blasts, sectarian attacks, tit-for-tat killings and the endless funeral processions as innocent victims of that violence were buried. Those tragedies – resulting from being in the wrong place at the wrong time – changed family histories forever. There were the bombastic paramilitary funerals where 'volunteers' – loyalist or republican – were buried with 'full military honours'. Their families, too, were devastated and their lives changed forever. There were the unforgettable photos or television footage of a body covered with a sheet on a lonely country road – the victim of a paramilitary 'execution', or of somebody shot by the British army. Who can forget the British reaction to Bloody Sunday in Derry, on 30 January 1972, when members of the parachute regiment killed 14 protesters. There was righteousness on all sides brought out so well in the paintings of the artist Rita Duffy.

Reviewing that terrible period, I have two personal thoughts. Firstly, there was what I believe to have been the futility of it all. It need never have happened. There was no need for 'war'. Armed violence was not inevitable – with the Armalite in one hand and the ballot box in the other. There was a peaceful democratic solution as laid out in the late 1960s – and throughout his public life – by the Nobel Peace-Prize laureate, John Hume. That prize is awarded for a person who has made 'the greatest benefit to mankind'. The author of this volume is in no doubt about the fact that, from his perspective the 'war' was unnecessary.

Secondly, I am of the view that – given the nature of the violence in Northern Ireland – there was nothing inevitable or deterministic about the signing of the Belfast Peace Agreement in 1998. That may have looked a faraway prospect in the late 1960s and 1970s as the Irish army provided support for a 'police-led counter-subversive campaign' in the fields and by-roads along a 300-mile border with Northern Ireland and elsewhere. That formed part of the unglamorous but necessary role of the Irish army in that twilight world of soldiering against subversion to protect the institutions and personnel of the state from armed attack. This book reveals part of the hidden history leading to the Good Friday Agreement.

I can still vividly recall the shock of learning about the murder of Garda Richard Fallon on 3 April 1970 following a bank robbery in Dublin. In all, a dozen gardaí died at the hands of subversives between

1970 and 1985. The chief prison officer in Portlaoise, Brian Stack, was shot by the IRA on 25 March 1983 and lived for 18 months following the attack. Peace did not come without a cost to servants of the Irish state.

There is an honourable tradition in this country of retiring from public or professional life while keeping one's counsel in retirement. This was determined by a culture of secrecy which enveloped public life during the early decades of the new Irish state. In that post-revolutionary world, the secrets of the civil war and of fighting subversion from the 1920s to the 1950s were rarely written about by either politicians, civil servants, soldiers or gardaí. But that tradition has been long since broken. Col. Dan Bryan, head of Irish Military Intelligence (G2), deposited his papers in the UCD Archives. Col. Maurice Walsh has published *G2 – In Defence of Ireland: Irish military intelligence 1918–1948* and Capt. James Kelly published a number of books on his experiences. Hopefully, after the publication of this volume, other retired officers will either publish monographs or leave their personal papers and reminiscences to Irish Military Archives.

Lt. Col. Harvey would be first to admit that this volume is not the last word on the wide sweep of Irish history reviewed. Besides bringing a great deal of new evidence to light from this hitherto unique soldiering perspective, this volume indirectly calls attention to the salient fact that so much of the Irish War of Independence, the Civil War, World War Two and the earlier IRA border campaigns has been lost. While there is still time, the same mistake ought not to be made about 1968 onwards. There ought to be a concerted effort to interview the gardaí and soldiers involved in policing and soldiering against subversion. This would also involve the preservation of garda logs and military patrol records, the archives of border garda stations and the archiving of captured subversive literature. There is the need to undertake an oral history or a Bureau of Military History-style witness statement record. More specifically, the relevant records in digital format of different government departments need to be centralised on a data base. Those sources ought to be coordinated and held in a central repository – the Military Archive.

This book will engage the reader from the first sentence of the prologue which recounts the events surround the kidnapping of the industrialist, Tiede Herrema, in October 1975, followed by the interception of the gun-running ship, *Claudia*, in 1973 and finally the Dublin and Monaghan bombings in 1974. It would be hard to choose three more significant events with which to focus the mind of any reader. For the generations who lived through those decades, the events are a stark reminder of what quickly became the new 'normal'. For a younger generation, this volume will provide you with an insight of what it was like to soldier against subversion for decades. A chronology and list of abbreviations have been supplied.

In reading the text, I am reminded of the terrible cost of 'the Troubles' to those living on this island and in England. Over 3,000 needlessly wasted lives thanks to the dictates of the respective warlords! The long-term cost of that carnage will no doubt be evident in what will hopefully be a future Truth and Reconciliation process. But there is also, notwithstanding the final peace agreement in 1998, of nearly thirty wasted years. Ireland and Britain joined the European Economic Community (EEC) in 1973. So much energy, resources and creativity in both countries went into responding to the threat of subversion in Northern Ireland. So much money, which might have been deflected to education and job creation, dissipated. The lives of over 3,000 people – who would have contributed to the commonweal – lost. Reading Lt. Col. Harvey's book will – for those with an open mind – de-romanticises the decades of subversion now glamorised by republican revisionists.

Dr Dermot Keogh is
Emeritus Professor of History,
University College Cork

Preface

From an Irish Defence Forces perspective, it was manpower, equipment, procedures and training that made Internal Security Operations possible during the Troubles. Skills, expertise and experience made them successful. Organisationally, it was all about capacity and capabilities; operationally, it was all about command and control; individually, it was all about commitment and courage. Soldiering against subversion required dedicated people prepared to withstand difficulty and hardship, poor pay and conditions, and yet be prepared to risk their lives in the process. The 'What' of government security policy was the preserve of the politicians, the 'How' of its implementation the problem of the security forces.

The North of Ireland had begun to fall apart, and from a starting point of chronic underinvestment and lack of preparedness the Irish security forces, despite the pressure of events, had to prevent the Republic going the same way. Mostly, this security forces' involvement was undramatic and their presence, posture and persistence went largely unnoticed and certainly unheralded, yet it was absolutely crucial. To disrupt the danger and threat from the IRA, to counter the fear and intimidation and to reduce the harm and hazard from the 'balaclava bandits' required competent people with a serious purposefulness. In the case of the Defence Forces, this critical commitment was neither adequately remunerated nor acknowledged. The Troubles were grim, forbidding and severe times, best forgotten and put out of mind; only omitted along with them has been the unwavering loyalty, the steadfast reliability and the staunch patriotism of the Defence Forces. To read this book is to understand the need for an army.

I began working on *Soldiering Against Subversion* two years before the fiftieth anniversary of the outbreak of the Troubles, generally regarded to be 5 October 1968, and it is a book about – in a word – recognition. The recognition, as genuine, valid and worthy, of the contribution of the Defence Forces to the Irish State during the period.

For the first time, it describes this involvement from the point of view of the Defence Forces, a slant largely absent in accounts to date. It places their extensive effort in context and presents a reasoned analysis of the Aid to the Civil Power application against the alarmingly chaotic and disorderly rhythm of the continually challenging circumstances presented from 1969 to 1998. This book is necessary because it is too easy to forget those difficult days and it is dangerous to do so, because the complexity of the fractured identity that was at the essence of the Troubles in a sense still remains to be resolved today. The Defence Forces played a crucial part in its containment.

The Defence Forces defended Ireland, protected its people and secured the safe functioning of the State's institutions against those who wished to undermine it. The Irish Republic was a sovereign independent state, with an elected parliament and courts, police and army to enforce the rule of law. The Provisional IRA (PIRA) sent out foot soldiers to wreak havoc, bomb indiscriminately, and kill without compunction. They had to be stopped and the Defence Forces contributed hugely in this regard. Ex-Taoiseach Liam Cosgrave put it succinctly, and for all his retired life was consistent in his conviction, that 'except for the Garda Síochána and the Defence Forces there would have been no state'. To further explain the role of the Irish Defence Forces during the turbulent period of the Troubles, I sought the advice and assistance of those who were there, real experiences from Irish soldiers putting themselves in the line of fire in defence of the State.

What or who caused the Troubles will be an enduring historical argument to be debated for decades to come. However, the hard fact was they had dangerous and tragic consequences and the Irish Defence Forces had to deal with them in a rapidly deteriorating security situation. In order to curtail the impact of the violence, both perpetrated and threatened, they had to initially bridge equipment, establishment, experiential and expertise gaps and thereafter implement a highly nuanced Internal Security Policy. The role of the Defence Forces in maintaining the stability of the state was critical; the importance of having good people crucial. It is their voice that gives this account perspective and professionalism, and, in all its honesty, truth and detail, a large degree of authenticity.

To ensure this bone fide reliability accurately imparts a true sense of the situation, it was imperative that interviewees could do so without the constraint of knowing they would be directly quoted, so that they could more freely give an honest, correct, responsible, considered and not sensationalised sense of their experiences. I believe this to have been achieved. Many were happy to be attributed but, finally, whether recollections have been credited or not, the judgement to do so was mine. It is my sincere hope that additional historical research into these fraught and frightening times is conducted in future years so that the valuable contribution of the Defence Forces is recognised as it richly deserves.

Prologue

It was a mild mid-October morning in 1975 when 7-year-old Fionnuala Buckley stepped out of her front door at St Evin's Park, Monasterevin, Co. Kildare, in the carefree, lackadaisical manner of children happy in their familiar surroundings. Sent by her mother to the nearby local shop for milk for the family breakfast, she had only taken a few steps from the doorway when she suddenly stopped short. Standing in front of her in camouflage gear and a bulky flak jacket was an Irish soldier, cradling a large black rifle in his hands and with a radio set on his back, the 3-foot long antenna pointing towards an otherwise normal sky. It was a lot to take in for the little girl, especially when she noticed he was not alone. There were other soldiers around, having taken up covering positions overnight behind garden walls, at the corners of houses and in the recesses of nearby doorways. Fionnuala's familiar surroundings were suddenly frighteningly unfamiliar; there was uncertainty in her normally certain world and her safe and sheltered surroundings no longer seemed so secure.

Unsure what this sudden appearance of the soldiers meant, Fionnuala sensed something serious was happening. The normally sedate atmosphere of the Park was now one of stark alarm and she turned around, heading back indoors to tell her mother, Breda, what she had seen. Preoccupied with getting breakfast ready and not understanding what her daughter was getting at, the unaware Breda told her to 'get back out and get the milk'. However, anxious and concerned, Fionnuala persisted with her story until, convinced that something was wrong, Breda herself ventured outdoors, taking in the strange scene for herself. Outside a cordon of serious-looking soldiers were focusing their attentions on a nearby house, the atmosphere apprehensive.

Venturing out, Breda joined her neighbours, who were congregating together on a corner at a safe distance from the incident unfolding before them. Overnight, the siege of 1410, Saint Evin's Park had begun. The Gardaí (police) and armed soldiers had surrounded the house, blocking access to the area, after provisional IRA man Eddie Gallagher and his accomplice, Marion Coyle, barricaded themselves into the upper storey of the semi-detached Park house, together with their kidnap victim, Limerick-based Dutch industrialist, Dr Tiede Herrema. A nationwide search operation had eventually led to this rural town in Co. Kildare. The siege had only just begun, but in the nearby Irish Defence Forces Curragh Camp soldiers were planning, making preparations and practising for a possible house assault. The Troubles, the Northern Ireland conflict, had suddenly, shockingly, arrived to a shaken Monasterevin.

***

Two and a half years earlier, in darkness and with a heavy Atlantic swell and rough seas prevailing off Helvic Harbour, south-west of Dungarvan, Co. Waterford, the mission for the Irish Naval Service was to locate, shadow and then intercept what intelligence services suspected was a ship approaching Ireland carrying a cargo of arms for the Provisional IRA. 'Operation Dandelion' was set in motion and three Irish Naval Ships, the LÉ *Deirdre*, LÉ *Fòla* and LÉ *Gráinne*, positioned themselves to spring a trap inside Irish territorial waters. But first it was a waiting game, surprise would be the key to success. The southern coast from Cork Harbour to Carnsore Point was already well covered, and for now it was all about remaining in position, watching the radar screens and preparing to intervene as circumstances dictated.

For a day and a half nothing happened, then a shadowing aircraft radioed a probable sighting, which LÉ *Fòla* confirmed four hours later on the 12-mile limit off the Saltee Islands. The net began to close. All three ships 'blacked out', hiding themselves from the approaching vessel, and at maximum radar range kept the approaching MV *Claudia* under surveillance throughout the night. *Claudia* made no move into territorial waters for the whole of the following day. Then after sunset, LÉ *Gráinne*'s radar picked up a small contact leaving Helvic Harbour and merging with the MV *Claudia*. Twenty-five minutes later it was time to spring the trap. 'Action Stations' were sounded on all three Irish Naval ships and LÉ *Fòla* and LÉ *Gráinne* were ordered to close in on the targets. Within the hour the Irish naval pursuers dramatically revealed their presence by suddenly switching on their navigation lights, and the trap was successfully sprung.

The 290-tonne Cypriot-registered MV *Claudia* was boarded and no resistance was offered. However, the smaller boat made a run for it and zig-zagged away from the scene to make boarding more difficult. LÉ *Fòla*, whose signal to stop was ignored, fired a warning shot over the vessel with LÉ *Gráinne* adding three more rounds, before putting a Gemini dinghy and boarding party into the water to pursue. The officer in charge of the boarding party fired several shots from his pistol before the smaller launch was taken in charge and its three occupants detained. Before midnight on 28 March 1973, it was all over and 5-tonnes of assorted arms and ammunition were seized. The MV *Claudia* was escorted to Haulbowline where it was unloaded; its deadly cargo transferred to Collins Barracks, Cork and placed under guard. On 29 March, the Minister for Defence, Mr Paddy Donegan TD, and the Chief-of-Staff, Major General TL O'Carroll, were flown to Haulbowline by Air Corps helicopter and congratulated the assembled ships' crews. This vital interception operation denied the Provisional IRA weapons, and lives were saved as a result.

✶✶✶

On Friday, 17 May 1974, close to 5.30 pm, three car bombs detonated without warning within ninety seconds of each other in Parnell, Talbot and South Leinster Streets, Dublin. As each device detonated, within milliseconds the explosive material was converted into massive volumes of gas and heat causing a pressure effect that instantaneously released energy in a shockwave, resulting in indiscriminate damage, burns and injury to anyone or anything in the surrounding area. With a blinding flash and a deafening roar, the metallic frames of the cars disintegrated, sending flying shards of glass and metal shrapnel into the air that sliced through bodies, tore through flesh and ripped through bone. Rubble mixed with wreckage, debris, bodies, blood and separated limbs lay everywhere, and amidst the dead, the dying and the maimed there was utter shock, disbelief, screams and terror.

Ninety minutes later a fourth car bomb exploded in Monaghan town. Thirty-three innocent people were killed, one an unborn infant, and 258 were maimed in what was the single biggest loss of life in any one day of the Troubles. This was not Beirut or Belfast; instead the

Dublin–Monaghan bombings remain the longest unsolved murder case in Irish history.

✷✷✷

It was a beautiful sunny summer's day as the joint army/Gardaí patrol responded to reports of suspicious boxes on unapproved roads off the main Cavan to Clones road on 8 June 1972. Sitting on the border road was a sturdy wooden crate, 10-metres in front of which was a rudimentary makeshift wooden sign with a primitively hand-painted four letter word: 'Bomb'. It was all rather simple and basic in appearance. There was no Defence Forces Explosive Ordnance Disposal (EOD) team stationed in the area, and having sealed off the area, Garda Inspector Samuel (Sam) Donegan and Second Lieutenant John Gallagher approached the box. A cord was attached to the crate, long enough to be pulled at from a distance and set off the device. Inspector Donegan pulled on the cord, toppling the crate into the ditch next to the road. Approaching gingerly, on inspection the crate was found to be empty; it was a ruse, a deception, a hoax bomb. Proceeding on to Legakelly Lane, Drumboghanagh, approximately 300-metres away, Inspector Donegan and Second Lieutenant Gallagher approached the second crate. Standing side by side, Inspector Donegan bent forward to examine it more closely when suddenly the crate exploded. Second Lieutenant Gallagher suffered severe leg injuries, but Inspector Donegan took the full force of the bomb. Rushed to Cavan Surgical Hospital, Inspector Samuel Donegan died five minutes before midnight without regaining consciousness.

✷✷✷

The border and bombings, the arms seizures, searches and sieges and more, made up the lengthy, very full chronological catalogue of incidents which occurred throughout the Republic of Ireland during the three decades of the Troubles. When listed by themselves, they are a collective record far more extensive than first imagined; far more comprehensive than first considered; far more involved in their detail than first thought, and the contribution of the Defence Forces was far greater than first appreciated or understood.

Once over, the years of the Troubles were considered a period probably best forgotten. Many features, facts and events were put out of mind, with the priority being to move forward and look to the future. An unconscious consequence of this, however, was that the Defence Forces' efforts and input in maintaining the stability of the Irish State, which many who have served feel has been minimised, overlooked and disregarded. This necessary defence was an enormously demanding and elongated effort, witnessing the difficulties and dangers of exposure to a sometimes highly charged atmosphere. More frequently, the period was an extended but very necessary operation filled with the grim drudgery of laborious and unspectacular security duties, poor pay and conditions and extended periods away from family. Notwithstanding, it was a role which gave the Defence Forces a very real purpose and their contribution is one sacrifice, of stoic calm and uncomplaining loyalty to the State, and a proud unswerving service to the nation. This is that already forgotten story.

PART 1

BEGINNINGS

CHAPTER 1

Troubled Times

The calling out of taunts, catcalls and jeers gave way to the throwing of stones, bricks and bottles, but it was the petrol bomb smashing full-square onto a Shortland armoured Royal Ulster Constabulary (RUC) vehicle, setting it alight, which gave rise to the loudest roars and cheers. The RUC men quickly evacuated the vehicle, its tyres, bonnet and roof ablaze as after a day of mounting tension Derry's Bogside area erupted into a running battle between Catholic nationalist youths and the predominantly protestant police force. The staging of the Apprentice Boys' parade had been contentious; there had been an expectation of trouble and the tension had been building for some time. As the Northern crisis worsened, Taoiseach Jack Lynch sent his Minister for External Affairs, Dr Patrick Hillery, to London to meet Michael Stewart, Secretary of State for Foreign and Commonwealth Affairs. Hillery expressed the Irish Government's grave concerns about the prospect of holding an excessively large Apprentice Boys' parade on 12 August 1969, deliberately routed through Catholic areas, and urged that it be banned, or at least confined to Protestant areas, that no partisan B-Specials (the RUC Auxiliary police force) should be allowed to be deployed and that British Government observers should be present to exercise a restraining influence on events. In reply, he was told that it was a matter for the Stormont and London Governments not Dublin, that it was better to control than ban the parade and that the parade was to follow the less provocative of the two routes.

What followed bore out the Dublin Government's misgivings and the London Government's misjudgement. Westminster's misguided policy on non-interference in Stormont's five decades of misrule was about to unmercifully misfire.

A strong RUC force had been drafted into Derry and the Catholic Bogsiders were fearful that its deployment would not be impartial; that instead it would be extreme and uncompromising towards them. The initial disturbances flared in Waterloo Square during the late afternoon, towards the end of the parade when sections of the Catholic and Protestant crowds faced each other. The RUC and its part-time reserve – the feared and hated steel-helmeted, shield-carrying, baton-wielding B-Specials – forced the stone-throwing Catholic youths back towards the Bogside, a nationalist area in Derry. After two hours of stone throwing between the two sides, charge and counter charge, advance and retreat up and down William Street, approximately a quarter of a mile into the Bogside, the RUC made its move.

The feared eruption of rioting and street violence escalated quickly, progressing into an unprecedented sustained exchange that developed with heightened intensity, the residents inflamed by the naked aggression of the RUC, the B-Specials and the Protestant mob following behind them. The brutality of the B-Specials was nothing new for the Bogsiders; eight months previously, in January 1969, they had launched a limited but nonetheless fierce foray and the residents had not forgotten the experience. This time they were ready, prepared and expectant. Moreover, they were organised and resolute. A reaction was planned and a defence arranged, their nervous suspension turned to a pragmatic tenacity. With the clashes continuing, when the physical weight of the mob swarmed into the Bogside proper they were met with pre-prepared rudimentary street barricades. Now the atmosphere changed as roused by the unrestrained RUC incursion, the besieged Bogsiders responded. Young and old, hundreds came to defend the Catholics against the RUC, more especially the untamed, predatory brutish B-Specials. The disturbances already mounting, the situation was, further inflamed when the RUC opened fire with baton rounds (rubber bullets) in response to the Bogside Defence Association's plans being put into effect, and they pressed boldly forward in their wake. It was close-quarter action with man-to-man exchanges.

The stakes were high and the assault sustained; any momentary lapse in the Bogsiders' defence could be quickly seized upon. The exchanges became heightened and their ferocity resembled a modern day medieval pitched battle, with sheer brute force against the defenders' stubborn will. Blood was spilled, bones broken and heads split; there were injuries on both sides and an unyielding defence fought back against incessant attack. The manning of the barricades remained steadfast and the defence endured; the Bogside remained intact. The Bogsiders were determined that the RUC were not getting in, and the defence was greatly aided by the advantageous height afforded by the Rossville flats, from the roof of which defenders rained down stockpiled stones, bottles and petrol bombs onto the RUC. The RUC had a response of their own, firing large quantities of tear gas (CS gas) canisters into the fray. The use of CS gas distinguished the RUC as the first police force in Britain to use 'war gas' against its own population. The result was a large lingering cloud of tear gas that covered the Bogside, causing respiratory problems for children and the elderly. Notwithstanding, the RUC were kept at bay. The 'Battle of the Bogside' lasted from 12 to 14 August, and at the same time the disaffected Catholic community across Northern Ireland took to the streets to ease the pressure in Derry. There was serious rioting in Belfast particularly, but also elsewhere.

Stormont had ignored decades of demands by the Catholic Nationalists for equality and inclusion. For years, the requests for reform from the 35 per cent minority population solicited no reaction. Disenfranchised, discriminated against, and dispirited that their grievances were continually unrecognised, it was not until the 1960s, when an era for change worldwide saw the Catholic nationalists dispel their demoralised position and create a non-violent Civil Rights movement. This aroused unionist fury and there was a backlash of violent counter-demonstrations with partisan participation, particularly by the RUC and more especially by the B-Specials. The hint of change alone gave vent to a pent-up deeply felt exasperation underpinned by fear and frustration that the Catholic Nationalist minority's demands for civil rights would cause unstoppable momentum towards reform, in turn leading to a United Ireland.

The Six Counties came into being by partition, an administrative division of the country of Ireland and part of the Treaty negotiations after the Irish War of Independence. The Government of Ireland Act 1920 first fashioned the six north-eastern counties into a Northern Ireland mini-state, and gave the Unionist population an overwhelming and unyielding hold on power, with a Unionist government and legislative shorn up by its own armed police force, the Royal Ulster

Constabulary and the part-time B-Specials, who utilised the wide-ranging powers of search and arrest and detention without trial contained within the provisions of the Special Powers Act 1921. The commonly found sectarianism of the Unionist regime had been legitimised. Even the outcomes of local elections favoured the Unionist candidates, because the electoral constituent boundaries were shaped to ensure this happened. Catholics remained powerless and politically excluded for decades, despite being a sizeable minority and even, as in Derry, where Catholics held a majority.

The 1960s was a time for change the world over, and it was to be a time for change in Northern Ireland also, only the Unionists remained steadfastly unmoved. Foremost amongst them was the Reverend Ian Paisley, who vociferously opposed what he referred to as any 'sell out to the powers of Popery and Republicanism', referring suspiciously to the exploratory reform of conditions for Catholics by the Prime Minister of Northern Ireland, Captain Terence O'Neill. Provocative, trouble-seeking and confrontational, with the prevention of change uppermost, this active intransigence was evident during the 1964 British General Election. Northern Ireland had a dozen seats at Westminster, all Unionist held. However, West Belfast, with its large Catholic population, potentially held the possibility of a seat for Nationalists. When an Irish tricolour was placed on show in the window of the election office of the republican candidate, the belligerent Paisley threatened to lead a march to remove the flag. The RUC chose instead to remove the flag themselves, and in turn later to seize the flag's replacement; the reaction to which was two days of rioting on Divis Street. Two years later, 1966, was the fiftieth anniversary of the 1916 Easter Rising and this helped colour the mood again when British Prime Minister Harold Wilson called a General Election for just prior to Easter. On this occasion, Gerry Fitt, founder and the first leader of the Social Democratic and Labour Party (SDLP), won the West Belfast seat and there was a Nationalist presence in Westminster. Nationalist grievances began to be heard, despite a heretofore House of Commons convention which 'prevented' questions about Northern Ireland being raised at Westminster – because when it came to Northern Ireland, you never asked a question unless you wanted to know the answer and the British parliamentarians did not want to hear the answers; the responses could only have represented the retarded social, economic and political reality of the dysfunctionality of the dynamic in Northern Ireland at play, intended to oppress the Catholic Nationalist minority.

A year later, Bernadette Devlin won a by-election for Mid Ulster on a Unity platform; now there were two Nationalist voices in Westminster. The nationalist Catholics were asking the same old questions; this time however they were determined to receive new and different answers. The nationalist Catholic cry for civil rights was eclipsing unionist intransigence. Times were changing and they echoed the modern drumbeat of the 1960s. The US had an Irish-American president, the civil rights movement in America was in full flow and it was an era of liberalisation. But the Unionist response was to march to the beat of the 1690 Battle of the Boyne, a seventeenth-century victory of Protestant William of Orange over the Catholic King James. Instead of participating in and otherwise contributing towards managing the change, the Unionists dug in. The extreme Unionist answer to Catholic civil rights demonstrations was counter demonstration. The enormity of the challenge remained and brought the communities into contention instead of compromise.

A newly emerging political activism articulated the voice of the more confidently assertive Catholic collective and self-consciousness. These young, modern-minded and, for the first time, university-educated, world-aware, and media-savvy cadre of Catholic representatives and spokespersons began to cogently argue the Catholic Nationalist case, correctly and rightly framed in terms of being a civil rights issue. Worryingly for the extreme elements of Unionism, this agitation articulated a self-evident institutionalised victimhood of the Catholic minority; the only correct response to which was reform, but instead the Unionist extremists were unwilling to compromise, fearful of a loss of influence over sole control of Northern Ireland affairs. The pulse of Northern Ireland's politics had begun to change; Catholic nationalists were aware of it and the Unionist hard-liners, resentful, moved to block it.

The Northern Ireland mini-state endured, specifically designed through partition, and partisan Unionist interests, control and power thwarted reform, representation and the right to democratic process. This led directly to injustice, intimidation, discrimination and deprivation of the Catholic Nationalist minority, who continually suffered discriminatory treatment when it came to housing, employment and electoral politics. The 'hands off' approach of the British government in London was a conscious stratagem to ensure that Northern Ireland stayed off the Westminster agenda; a blind eye was turned to a territory they held claim over, yet where similar standards of governance to the UK they knew did not apply. In Northern Ireland, to be a Catholic Nationalist was to be made wholly disadvantaged. An entrenched inter-communal distrust, bitterness and hatred arose from many years of disdainful unimaginable bigotry and neglect.

There were no signs that the Unionists had the inclination or interest to ameliorate the atmosphere – even belatedly. Different choices could have avoided the decline that was to come and lives could have been saved from the decades of bloody, protracted political violence that followed. In Northern Ireland, the weight of the past – of unsettled history, unreconciled identity and untolerated tradition – endured and ancient enmities, deep-seated mistrust and pernicious prejudice persisted. Necessary reform of even-handedness in local government affairs was not forthcoming or arrived too late. Implacable and ideologically opposed elements to end the gerrymandering sought instead to perpetrate the disenfranchisement of Catholics and the discrimination continued. Worse, orchestrated violent counter-demonstrations turned the already deep dividing line between Catholic Nationalists and Protestant Unionists into a pandemonium that could easily have unbalanced the stability of the entire island.

CHAPTER 2

Border-Bound Beginnings

*I*t is with deep sadness that you and I, Irishmen of goodwill, have
learned of the tragic events which have been taking place in
Derry and elsewhere in the North in recent days.

Irish men in every part of this island have made known their
concern at these events. This concern is heightened by the realisation
that the spirit of reform and intercommunal co-operation has given
way to forces of sectarianism and prejudice. All people of goodwill
must feel saddened and disappointed at this backward turn in events
and must be apprehensive for the future.

The Government fully share these feelings and I wish to repeat that
we deplore sectarianism and intolerance in all their forms wherever
they occur. The Government has been very patient and have acted
with great restraint over several months past. While we made our
views known to the British Government on a number of occasions,
both by direct contact and through our Diplomatic representative in
London, we were careful to do nothing that would exacerbate the
situation.

But it is clear now that the situation cannot be allowed to
continue.

It is evident, also, that the Stormont Government is no longer in
control of the situation. Indeed, the present situation is the inevitable
outcome of the policies pursued for decades by successive Stormont
Governments. It is clear, also, that the Irish Government can no
longer stand by and see innocent people injured and perhaps worse.

It is obvious that the RUC is no longer accepted as an impartial
police force. Neither would the employment of British troops be
acceptable nor would they be likely to restore peaceful conditions –
certainly not in the long run. The Irish Government have, therefore,
requested the British Government to apply immediately to the

United Nations for the urgent despatch of a Peacekeeping Force for the Six Counties of Northern Ireland and have instructed the Irish Permanent Representative of the United Nations to inform the Secretary-General of this request. We have also asked the British Government to see to it that police attacks on the people of Derry should cease immediately.

Very many people have been injured and some of them seriously. We know that many of these do not wish to be treated in Six County hospitals. We have, therefore, directed the Irish Army authorities to have field hospitals established in County Donegal, adjacent to Derry and at other points along the border where they may be necessary.

Recognising, however, that the reunification of the national territory can provide the only permanent solution for the problem, it is our intention to request the British Government to enter into early negotiations with the Irish Government to review the present constitutional position of the six counties of Northern Ireland. These measures which I have outlined to you seem to the Government to be those immediately and urgently necessary.

(Taoiseach Jack Lynch's televised address to the nation, 13 August 1969.)

In response to the riots in Derry, the Irish Taoiseach, Jack Lynch, gave a carefully measured broadcast to the nation after presiding over an emergency cabinet meeting which saw Government ministers recalled from their summer holidays to discuss, then determine, an appropriate Irish Government response to the deteriorating situation in the North. There was an imperative to act, yet an equal imperative not to overreact.

Well below its peacetime strength, possessing only antiquated equipment and little reliable transport ability of any note, and with no permanently occupied military posts north of a line from Galway to Gormanstown camp in County Meath, the Defence Forces were ordered northwards:

We were a mostly barrack-bound army, sedentary, domesticated, old and as obsolete as our equipment. There were officers and soldiers still in service who had first-hand involvement in countering IRA campaigns during the Emergency and in the late 1950s. Little or none of this was ever mentioned, however. Idle and inept, would – if brutal honesty were called for – aptly describe us. Overseas service with the United Nations, however, had been our escape to professionalism and a new, totally different, emphasis on soldiering emerged. The experience of the Congo was a shock, and this outward-looking emphasis was further developed with UN service in Cyprus. Both significant involvements were a great education for us, because among the UN contingents were people from other armies who had actual war-fighting experience – during World War II and the Korean War.

The standards that we operated with, and under, led to a raising of our own standards, an increase in invaluable experience and an improvement in equipment. Despite all this, in 1969 the army was still very small, largely inactive with antiquated transport, deficient in resources and no defence policy or direction. In short, neglected. Skeletal if you like, but one without the bones of a proper framework or the flesh of any fighting capability – at best a light infantry force. Defence was the victim among government departments and very little of [the] scarce money [available] was spent on it. Conditions were unsatisfactory, pay was poor. It was choked by civil service control and lacked any perceived purpose. Ill-prepared, with a deferential, weak leadership who all too readily bowed to pressure from politicians.

The North was a powder keg set to blow, and August 1969 was a time of enormous tension and pressure. There was a great and growing unease, anxiety and concern about the immediate future, and the highly volatile and uncertain security and political situation was the context within which a neglected and unprepared Defence Force was directed to act.

There was an unprecedented urgency throughout the Defence Forces. Jack Lynch's address to the nation was complemented by an order for immediate action and so the Defence Forces apparatus kicked into life, the organs of command and control stirred themselves and the military's main effort was directed towards getting troops to the border in the north west to set up field hospitals.

The first phase was to consolidate the maximum available transport assets spread throughout the Western Command area to get the vehicles in and get convoys of troops and equipment out. The staff of Western Command Headquarters, located in the centre of Ireland at Custume Barracks, Athlone, Co. Westmeath, had to coordinate the details to meet the demands of their sudden new circumstances:

> The many necessary land-line phone communications to outlying barracks within the command had to be channelled through the Barracks switchboard on the one external line out, for which there was great demand. The frustration was immense, the progress impeded, headway [was] hindered, advance obstructed and the time factor critical. The transport need was a priority: stores, troops; all kinds of equipment were needed and the means to get them to where needed had yet to be assembled, and great difficulty was being experienced in doing so. An added difficulty, once the land-line phone line became available, was actually making contact with the individual unit transport officers in the different barracks; [if] they not at their desks, [but] instead [were] outside in the transport yards or elsewhere. You then had to hang up and wait your turn in the queue for the external land-line again. There were bigger ... concerns, however, as a picture soon emerged regarding the actual roadworthiness of much of the transport fleet. There were multiple breakdowns. The antiquated vehicles were not even making it to Athlone, and of those that did, [many] broke down on the way to Donegal.

Not all of the transport was unserviceable or broke down, and the convoys – even though they made faltering progress – eventually arrived to their destination.

Also heading northwards, and ultimately for locations along the border but from far further south, were units from the other command formations: South, East and Curragh. They moved in convoys from as far away as Cork city and county and also, as it happened, from Arklow, where the Curragh Command's 3rd Battalion 'The Bloods' were on Summer Camp. Border-bound were what was to become four *ad hoc* 'cobbled together' company-sized infantry groups. The newly designated 14th, 15th, 16th and 17th Infantry Groups were to deploy to border areas, including the towns of Dundalk, Castleblayney, Cootehill and Cavan, to participate in what was to be a very complex operation:

> I was on 'Exercise Shanagarry' in East Cork and we were aware that matters were becoming hot in the North, and one night, very late, while asleep I remember being awoken by someone telling me I must report back immediately to my unit, the 1st Motor Squadron in Fermoy, Co. Cork. I arrived there in the middle of the night (early morning 14 August 1969) to find the camp a hive of activity. The unit had been placed on '12-hours' notice to move' to the border. I remember as a young officer being impressed watching the army system kick in from a logistics point of view. Trucks arrived from Collins Barracks, Cork, to the camp's main gate, the drivers descending from the cab of the truck, handing over the vehicles' keys and log book and receiving in return a signature for them and a travel warrant for public transport to return to Cork City. We took our allotment of 1st line ammunition from holdings stored within the camp; the balance was removed into Collins Barracks, Cork. The entire unit was mobilised.
>
> The 1st Motor Squadron was an ideal unit to send. We had 'wheels' (vehicles), [and] were loosely self-contained as an already integrated entity. It was the correct company-size strength of 140 and we had recently been on Summer Camp where we had to build a camp, run it and on completion strike (deconstruct) it. Whilst on camp we rehearsed checkpoints (CPs) moving in bounds and such like; ideal preparation, but as it happened, completely unintentional preparation for what lay ahead. All this on the back of two exercises: 'Exercise Shanagolden' (for the FCÁ) and 'Exercise Shanagarry' (1st Brigade). The older, sick and more infirm troopers (soldiers) of the unit were to be left behind and along with the 11th Battalion FCÁ headquarters staff would act as a fire piquet for the camp.
>
> Having completed our arrangements we gathered somewhat excitedly for a departing conference and whilst waiting for the Southern Command Intelligence Officer to arrive we began

wondering among ourselves [if we] were going in (to the North)? What will be there? What are we to do if we come face to face with the B-Specials, or even the British army? Are we to take them on? The briefing was short but intriguing. The last order we received was: 'Get to Mullingar, bed in and wait for sealed orders.' There was concern about the availability of relevant maps and when we raised questions about this we were told, 'with the sealed orders would be maps' and with that we were on the move.

We passed out through the gates of Fitzgerald Camp, Fermoy, late afternoon 14 August 1969 at 4.30 and [when] we turned left onto the main Cork to Dublin road there was a large crowd of family members, townspeople and well-wishers there to say goodbye and cheer us off on our way. This was repeated again as we passed through Mitchelstown and it seemed ever increasingly so by even larger crowds as we went through the various towns along our route until we came to Portlaoise and Mountmellick, where what seemed like huge cheering crowds greeted us. On our arrival to Columb Barracks in Mullingar we found turmoil reigned as troops coming together to form the Infantry Group were arriving in and shaking out, accommodated mostly in tents. The sealed orders from Dublin arrived also, placing us on a 'half hours' notice to move'.

Meanwhile, the night of 13–14 August saw the continuation of the Battle of the Bogside in Derry and the spread of street violence, clashes and large-scale rioting across the North, especially in Belfast where the situation had tragically and alarmingly led to loss of life and the burning out of Catholic families from their homes, along with much disorder and dislocation elsewhere.

To ensure that this unrest, unsettledness and insecurity was contained and the strife did not spread into the South, troops were directed to head for the border immediately:

On the cessation of the Taoiseach's address, we headed for the border that same night in old 1951 Bedford trucks and clapped out Land Rovers from Custume Barracks, Athlone. I was company commander of 6th Infantry Battalion Company, which was scrambled together, and we left Athlone at 10 pm heading to Donegal to be prepared to protect the Field Hospitals we were to establish. There was a certain hype, expectancy and excitement also prevailing, that perhaps we might be crossing the border. With this playing on the back of my mind I stopped the convoy outside Boyle, Co. Roscommon, and did a thorough check through the ammunition to discover that no 84 mm anti-tank or 81 mm mortar rounds had been loaded. Arriving in the early hours, we began setting up 'Camp Arrow' in an open field in darkness on the Letterkenny to Ramelton road, close to the border. I was concerned that we had no Force Protection measures in that open field and were not left position checkpoints on the road frontage running outside along the camp's boundary with the roadway. And so to set up camp, the soldiers and non-commissioned officers (NCOs) had two man bivvies, the officers were in larger eight-man tents, wherein stores were also placed. The first hours were fairly *ad hoc*, and with two more infantry companies expected; one from the East and one from the South, we had to prepare accordingly. They did arrive the next day, but by a bit of good fortune, the 4th Engineer Company were on Summer Camp in nearby Finner Camp and they assisted greatly in getting latrines and other such necessities, even managing to set up a working television on an outside pole in the middle of the field. The support weapon ammunition, ponchos and other equipment began to arrive in, as did the First Line Reservists, even some from England, supported by their English employers. There we sat, keeping a low profile, not conducting any patrols. After a number of days we began to question what we were doing there. Among the priorities: getting mass organised for the 15 August became regarded as one more important than others.

Control of the border in its own right was identified early on as being important, so along with the setting up of Field Hospitals – in reality First Aid stations, three of which were established on the main Donegal to Derry road and a fourth in County Cavan – it was important that the Irish Government retained its state territorial authority and the power to direct, influence or restrain movement across it. The highly volatile and uncertain political situation was the overall context within which the Defence Forces were directed to act. The circumstance for the Irish Government unfolded as an unprecedented crisis; developed north of the border in a manner over which it had no jurisdictive control. Internally there were those, some Government ministers amongst them, suggesting the seizure of the moment to end partition by directing the Defence Forces across it. Jack Lynch had received the wise counsel of the Governor of the Central Bank, TK 'Ken' Whitaker, who advised that the Republic take over neither Britain's financial contributions, nor the task of keeping order by controlling the border.

There were those, primarily Sinn Féin, who were advocating such an intervention to crowds in Dublin. Scuffles broke out, punches and kicks were thrown and there was a lot of pulling and dragging; a crowd dynamic was whipped up and a mob mentality aroused. The inevitable clash erupted – not a fully fledged fight, more a confused struggle – but there was a roughness to it all the same. The non-violent demonstrators had marched from outside Dublin's General Post Office (GPO) on O'Connell Street where about 3,000 people had gathered initially and been addressed by the President of Sinn Féin, Tomás Mac Giolla. He raised cheers when he announced that IRA units had 'defended with guns, Belfast people under attack, that the IRA were the only ones present to protect the people and that it was time for action'. From among the crowd, 'volunteers' for active service were recruited from the platform, whereupon he pointed out that the army had the weapons needed to protect the people in the North and that if the (Irish) army were not prepared to use their weapons then they ought to give them to the volunteers, who would. He then encouraged the crowd to accompany him to Collins Barracks, Dublin, where upon their arrival he demanded that the Collins Barracks garrison protect the people of the North or else hand over their guns to the volunteers, who were ready to do so. They began chanting: 'Give us guns, give us guns', and with that a scuffle broke out with the attendant Gardaí and the scene became an unpleasant and threatening one for a time, before the crowd realised they were not getting guns on this occasion and dispersed.

The following evening (16 August) also saw some disturbances, again initiated after a meeting outside the GPO, this time under the auspices of The National Solidarity Committee. Hostile and ugly scenes followed when a crowd of 2,000 marched on the British Embassy in Merrion Square outside which the street was cordoned off by Gardaí, as there had also been protests the previous evening. On arrival at the cordon, the marchers started throwing stones, with bricks and bottles being added as the disturbance continued. The Gardaí responded with baton charges, causing the crowd to eventually disperse and retreat into Clare Street, only for them to erect a makeshift barricade outside the Mount Clare Hotel. Fires were set, windows broken and cars vandalised. In all, fourteen Gardaí were injured during the disturbances but the Embassy remained intact.

Whilst this was ongoing, not too far away in St Stephen's Green three Nationalist Stormont MPs arrived at the offices of the Department of External Affairs (Iveagh House) requesting to speak with the Taoiseach. They were there to obtain weapons for beleaguered Catholics in Belfast's Falls Road area, where the B-Specials and extremist Protestant mobs were running amok attacking nationalists, burning rows of houses and injuring scores of residents. Three people had been fatally shot, and with the number of displaced people growing the situation was deteriorating alarmingly, eclipsing the uproar and rioting that was witnessed during the Battle of the Bogside:

> I was Quartermaster for a large FCÁ Camp (second line, part-time reservists) in Gormanstown Camp, Co. Meath, when mid-morning at the camp's end – and organising the FCÁ out, and refugees in – I emerged from my office to find the camp suddenly 'chock-a-block' full with army vehicles and hundreds of troops. Enquiring as to what was happening, I was glibly told: 'Oh, we're from the Brugha (Cathal Brugha Barracks, Rathmines, Dublin) and now we're the 16th Infantry Group going to the Border.'
>
> Their arrival was a total surprise to me and the sudden presence of possible extra mouths to feed immediately triggered my quartermasterly instinct and mind-set and I decided I needed to know if they were expecting to be fed. To this end I boldly interrupted an officer's briefing in progress and requested of the officer-in-charge were he and his men staying for lunch, to be told they were and [I was] thanked for my seeking clarification on the

matter. Then was added: 'But I want the Point Platoon fed first.' I had never heard the expression 'Point Platoon' used before and discreetly enquired as to who and what were his Point Platoon? I was informed that they were a recently passed-out recruit platoon and the only platoon to have combat uniforms!

It is often said that the truth comes out in a crisis. Such truths that the Troubles were set to expose, however, had yet to be revealed. The Irish Government would face unprecedented challenges as the various strands of the circumstances played out dramatically. One element which became starkly obvious early on though was a lack of foresight: aware of a growing political problem on its doorstep, the Defence Forces were grossly unprepared for its outbreak and the early days of the crisis – a period of considerable danger – proved to be a time of great difficulty. There was great uncertainty; no one was sure what might happen next; and there was no planning contingency, no resources were available and no organisational preparations had been made. Yet the need for action and a speedy response to the eruption of the Troubles was paramount. Nine years previously, the Defence Forces had received a serious jolt when they were suddenly tasked by the United Nations to provide a response for overseas troop participation in the Congo. This overseas involvement was to prove to be the single most significant development in the history of the Defence Forces. Nearly a decade later, the Defence Forces remained undermanned, underarmed and underfunded, only now it was facing a severe test at home; the mission to contain a situation which, if unaddressed, could possibly lead to a civil war on the island of Ireland.

Along with the setting up of field hospitals and refugee stations, and coordinating the northward movement of Irish troops to the border, a prudent, logical contingency to explore was the possibility of a drastic humanitarian crisis, with an extraction operation *in extremis* if necessary. If the violence in the North escalated, should Irish troops on the border move into the Six Counties to extricate nationalists from attack and significant loss of life, or to facilitate the rescue of wounded and terrified portions of the Catholic population? A judicious proposal, it was contingent on the operational and logistical capability to execute it. However daringly audacious, morally justified and politically righteous, it would need to be rigorously feasible, and the Irish army in its current state was not in a position to respond to such a scenario.

There were, however, some who recklessly advocated this course of action. The Taoiseach, Jack Lynch, was not one of them and he again requested Dr Patrick Hillery, the Minister for External Affairs, to travel to London to propose the setting up of a combined Irish and British military peacekeeping force, or alternatively a United Nations one. Unsuccessful with the British Government in London, the Irish Government continued to internationalise the Northern Ireland crisis and Patrick Hillery travelled to the United Nations Headquarters in New York in an attempt to raise the Northern Irish situation as a motion on the UN Security Council Agenda. This initiative was not necessarily to actually achieve such an outcome, it was deemed an internal matter for the United Kingdom, but to create worldwide awareness of the matter, which was certainly achieved.

The British had overall responsibility for the situation in Northern Ireland but understood neither the problem nor the place. The Northern Irish Unionists understood the problem, but had no desire to reform, and the Northern Irish Nationalists had a strong case for reform but had neither the voice nor the platform. The Irish Government had no jurisdiction but had to contain the crisis from spilling over into their territory. Not only were they challenged externally, there were internal problems to be controlled also, not just within the country but in the very Cabinet itself. Arising from all of these convoluted causes, courses and consequences of the crisis, there were other difficulties to be dealt with. There was shock and outrage from the Irish public and claims of interference in their internal affairs from the British; there were cries for arms from beleaguered northern nationalists and calls for an Irish army incursion from some Government ministers. Throughout the Republic there were 'Forty Shades of Green', an expression taken from a Johnny Cash song to express a range of Republican feelings, some of which were fast changing. The Government, the Gardaí and the Defence Forces had to tread a very fine line, yet were still unaware of just how fine it was to become. Captain Noel Carey (Retd.), hero of the Defence Forces involvement in Jadotville in the Congo, recalls:

We were convinced we were going in. We were personally ready to cross the border [and] Jack Lynch's televised address at 6 pm earlier in the evening, together with the prior memorable television news clip of a hate-filled RUC baton charge of a peaceful civil rights march (on 5 October 1968 in Derry's Duke Street, when RTÉ cameraman Gay O'Brien filmed images that were broadcast around the world) were uppermost in our minds. Twenty trucks left Custume Barracks, Athlone, that night. We left ten of them on the side of the road, broken down, as we travelled northwards to Finner Camp, where we overnighted.

At a conference the next morning, we were informed we were going to locate in a selected campsite called 'Camp Arrow' outside Letterkenny near the border, of which I was made Camp Adjutant. Shortly after arriving, I remember we were all standing there in a large empty green field ... with officers in their super-fines, NCOs and men in their bull's wool uniforms, until trucks arrived from Athlone with tents and we then set about erecting them. Later that day a rag-tag cobbled together company arrived from Collins Barracks, Cork, under Commandant Jim Flynn. They had been on Summer Camp in Cork. Another similarly quickly assembled Company, under Commandant Ned Dineen, arrived from the Eastern Command later again the same day. Brigade Headquarters were set up in Rockhill House.

There was a lot of comings and goings that day as we set about organising ourselves. We were greatly aided by an engineer unit under Captain Walter Rafferty, who very quickly erected a temporary cookhouse, latrines, dining areas and washing facilities. We had no support weapons (mortars and anti-tank weapons), or ammunition; however, this arrived at 10 pm with the armoured cavalry unit. I remembered their first vehicle on arrival in through the camp's gate drove straight through the commanding officer's tent. Nor was the drama over just yet, because early the next morning we got news that the international press were on their way to visit the camp and our main concern was to hide from view the newly arrived support weapon ammunition. This we tried to do with tarpaulin canvas strip lengths, which kept slipping off the ammunition boxes. Matters thereafter settled down.

The first morning, the cooks – however they managed it – even had a breakfast prepared. Lieutenant Colonel George Murphy was Officer Commanding and Commandant Tom Gleeson was the second-in-command. Commandant Dermot Byrne was Company Commander, Western Command Company, and Captain Joe Fallon his second-in-command. It was the first time since 'The Emergency' that a full battalion was on the ground. There were between 600–700 men in Camp Arrow. Our equipment was outdated, we had no combat uniforms, no wet gear, no sleeping bags and our radios were primitive. The helmets were of First World War era and our webbing was from the Second World War times – in a word 'ridiculous'.

Notwithstanding, we were mentally prepared and very willing to cross the border, especially when the support weapon ammunition arrived. Within a few days delegations came from Derry, two separate groups, the first wanting weapons – to whom we replied that we had no authority to give them any. The second was a larger group; they shouted and roared at us disparagingly for not going into Derry. We had a concern for how our fellow nationalists were being treated, brought up as we were on a definite dogma that the 'Irish' were nationalists only, and felt that we had justification to go in. It was all very polarising and upsetting.

Time passed, the weather deteriorated, the excitement waned, [and] there was less and less contact with and between Command and Brigade Headquarters and ourselves. Some discontent emerged among those of the First Line Reserve, especially those who had come back from England. They wished to return home but were refused permission. The weather deteriorated into October and units rotated up those unit personnel who had yet to come to the border until the companies from the South and the East went back to their commands, leaving the 6th Battalion only in situ in Camp Arrow.

The tents began leaking, the morale deteriorating somewhat and in early December the field hospital returned to Custume Barracks, Athlone. When this was pulled out we moved into Rockhill House, from which we patrolled along the border with the Garda. We received visits and inspections from higher headquarters but there was an unrest stirring within due to a lack of information on what was likely to happen and this was driving us mad.

We rotated back to Athlone in mid-December and were very glad that the Second Line part-time reserve, the FCÁ, were allowed to do Barrack guard duties; this was a great relief to us. The Battalion gradually identified people from the border areas who wanted to go there in proximity to where they were originally from. It took a year to a year and a half to settle down. It was a critical time in the army because we did not know what was going to happen.

CHAPTER 3

The British Army Blunders

With severe and prolonged rioting in Derry, Belfast and elsewhere across the Six Counties, the Irish army was already moving towards the border. The British Prime Minister took the decision to hurriedly draft in British army elements from the mainland to reinforce the token military presence garrisoned there and together they patrolled the streets across Northern Ireland to prevent a breakdown of law and order. At 5 pm on 14 August 1969, 300 British soldiers of the 1st Battalion, the Prince of Wales Own Regiment of Yorkshire, reinforced by a Company of the 1st Battalion, the Royal Regiment of Wales, having earlier arrived in Northern Ireland on the HMS *Sea Eagle*, entered the Bogside in Derry. Meanwhile, three companies of the 2nd Battalion, the Queen's Regiment, and two companies of 1st Battalion, the Royal Regiment of Wales, deployed into Belfast.

The following day, Brigadier Peter Hudson, Officer Commanding 39th Infantry Brigade, toured the areas and determined reinforcements were required. Later that same day the first elements of the 3rd Battalion, the Light Infantry, began to arrive. 'Operation Banner', the British army campaign in Northern Ireland, was underway. By early September, 6,000 British troops were in Northern Ireland.

They were there to quell any further intercommunal violence and at first were welcomed and accepted in the embattled Catholic areas of Belfast and Derry; their presence even perceived as likely to back the political reforms insisted on by London. In mid-October 1969, the decision was taken to disband the B-Specials and replace it with the Ulster Defence Regiment (UDR). This, however, was to be a part-time element of the British army. The Unionists were deeply shocked, but it was deemed that the B-Specials represented Protestant repression and needed to be reformed. However, the move enraged Protestants, resulting in serious rioting along the Shankill Road area. Shots were fired at the British army and over twenty soldiers were wounded overall after riot squads moved in and made arrests. The British army presence in the North was regarded as a huge relief by Catholics, who happily furnished tea and biscuits to the troops. This honeymoon was not to last, however, and the pre- and post-Christmas period was to prove to be the lull before the gathering storm.

During Easter 1970 (1 April) at the edge of Belfast's Catholic Ballymurphy housing estate, trouble broke out between two sets of rural groups and the Royal Scots intervened between them. However, instead of 'holding the line' between both sets of protagonists, they waded in against the Catholic residents with batons and indiscriminate volleys of CS gas to quell the stoning, rioting behaviour and continuing disorder. If not a key turning point, it was perhaps the beginning of a radicalising moment whereby nationalists began to view the British army as an instrument to perpetuate the status quo in favour of Protestant loyalists; a view reinforced on 27 June by their non-interference, despite requests in advance to do so, in the Catholic Short Strand enclave amid an armed attack by a loyalist mob, a defence which included the armed protection of St Matthew's Church – an event in the sub-culture of the Troubles that marked the rebirth of the IRA. Earlier that month was also to see a change of government in Westminster when the Conservative Party under Edward (Ted) Heath came to power.

Traditionally, the Conservatives were more closely allied with and supportive of the Unionists, and the Stormont Government in Northern Ireland now found themselves with the twin advantages of being fully supported by London and with British troops at their disposal. Brian Faulkner, Prime Minister of Northern Ireland, favoured the prioritising of security to that of political reform, and as a result the British army, at the behest of the Unionists, were directed to nullify the fledgling IRA. This push for harder security measures addressed the symptoms rather than the root cause of the Troubles, and was to later include internment without trial of over 300 people suspected of being involved with the IRA.

When the Troubles initially broke out in August 1969, the IRA had few members, fewer guns and hardly any money. The organisation was unable to adequately defend Catholic areas against the 'Protestant Pogrom', as it was considered in some quarters. Those few remaining individuals were taunted by graffiti daubed on walls publicly denouncing and condemning the IRA as standing for 'I Ran Away'. Discouraged, and disheartened after the failure of 'Operation Harvest', the border campaign from 1956 to1962, the leadership had taken to the pursuit of a more political campaign advocating the merits of advancing a Marxist–leftist policy. After August 1969 a more militant element emerged, and in December 1969 there was a split in the organisation resulting in the pre-existing, more politically inclined, 'Official' IRA and the more extreme, militantly active 'Provisional' IRA. A strained stand-off existed between the Provisional IRA (PIRA) and the British army; though this was actually part of the Provisional's strategy of 'phased or staged engagement'.

The first engagement – defensive in nature and an opportunity to redeem themselves in the eyes of the Catholic community in Belfast – occurred on the evening of 27 June 1970, when a loyalist Orange Order band and their supporters marched through the Short Strand/ Ballymacarrett area of East Belfast. On their return from the main parade, violence erupted as the march entered the Catholic Springfield Road area.

The River Lagan, the Newtownards and Albert Bridge Roads enclosed the district on three sides and existing within the boundary was a hugely outnumbered Catholic enclave. Theirs was an uncomfortable existence and the spectre of conflict often hung over them. Protection was problematic and withdrawal was difficult, and if attacked they knew they simply had to stand their ground. With the British army and RUC deployed nearby, but unhelpfully not intervening, it fell to those within to prevent being burned out of their homes. Armed PIRA men moved into positions distributing themselves throughout the district, including taking up the advantageous aspect afforded by the tall tower steeple of St Matthew's Church, granting them excellent fields of observation and fire.

When repeated, determined incursions by loyalist mobs were in progress, those in the steeple responded with unyielding defence. The five-hour firefight prevented the Protestant mob from being able to position themselves to hurl petrol bombs. The march had become a riot then transformed into a gun battle, and the spirited and energetic defence of the Provisional IRA saw the attack wither. It was PIRA's first major action and an enormous propaganda victory; successfully defending a vulnerable Catholic enclave from an armed, aggressive loyalist mob. The following day, loyalists expelled 500 Catholic workmen from the nearby Harland & Wolff shipyard and the months of June and July 1970 were to witness a series of blunders by the British military, mostly at the behest of the Unionist regime in Stormont, with an all too willing and emergent Provisional IRA capitalising on the mistakes and plunging Northern Ireland into three decades of armed conflict.

The insensitivity of The Falls Curfew was one such event that played directly into the Provisional's hands. On 2 July 1970, an arms find in a house on Balkan Street and the resultant repercussions over the following three days were to see a turning point in the initial rapport between the Catholic community and the British army. Following a tip off, a British army patrol of five or six vehicles was despatched to the Lower Falls area, where a quantity of arms and ammunition was discovered in a house on Balkan Street. As the British troops started to withdraw, they came under attack from local youths who pelted them with bottles and stones. With the British platoon besieged in the middle of The Falls, reinforcements were sent only to be cut off by rapidly constructed barricades and suddenly an entire company was stranded in the same area. In turn, two companies were despatched to their rescue and they were forced to fire CS gas at the rioting crowds. By late afternoon, the Falls was in chaos as more troops were sent in to rescue the rescuers.

The residents claimed the unfolding of the confrontation was more systemic than reactionary, and that after days and nights of rioting and gunfire the army imposed an illegal curfew on the Lower Falls area of Belfast, putting the area in lockdown as an extended cordon line perimeter surrounded and enclosed the Catholic nationalist area for 36 hours. In conducting searches, residents complained bitterly that the army had been abusive and it was believed they caused unnecessary damage: ransacking homes, ripping up floorboards, breaking furniture and cracking open the plaster on the walls. The area being predominantly Official IRA, the two branches of the IRA fought the British army with gunfire, petrol and nail bombs. Four people were killed – three shot and one knocked down, pinned by a military vehicle – and by its cessation approximately 100 weapons and quantities of ammunition were seized. At the conclusion of the curfew, the army brought two

Unionist Ministers, William Long and Captain John Brooke, into the area in the rear of a military vehicle to demonstrate their effectiveness. However, it only really ended when hundreds of women descended on the area with food, forcing their way through the cordon and leaving, it has been claimed, with IRA weapons concealed in prams and in their clothing.

Dr Patrick Hillery, the Republic of Ireland's Minister for External Affairs, also visited the area, much to the outcry of the Unionists. The 'Falls Road Curfew' was an act of monumental stupidity as it generated a sense of alienation among the Catholic community. Trust was lost and the conviction that the British army were irredeemably pro-Unionist was copper-fastened. The year-long honeymoon between nationalist Belfast and the British army was at an end.

The Provisional IRA gained enormously from those early errors of judgement and was hurled headlong, beyond its expectations, towards embarking on the beginnings of its 'offensive stage'. For a propaganda effect to be sustained you have to demonstrate its achievement in real terms; the young were vulnerable to the Provisional IRA's propaganda, and these idealists in many cases became somewhat blinded by it. The Provisional IRA believed that violence was a necessary part of the struggle to rid Ireland of the British and aimed to enthuse public support for their 'cause' and encouraged people to believe that now was the moment to end partition. They believed that 'one big push' was all it would take and by escalation of the military campaign this was certain to be achieved. 'Escalate, escalate, escalate' became PIRA's mantra.

The blunders and misuse of military resources by the Stormont Government, and by extension Westminster, caused the total alienation of the minority Catholic population from the Northern Ireland system, granting the Provisionals an opportunity to take hold. This all resulted from the Unionists' unwillingness to compromise. A previously all but extinguished IRA had been handed a platform of opportunity – gifted a 'cause' – and the momentum of its initial campaign was accelerated beyond its expectations by sheer bloody-mindedness.

A visibly larger, stronger, more self-convinced Provisional IRA now took on the British army. Gun and bomb attacks became more frequent and ever more audacious and a battle of wits began between PIRA bomb makers and the British army bomb disposal teams. The Provisionals were soon getting the better of the street exchanges and British soldiers were now targets, whether they were on-duty or off-duty. For the British army, operations in Northern Ireland were a very different type of conflict to what they were trained for. The street fighting was as dangerous as any overseas foreign theatre, but there were no front lines and on any given day the 'battlefield' might be a street, a housing estate or a rural lane. The Provisional IRA could launch an assault, an ambush, a sniper attack, or a bomb explosion, then blend into the background by turning into an alleyway or a building, switching instantly from active hostility to just another person walking down the street – invisible and unknown.

For the British soldiers living conditions were poor, cramped makeshift barracks located in old factories and school buildings. These too were subject to attack, and there were daily hardships and dangerous demands on the individual soldier. Almost every day of a British soldier's deployment to Northern Ireland was challenging, with high levels of street violence, riots, bombings and shootings, fatalities and being wounded not uncommon.

During the first six months of 1971, the idealists dedicated themselves to a desperate and deadly cause and the urban guerrilla offensive of the Provisional IRA concentrated heavily on 'British' economic targets as well as British troops. With the British army directed to pursue a military victory and the nationalists prepared to fight them, Northern Ireland was bloody, violent and politically stagnant. Through Stormont's lack of reform and inaction towards equality, feelings of frustration, despair and grievance flourished in young Catholics, leading many in the community to join the IRA, which they saw as the only remaining option to change society in Northern Ireland. British politicians claimed that Northern Ireland was an integral part of the United Kingdom, while the Irish asserted that a small island, geographically, if not historically, ought to be an undivided state.

***

When he stepped off the aircraft at RAF Aldergrove in November 1972, Edward Heath was the first British Prime Minister in fifty years to visit Northern Ireland. The British were absentee power holders, but the authority they exercised in Northern Ireland, via the British army, was a power without responsibility. Brian Faulkner, Prime Minister of Northern Ireland and head of the province's security committee, claimed that Belfast was as British as Bristol or Birmingham. Faulkner pushed for tough action against the 'thugs and murderers' of the Provisional IRA, and despite the misgivings of the General Officer Commanding of the British army in Northern Ireland, Lieutenant-General Harry Tuzo, who cautioned against it, Faulkner was granted authority to introduce internment without trial in August 1971.

Between 4 am and 7 am on 9 August 1971, 'Operation Demetrius' was executed and thousands of British soldiers, accompanied by RUC Special Branch detectives, swooped on addresses throughout the North, raiding houses and making arrests. Of the 342 individuals initially detained, 104 were released and the remaining 238 were jailed in Crumlin Road Prison in Belfast or on the Prison Ship *Maidstone*. Front doors were splintered, men and youths dragged from their beds, screaming wives, mothers and children roughly manhandled. It was an ill-conceived policy, poorly executed and one-sided. Few senior Official or Provisional IRA men were rounded up, since the RUC was operating with out-dated lists of suspected IRA members and many young members were unknown to them. Strikingly, no similar attempt was made to arrest Loyalist activists. Undertaken with the aim of smashing the newly emerging IRA, instead it imposed the gunmen on the people within nationalist 'no-go' areas. Riots and disturbances followed and thirteen people died on the first day of Internment. Overall, twenty-four people were killed in three days. Many refugees fled to camps south of the border and by mid-August an estimated 6,000 people had sought refuge in the South. Lieutenant Colonel Diarmuid O'Donoghue (Retd.) recalls:

When the Troubles started, I was holidaying in the 'Long Strand' near Rosscarbery, Co. Cork and a Garda arrived to say he had been contacted by my then Company Commander, Michael Minihan, and I was to report immediately to my unit in Dublin. Thereafter, I served six months in Castleblayney in Co. Monaghan. On this later occasion, whilst serving in Gormanstown Camp, I was catering officer for an FCÁ Camp and on the eve of its conclusion I was looking forward to once again holidaying in West Cork. However, suddenly the gates of the camp opened and refugees from the North – women and children for the most part – six abreast, came streaming into the camp. It seemed like hundreds of homeless, tired, distressed and worried people presented seeking shelter, security and sanctuary. I can honestly say we did our best for them. It was to be three further weeks before I managed to go on holiday.

Internment failed to achieve the propaganda aims of the authorities, and furthermore a number of detainees were mistreated. The fourteen 'hooded men', as they were to become known, experienced 'Five Techniques' used on them during interrogation, including hooding, sleep deprivation, white noise, starvation, standing for hours spread-eagled against a wall leaning on their fingertips, all the while accompanied by continual harassment, blows, insults and questioning. Some were forced to run the gauntlet between lines of baton-wielding soldiers and a few were taken up blindfolded in a helicopter (actually hovering only a few feet off the ground) and told they were going to be thrown out. In 1976, the Irish Government took the issue to the European Commission of Human Rights and in 1978 the European Court of Human Rights found the British Government guilty of using inhumane and degrading treatment. In Northern Ireland, the consequence of internment was to escalate the chaos and the level of conflict.

Brian Faulkner's aim of using internment to end the violence by flushing out the gunmen did not work. On the contrary, the Provisionals' benefitted from internment, rather than being crushed by it. The use of the British army as part of a policy prioritising a security approach over that of political reform, to nullify the fledgling Provisional IRA, backfired badly. Internationally too, the television images of the Troubles were of explosions, streets full of broken bricks and bottles, and burnt-out barricades; footage of rioting crowds, yelling and cursing in the midst of swirling clouds of CS gas as soldiers charged from behind a barrage of baton rounds, were all illustrative of a worsening situation. From July 1971 to year's end saw a sharp increase in Provisional IRA activity. There were increased killings (140 people died in the four months after internment) and increased bombings as the Provisional IRA stepped up both the intensity and extent of its campaign, accelerating its policy of escalation.

On Sunday 30 January 1972, soldiers of 1 Para (1st Battalion, Paratroop Regiment) under Lieutenant Colonel Derek Wilford entered the Bogside area of Derry to police a Northern Ireland Civil Rights Association march and by the day's end had shot twenty-seven unarmed people, fourteen of them fatally. The procession was near the Rossville flats when the army's 'arrest operation' was mounted. It was one of the British army's most controversial operations ever undertaken, and has since become known as 'Bloody Sunday'. Outweighing any previous blunders, it was as inexplicable as it was incomprehensible, even for Northern Ireland. Overwhelming in its enormity, Bloody Sunday left the nationalists overwrought and inflamed and incited an already incendiary situation. Causing widespread shock and anger, 15-year-old Don Mullan, who was part of the rally on the day, described the situation as he saw it:

> I participated in the civil rights march that day, my first ever, and was standing only 2-feet away from 17-year-old Michael Kelly when he was fatally shot. I can still hear him gasp as a ricochet bullet punctured his flesh. An instant later, confusion and terror reigned as a rubble barricade began to stir dust as bullets thundered into it. I am still unable to recall accurately the events of those horrific moments of my adolescence. I [remember] people to my right crying out and falling close to me at the barricade. Then suddenly, the wall of an apartment above my head burst, showering those below with brick and mortar. A primeval instinct took possession of me and unashamedly I started running home to safety. 'Son, what's happening?' a woman's voice called. 'There must be at least six dead,' I shouted back. Her face registered disbelief, but I did not stop to convince her.
>
> The following day, my best friend called for me and we retraced our steps. I remember pointing to the bullet marks on the wall above where I had been the previous afternoon. We looked with incredulity at the bloodstains on the pavements and by the barricade. Across the road in a first-storey apartment, one window

had six bullet holes with cracks spreading out like webs. The blue and white Civil Rights banner that had led our procession the previous day was now heavily stained with the blood of Barney McGuigan, a father of six children, who was shot while holding aloft a white handkerchief as he had cautiously made his way to the aid of a fatally wounded man. He was killed by a shot in the back of the head.

On the day of the funerals, my friend and I stood silently together in the cold rain that swept over Derry as cortège after cortège slowly made their way towards the cemetery gates. We were numb, confused and increasingly angry.

Over thirty years later, I would sit in the public gallery at Central Hall in Westminster, as 'Soldier F' of the Parachute Regiment in 1972 admitted under cross-examination that in addition to three other people he had also killed Mr McGuigan. Memories of that tragic day still give rise to anger and outrage within me.

Bloody Sunday was a bitter experience, especially after the whitewash of the Widgery Tribunal. The atmosphere began to change dramatically as a direct consequence. Boys that I played football with were making other choices. The IRA had many willing recruits thereafter and, well, honestly, I considered making that choice too.

The Creggan Estate in Derry was to become a Republican stronghold, but in my childhood it was not a rabid anti-British or anti-English environment. So the big question is why and how it became so? And it was not because my community was born with a genetic defect that made us prone to violence.

Following unrelenting street disturbances in August 1969, the British Army was ordered into the streets of Belfast and Derry. In the early days they engaged in various community liaison projects. It was not unusual for local soccer clubs to line out against regimental teams. I also recall on one occasion a British Army band, I think, Royal Marines, coming to our school. We gave them a rapturous welcome, preferring their percussion and brass to English, French and Maths. In May 1970 our school was the first in Northern Ireland to be offered an Adventure Training Course by the army with ten places at Magilligan Camp, about 25-miles from Derry, which included rock climbing, hill-walking, canoeing, orienteering and expedition work. Magilligan Camp was later to become a detention centre for internees in August 1971 and the theatre for an ominous encounter between unarmed Civil Rights [Association] demonstrators and 1 Para the week before Bloody Sunday 1972.

The Falls Road Curfew, the introduction of internment without trial, and especially Bloody Sunday were to have powerful, cumulative and long-lasting repercussions over the following three decades. At the time, anger, alienation and abhorrence drove a wedge between the British army and the Nationalist Catholic community, who felt that 'the Paratroopers murdered 14 civilians on Bloody Sunday, but the Widgery Report (a British inquiry into the Bloody Sunday shootings) murdered the truth'. Trust and faith in the British army was lost, and for the Catholic community alienation became habitual and the State proved unsympathetic. Prior to these events, the Provisional IRA had nominal support, minimal backing and negligible encouragement. Afterwards, however, attitudes hardened and entrenchment followed.

CHAPTER 4

The Provisional IRA Emerges

The danger now was that PIRA's campaign of terror could lead to a backlash and ultimately civil war, first in Northern Ireland but then spilling across the border, engulfing the entire island and population. As it stood, the situation in Northern Ireland was already very dangerous. Different groups of Republicans and Loyalists, all unlawful organisations, raised stark issues for the Republic. The security of the State was threatened by these small unrepresentative self-appointed groups without any mandate from the electorate. They had taken it upon themselves to conduct their campaigns and counter-campaigns of violence, causing death and destruction. They were attempting to dictate to the democratically elected government representatives of Irish society what policy to pursue. By organising themselves into private armies, their use of physical force, intimidation and coercion caused the State to have to actively defend democracy or succumb to their anarchy.

Half a century of discrimination in the North had given rise to the Civil Rights Movement, the response to which was violent counter-demonstration and mob attacks into Catholic areas of Derry and Belfast. Many one-time residents sought security and shelter elsewhere in the North and some across the border in the Republic. Barricaded 'no go' areas sprang up, and to begin with the communities were organised by local defence committees. However, the IRA, once long gone, began to re-emerge as the 'old-timers' within the organisation were quick to recognise the potential that the crisis offered, especially with the appearance of British troops on the streets. These '69-ers' saw the opportunity to reinvent themselves and initiate a new campaign. It was a moment to be seized upon and they grasped it wholeheartedly.

The Provisional IRA's strategy was to target the Stormont regime and force the British protecting power to use its own troops in counter-insurgency operations. The measures taken by the British troops would then operate to keep the political temperature of the dissident community at a level favourable to the Provisional IRA.

Catholic Nationalists, already externally under siege, were now to come under the internal influence of the Provisional IRA. Catholic youths were vulnerable to Provisional IRA propaganda, and were ripe for radicalisation. The veteran IRA recruiters gave Catholic youths a 'cause' in defence of their own areas. Unfortunately, the uncompromising Unionists and the British army played right into the narrative in a way unimagined by their recruiters. Young men and women were driven into PIRA and sympathy was generated for them and their military across the Catholic communities.

Now community-based with widespread support, PIRA generated a reputation that ensured even those opposed to them would not cross them. The lack of real access to Catholic communities made it difficult for the RUC Special Branch to identify members. Rotation of British army units unskilled in counter-terrorism made the army a very blunt instrument. Those who called for stronger military action, the commitment of more troops, internment without trial, curfews and the like, ought to have borne in mind that they were behaving as the Provisional IRA's strategy called for them to behave.

These measures brought mounting costs: moral, military, political and psychological; and it was these, not the insurgent operation itself, which was expected in due course to modify the political will of the protecting power – the British. Thus, every measure of military escalation was, in a sense, a success for those who provoked it – PIRA.

The Provisional IRA was highly organised. Overall charge was executed by the seven member Army Council, an army executive which in turn was elected by the General Army Convention (GAC). Made up of delegates from the brigades, the GAC met infrequently and the Army Council was considered by republicans to be the *de jour* government of Ireland. The Chief-of-Staff (appointed by the Army Council) was supported by General Headquarters (GHQ) staff, comprising of a Director of each department: Intelligence, Operations, Training, Engineering, Finance, Security, Publicity, Research and the all-important Quartermaster.

Territorially, there were two commands: Northern and Southern. The 'War Zone', Northern Command, comprised eleven counties (the Six Counties and five border counties) and Quartermastering Support. Southern Command was comprised of the remaining twenty-one counties, and was involved with all the provisioning, supplying and logistical facilitation of operations, both in the War Zone, England and Europe. Training, bomb-making, financing, weapon importation, storage and transportation and anything else in producing the capacity to sustain the 'cause'.

There were a number of consciously constructed operational phases and evolving game plans which gave the Provisional IRA purpose, direction and momentum over the years of the Troubles:

- Defence ('Area Defence')
- Offence ('One Big Push')
- The 'Long War'
- Bombs, Bullets and Ballot Boxes
- Dirty War
- Stalemate, Standstill and 'One Final Push'
- Peace Process
- Bombing Britain
- The Good Friday agreement

The 'Quick Victory' of the early 1970s was not realised and a war of attrition took hold. There were several other critical periods during the conflict and many changes occurred as PIRA were faced with rapidly changing political realities. Sometimes the military establishment were at odds with its political masters, with all sides becoming more sophisticated over time.

If the British security forces were combatting terror, then their Irish counterparts south of the border were mounting a containment operation. The Provisional IRA killed 15 people in 1970, 89 in 1971 and in 1972, the worst year of the Troubles, the so-called 'Year of Victory', – they killed 243 people in a concerted and terrifying shooting and bombing campaign.

The televised rioting, the burnt-out Catholic homes, internment and Bloody Sunday all became rallying points around which PIRA built a support network for fundraising and arms supply – particularly in America, but elsewhere also. It was all powerful propaganda, and recruits, arms and money followed.

✷✷✷

The hard fact is that in guerrilla war the enemy holds the initiative for large parts of the time and information is the key to his defeat.

(Lieutenant General Sir Harry Tuzo, GOC Northern Ireland, 1971–3.)

The British army implemented the political will of the Stormont and Westminster governments in arresting and detaining IRA suspects during 'Operation Demetrius' on 9 August 1971, a course of action advised against by Lieutenant General Tuzo. However, a British army Press Officer with 39 Infantry Brigade stated at the Operation's beginning: 'Today is the beginning of the end of the IRA … without the head the body will simply thrash around and eventually die ….' However, many IRA leaders had slipped the net and internment soon became an unmitigated disaster. Violence escalated and 'for every one we picked up, we have recruited 10 for the IRA'. A new generation of republicans had taken up the struggle.

As well as being 'at war' with the British, the IRA was also at war with itself; following the December 1969 split between the 'Red' Marxist Official IRA, under Cathal Goulding, and the 'Green' militaristic Provisional IRA under Seán Mac Stíofáin. The Provisional IRA was convinced that only physical force would drive the British out of Northern Ireland, a campaign that went into overdrive during 1971 and reached its peak in terms of deaths in 1972, when the Officials (or 'stickies' as they were known because that was how they applied the Easter Lily emblems on their lapels at Easter time, the Provisionals preferring to use a pin) called a ceasefire. But not before they had bombed the headquarters of the Parachute regiment at Aldershot, England, killing seven (including five canteen staff members) in reprisal for Bloody Sunday.

By any normal standards, 1972 was a grim year in terms of bombings, shootings and the number of fatalities. In July alone there were 200 explosions, 2,800 shootings and 95 deaths. But for the Provisional IRA, now sixteen months in existence, it gave cause for great self-belief, not least their 7 July secret high-level meeting with William Whitelaw, Secretary for Northern Ireland, in 96 Cheyne Walk, Chelsea, London. With Stormont abolished, direct rule (from London) was instigated and law and order was firmly placed under British Government and military control. A ceasefire called on 26 June, then ten days old and holding, was the backdrop to the talks. The assembled delegation consisted of Gerry Adams, Ivor Bell, Seán Mac Stíofáin, Martin McGuinness, Dáithí Ó Conaill, Seamus Twomey and an observer, the Dublin solicitor Myles Shevlin. The meeting proved inconclusive, the Provisional IRA's demands were too much for the British, and the ceasefire was over within 72 hours. A confrontation occurred at Belfast's Lenadoon housing estate when Catholic families were prevented from being rehoused in vacated Protestant houses. The image of a British army Saracen armoured car suddenly ramming a truck piled high with the Catholic families' furniture was broadcasted widely and internationally.

The Provisional IRA sensed a final victory and they 'escalated, escalated, escalated' their campaign up yet another gear. On Friday 21 July, in what became termed 'Bloody Friday', they set off 22 explosions in 90 minutes, killing 9 people and injuring 130. This intended 'spectacular' bombing operation backfired badly on the Provisional IRA, though, as the British army were unable to deal with the many bombs in so short a time. It was the worst day in Belfast since the German blitz of 1941.

If 'Victory 1972' was not achieved and the movement's appeal was hurt badly by the bombings throughout the year, the Provisional IRA were relentless in maintaining their campaign, confident now of delivering 'Victory 1974'. The curious blend of open and guerrilla warfare continued as PIRA activists ambushes at crossroads, shot at 'opportunity targets', and sniped at soldiers on the streets, across walls and around corners. Local units suddenly appeared, engaged the British army, and then just as quickly melted back into the housing estates.

The Provisional IRA continued to enjoy popular community support and were proving to be a ruthlessly efficient guerrilla force and militarily, the British army were still struggling to come to terms with them. How deeply threatened then was the Irish State by these actions? Was the integrity of the Irish State more vulnerable to the danger than British sovereignty in Northern Ireland? Even with the initial confusion between 'the doves' and 'the hawks' within the Irish Republic's ruling party Fianna Fáil resolved, what kind of a security response could be mounted sufficient to match the violent vigour of the Provisional IRA? Curiously, the context south of the border was different, and while the Irish State had every reason to fear what the Irish Minister for Justice, Des O'Malley, described as 'the scourge of society' (PIRA), there existed a residual memory within the republican movement of what had happened during the 1940s, when de Valera's Fianna Fáil Government reacted strongly to the IRA threat. Six were executed and three left to die on hunger strike. Subsequently, in 1954, two years before 'Operation Harvest' or the IRA 'Border Campaign' (1956–62), the IRA introduced General Standing Order Number Eight as part of its operating policy:

> Volunteers are strictly forbidden to take any militant action against 26 County Forces under any circumstances whatsoever. The importance of this Order in present circumstances, especially in Border areas, cannot be over emphasised .... Volunteers arrested during training or in possession of arms will point out that the arms were for use against the British Forces of Occupation only.

In theory, PIRA were careful not to bring themselves into open conflict with the southern authorities, not out of concern for members of the southern security forces, rather to prevent any 'anti-IRA' sentiment from surging across the Republic and a reintroduction of the harsh measures used to deal with them. As it was, the Irish Government was already strengthening its arsenal of measures to deal with the IRA: using new legislation; the building up of the Defence Forces and the Gardaí; and the reintroduction of the Special Criminal Court (SCC) amongst them. However, the Provisional IRA was also building up its arsenal of measures, weapons most prominent amongst them.

On the outbreak of the Troubles, their previously dumped collection of guns and ammunition was unearthed from hides, taken from outbuildings or under grain in farmyard sheds and unwrapped from plastic bags, barrels and boxes. They were basic weapons but in good condition and capable of delivering the lethal effect they were designed and manufactured for: Lee-Enfield .303 (Mark 4) and US Garand .30 calibre semi-automatic rifles, Springfield carbines, Thompson and Sten sub-machine guns, shotguns, .22 rifles, .45 Webley revolvers and explosives stolen from quarries. The simplest bomb was sticks of gelignite taped together with a detonator and a length of fuse, but there was also a lot of information on explosives available in libraries, and IRA training manuals were updated and made available. Subsequently, homemade explosives were produced from readily available materials, much of it fertiliser-based. From very early on, the first consignment of modern ArmaLite rifles were delivered to the IRA and in September 1972 a huge shipment of RPG-7 anti-tank rocket launchers was successfully and secretively landed at Shannon Airport. Originally the plan was to land the shipment at Farranfore Airport in Co. Kerry but the runway was too short for the aircraft. These rocket launchers were used in a series of attacks along the border the following month.

With the Provisional IRA campaign going into overdrive in Northern Ireland, there was a constant need for weapons, and what could not be brought in could possibly be built. There were those in PIRA who were to prove highly proficient in producing prototypes and then perfecting them. At a more basic level, training camps were organised and established well away from the 'war zone': in Kerry, Mayo and other out-of-the-way locations. A five-day training camp model was developed where weapon and explosives familiarisation was conducted, as well as training participants in the characteristics and capabilities of the weapons available. Weapons would be disassembled, their working parts exposed and explained and then the weapon reassembled. This 'stripping and assembling' of a weapon demystified it and for many fed the fascination with guns that was an attraction in the first place. Safety precautions, cleaning, care and maintenance were next and then firing practise with live rounds. Any bad habits were corrected through instruction and the individual trainees for the most part reached a standard to be allowed to operate on the streets and in rural parts of Northern Ireland.

Security was an issue and keeping the exact location of the training camp hidden was always uppermost. Active measures were taken to avoid suspicion and discovery. Those attending camps departed from their homes by different routes and were collected at a central rendezvous from which they were transported in vans, minibuses with blacked-out windows and in the rear of cattle trucks. Products used at the camps – including food and drink – were made generic and any reference to locality on milk cartons, shopping bags etc. was removed. No local newspapers were permitted. If discovered, there were selected escape routes and rendezvous spots where the participants were to gather after the getaway was made. Sometimes specialised camps for explosive making or advanced weapons training were also held. Hundreds of trainees passed through the training camps and areas; all were prepared and most put what they had learned into action to perpetrate and continue the violence. Often, force was not only used for the furthering of the 'Brits out' aim, but also for its own sake. The constant continuum of thousands of small-scale attacks, shootings and bombings were of value to the Provisional IRA in keeping the low-intensity struggle contested, thereby maintaining morale amongst the active members by keeping them tirelessly committed. This also kept their focus and nurtured their ability – keeping it fit for purpose – and was an overt statement of prevailing strength to the community from which it drew its support.

Financing the campaign and the organisation was always a difficulty; by its own estimates the Provisional IRA cost £2 million a year to keep itself functioning. The funds required came from an assorted mix of sources; a levy on Belfast's black taxis, gaming machines, drinking clubs, extortion, defrauding the tax and social welfare, smuggling operations along the border involving petrol, cattle, cigarettes and diesel, as well as funds raised abroad – particularly in the USA – and of course bank and wage robberies in the Republic. There was a lot of criminality associated with PIRA and the professionalisation of the Provisional IRA's handling of its finances was to develop over the years regarding the administration and control of its earnings.

The production of money was one aspect of Provisional IRA activity; the production of fertiliser-based explosives was another. Ammonium nitrate was extracted from a process using Net Nitrate fertiliser mixed with gallons of water. When this was heated and the resultant residue mixed with diesel oil, this became the primary ingredient for PIRA bombs. This process produced a nauseating stench with sickening fumes, and together with the heat such facilities, often semi-derelict buildings in remote areas, were unpleasant places to work. The explosive material extract was collected regularly and transported to bomb factories to become the primary component in car bombs.

The Provisional IRA had the means, method and mentality to continue its armed struggle, taking the fight to the British on every occasion they could, convinced that victory was in their grasp. The military thinking of the Provisional IRA was to change over the years; the leadership became Northern-based, its structure was dramatically reorganised and its support base was broadened by blending the armed struggle with electoral politics. There were to be cessations, ceasefires, truces, campaign resumptions and decisive escalation of violence; more lives were lost in Northern Ireland, and the Irish State was required to go to great lengths to combat the real and sinister threat posed by the organisation.

CHAPTER 5

The Irish Government Shudders

An impromptu after-hours soccer match at Collins Barracks, Dublin, on 2 April 1970, involving the garrison's young officers on the quayside esplanade near the River Liffey is interrupted and an officer requested to report immediately to the Brigade Commander's office. On the way he is joined by another junior officer, both Lieutenants from the 5th Infantry Battalion, similarly summonsed from elsewhere on the barracks. Three senior officers were waiting for them in the Brigade Commander's office and the two Lieutenants were told to quickly get into uniform and that an already loaded convoy of trucks was awaiting their arrival in Cathal Brugha Barracks, Rathmines, Dublin. They were to command the convoy from there to Aiken Barracks, Dundalk, taking it on a given route from Dublin through Slane and Ardee to Dundalk. One of the former Lieutenants recalls:

> On arrival to Cathal Brugha Barracks, it became apparent that the convoy contained a large consignment of Lee-Enfield rifles, ammunition and gas masks. Unable to verify the exact quantities involved and the specific serial numbers of the rifles, I declined to sign [the] Issues and Receipt Voucher presented for my signature by the Ordnance Survey stores staff. That I was unable to check the correctness of the convoy's consignment was itself an irregular situation, but more worrying was the absence of any attendant armed escort party. The convoy was organised into two packets of three trucks each. The lead packet's first truck contained rifles, the second rifles and ammunition, the third ammunition. I sat in the lead truck. All three drivers were armed, as were their companions. However, in terms of security this was light or minimal. The convoy's second packet, to travel 15-minutes behind the first [and] commanded by the other officer, also had three trucks: two

containing gas masks and the third truck empty, [which] acted as
a spare in case of a breakdown. With a military police Land Rover
placed well out in front as a vanguard ahead of the first packet. I
briefed the drivers of the trucks to keep the truck behind in view.
That completed, we headed off on our northwards journey out of
Dublin's Southside to Aiken Barracks, Dundalk.

The specified route was not that most regularly taken to reach
Dundalk. Normally this involved turning right shortly after Slane
and proceeding to Dundalk via Drogheda. Having made our way
through the city and now beyond Slane, we were driving along the
prescribed irregular route and as the road was winding, twisting
and narrow, together with darkness having descended, it was
difficult to keep the truck behind in view. I was also distracted
by the fact that our radios were not working and concerned
with thoughts in my mind as to why we were here, that it was all
too easy to become intercepted by an armed body and was this
planned to happen? It was then that I noticed the third truck full
of ammunition was missing!

I ordered the driver of the lead truck beside me to pull over
onto the side of the road so that we could regroup and was shortly
joined only by the second truck. We waited and waited but no
third truck appeared. The Military Police Land Rover had lost
visual contact with us, so retraced its route and having located us
I directed them back to find the missing third truck. The Military
Police found the convoy's separate second packet of trucks but
there was no sign of the missing ammunition-carrying third
truck. Suspecting that for whatever reason the driver of the third
truck had mistakenly, or otherwise, taken the more usual, regular
route to Dundalk, I decided to phone Aiken Barracks, Dundalk,
to confirm that it had arrived. This, in the pre-mobile phone days,
required a pay phone and loose change. Both eventually found, I
got through to Aiken Barracks in Dundalk and ascertained that
… having mechanically struggled up the hill at Slane, the driver
[had] considered it prudent to travel the more familiar route to
Dundalk.

We proceeded to Dundalk on our given route and arrived at
Aiken Barracks. The Acting Post Commander, of Commandant

rank, ... was unhappy with the irregularity of the circumstances and was not prepared to take responsibility for the convoy, its content or to allow the consignment be unloaded, nor agree to provide an armed guard for it.

Having arrived to where [we were] ordered, albeit in unusual circumstances, I backed the six trucks up against each other, three abreast, and mounted our own guard. The acting Post Commander in Aiken Barracks was not happy. I, the Convoy Commander, was [also] not happy, the drivers now undertaking an overnight guard were not happy, the transport company unit who had provided the now not returning six trucks were not happy. All in all, for all involved, it was an irregular, unusual, unhappy situation and circumstance.

The gas masks were eventually emptied into a billet in the barracks and the three trucks released back to their unit. The three remaining trucks were left unloaded, the weapons and ammunition only taken off them two days later.

The 'Dundalk Arms Shipment', as it came to be called, and the likely intended release of arms and ammunition from army custody into Northern Ireland, had effectively been stalled. On hearing a report of the situation, the Taoiseach immediately insisted on the cessation of this unauthorised arrangement and the shipment of arms was cancelled. This unsanctioned effort to put Irish Defence Forces rifles and ammunition (obsolete but still deadly) into the hands of people in the North was a high level, but not governmentally authorised direction. The attempt to smuggle arms through the Defence Forces chain-of-command having failed, unbelievably a further clandestine ploy was revealed, but this too was fortuitously uncovered in the nick of time. Information was received about a surreptitious plot to bring a consignment of arms from the continent through Dublin Airport. A cloak-and-dagger episode of unparalleled gravity, it was a crisis within a crisis, the implications of which – if successfully executed, even in its very attempt – could have had a calamitous political effect. It might have completely undermined the diplomatic standing of the Irish Government and State. The 'Arms Crisis' was the greatest internal crisis since the Civil War in Ireland. With emotions throughout the country already running high due to the violent turn of events in the North, these were further legitimate concerns for stability in the South.

It appeared as if certain ministers were operating independently of Government policy on Northern Ireland. Two senior government ministers were sacked and a third resigned in sympathy. The two dismissed ministers were subsequently charged along with three others, one an Irish army Intelligence Officer, with conspiring to import arms. The 'Arms Trial' was a sensational development, though all the accused were acquitted. Previously, ill health had caused the prior resignation of a fourth minister and the early retirement of a parliament department General-Secretary. A hard-hit Irish Government had been engulfed in turmoil and it looked as if it might collapse and perhaps even unravel the stability of the State along with it. However, the government of the day faced down the volatility and upheld the law. They were not going to preside over a situation that would put the country at mortal risk, but as it was, the unprecedented challenges kept on coming.

On 3 April 1970, the murder of Garda Richard (Dick) Fallon had a profound effect on a southern public not yet inured to the violence that was engulfing Northern Ireland. Dick Fallon was the first member of the Garda Síochána to be murdered since 1942, when Garda George Mordant was shot dead by a wanted man he was attempting to arrest. It is believed that Chief Superintendent John Fleming, Head of the Special Branch, and Superintendent Phil McMahon went to the Department of Justice General Secretary with reports about the murder, likening it to the work of Saor Éire, a Republican splinter group. A reward of £5,000 was offered for information leading to the arrest and conviction of the perpetrators. Despite this offer, a detailed investigation and a wide sweep of republican suspects, nobody was ever convicted of the crime.

Garda Richard Fallon was one of three Gardaí responding to a call to check out the Royal Bank of Ireland in Dublin's Arran Quay when a cut telephone wire registered as an alarm fault. Two of the Gardaí got out of the patrol car and were walking towards the Bank's door just as the raiders were coming out, one of whom opened fire, killing Garda Fallon. On the day that he was buried, Dublin came to a complete standstill with 1,000 uniformed Gardaí lining the route. The group were believed to be responsible for a number of bank robberies and one member was blown to pieces as he was carrying a bomb along the Heuston Station to Connolly Station railway line near McKee Barracks. A second man was injured in the premature explosion. A relatively large crowd turned out for this funeral too, and it was an indication of some semblance of support for the IRA in the south. It was the nature and degree of this support, and perhaps more so its revolving nature, that was of concern to the Irish Government.

The intense political and sectarian rioting that took place in Northern Ireland during August 1969 caused outrage and anger; fright and fear; uneasiness and uncertainty. There was a sudden and sharp sensation of alarm, followed by concern and the awareness of a deep-seated patriotism. In the aftermath of the initial disturbances, with each wrong move of the British army deepening the crisis, a new emotive nationalism prevailed. How exactly this resurgent and impassioned patriotism was to find expression, in part or in full, had yet to be properly determined. The South was an independent state, but the painful reality of the attacks on Catholic homes in the Bogside and the Falls Road, the one-sided imposition of internment without trial, and the sheer awfulness of Bloody Sunday had to have a spill-over effect. Already the occurrences had proved to be a powerful recruiting force for PIRA, with other support mounting nationally and internationally. As well as recruits, money and guns were finding their way to the North while the political climate in the South was in danger of becoming a spectrum of the 'forty shades of green' of popular support for IRA.

The situation was developing from an atmosphere of ambivalence, arising from a latent newly reawakened nationalist sentiment. But what identity would shine through the ambiguity? The Irish Government had to shape and manage the situation to ensure this popular feeling did not manifest itself into large-scale violent militant republicanism. There was a danger that 'fuzzy thinking' in the populace about the depth and direction of its own nationalist identity did not play into the hands of the Provisional IRA. Those in the Dáil (Ireland's parliament), both in government and opposition, had a solid historical understanding of what had happened before – during the Civil War and the IRA campaign of the 1940s 'Emergency' – and some had personal political experience of the handling of the IRA's Border Campaign in the late 1950s.

On a personal level, many had lived those experiences and had long memories. They understood the value of peace and freedom and the price to be paid for it. They understood its fragility, and whatever happened they must preserve it. There was no need for them to be tutored in the necessity of holding the line to preserve the rule of law and to seek the ending of partition by peaceful means. They had a natural respect for the Defence Forces and the Garda Síochána having displayed loyalty to the State on a number of occasions since its foundation. They knew they were the ultimate defenders of the people's will, the State and its institutions. However, they also knew there were those whose thinking was very crude and dangerous, that an attitude existed among some that if Partition must end, and if blood had to be spilled, let it spill now, and get the matter finished with. The Government was adamant there must be no such flirtation with militant republicanism and its campaign of violence. There was strong anti-British feeling in many quarters and emotions were running high, a lot of genuine people were horrified at what was happening in the North and this had to be contained or it had the potential to cause serious trouble in the Republic too.

Nobody has the right under any guise to disregard the law as enacted by a freely elected parliament. Any illegal group so doing was challenging the government and the State's institutions first, but also the people themselves. The Provisional IRA and their supporters would willingly undermine this system of governance subverting the will of the people. The people were the State's centre of gravity, the 'hearts and minds' of the nation was the moral source of strength and the government was responsible for doing whatever would prevent the balance of public opinion tipping the wrong way. The Irish Government knew they had an onerous responsibility, sometimes without having corresponding control. The Government had to behave in a manner which would not make things worse for the minority in the North, nor to cause an even worse scenario for the Republic.

Externally, matters were critical and would remain so, internally the State could not countenance the presence of an illegal and armed body within its jurisdiction; its very existence challenging the government's authority to administer justice and exercise its power. It is both divisive and dangerous and Ireland has a bloody history and many haunting memories. There was, however, some tacit support for PIRA and the concept of 'a Nation once again' was very strong. There had been one in the past, but it possessed many versions: there were those 'sneaking regarders' and those with ambivalent attitudes, the sponsors, the sympathisers and supporters; there were the 'fellow travellers', who paid lip service; the 'public house patriots'; and there were those who physically and financially directly succoured and strengthened them. There was also the 'forty shades of green', the range of Republican support and sentiment that was constantly blurring.

At the sharp end, PIRA's operatives craved action and waged a guerrilla war. For their victims and their families there was no ambiguity and the Irish Government had to keep and maintain a credible grip on the feelings of the community. The Government had to mitigate the clamour for action and the demands for a more radical reaction towards the North. Nor could they countenance the desire to see a forced reunification. They had to portray a sense of responsible realism above the popular zeal. PIRA had received, propagated and capitalised upon the massive propaganda afforded by Unionist bigotry, B-Special brutality and British army blunders. The Provisional IRA's view had a salutary single-minded simplicity to it: create a desperate situation, make Northern Ireland ungovernable and the British would withdraw in exasperation.

Northern Ireland was a divided society from its formation, rooted in an ugly sectarianism where a necessary power-sharing situation was required but denied. The Provisional IRA had grasped the opportunity provided by the turmoil of the period, sinisterly exploiting the people as the circumstances unfolded and the Irish Government had to ensure that they did not unwittingly succeed in widening its grip into the republic. 'Tories out, North and South' was the Republican slogan and the Irish Government was in no doubt as to the damage that the Provisional IRA could cause. Yet neither could they be seen to approve of the British Government security initiatives and activities; they had to be seen to be taking a firm line with the British while also taking a similar position against the Provisional IRA. A balancing act was required externally for an internal audience; indeed trying to hold the governing party together from its own internal dissection was proving difficult. This was perhaps reflective of a wider dichotomy between some die-hards, who subscribed to the Irish physical force tradition, and those who favoured a consensual political approach. The tension within found voice at the 1971 Fianna Fáil Ard Fheis (the annual party conference) when a hot-headed party element gave full vent to the vitriol in chaotic, uproarious disorder. There were shouts and roars of both approval and disapproval; chants of 'We Want Jack' (Lynch to continue as party leader) and counter chants of 'Union Jack' (suggesting he was not sufficiently Republican). The commotion finally came to an end when a memorable and determined defence of the Party leader was made by Patrick Hillery, Minister for External Affairs, and cooler heads and composure won out; the wiser council progressing.

It was this wiser, more judicious and responsible common-sense course that was to underpin the Irish Government's approach to its security policy during the Troubles. Neither Westminster nor Stormont would talk politics with Dublin as they pursued a security solution. The Irish Government had therefore to pursue an approach tailored to the specific situation. The complexity of the conflict in Ireland was heavily influenced in the main by politics, but it was also sectarian and historic in character. There were a number of layers to the situation's creation, continued existence and potential solution. The first was to ensure the British produced a worthwhile political initiative, to move the Unionists from their traditionally intransigent stance. However, it is difficult to expel ignorance if you retain arrogance, none of which helped dampen public passions in the South nor prevented the Provisional IRA from exploiting them. A heavy-handed security policy would play into PIRA's hands, but Ireland had also to be defended and a firm, if not tough, stance was necessary. There could be no ambiguity about the pervading public ambivalence. There were no 'forty shades of green' here, the approach had to be moderated by an enlightened and unambiguous emphasis to dispel any sneaking sympathy.

***

The outrage that was Bloody Sunday was like a chord being struck in the national memory, stirring the psyche, and emotions were running high. A lot of people were horrified at the killing of unarmed demonstrators in Derry by the British army. However, there were those to whom the situation presented an opportunity and this was eagerly seized upon by a hard core of protestors outside the British Embassy at 39 Merrion Square, Dublin, on 2 February 1972. The troublemakers began hurling stones and bottles at the building as a hugely outnumbered cordon of Gardaí valiantly attempted to preserve order, inevitably in vain. Petrol bombs were thrown and some in the crowd clambered up onto the first floor balcony of the house next door, smashed the shutters of the Ambassador's room, poured in petrol and started a fire. The crowds obstructed the Fire Brigade from reaching the burning building or cut their hoses. As Des O'Malley, Minister for Justice, recalls:

> I was in my office in the Department of Justice. With me was the Minister for Defence, Jerry Cronin, the Chief-of-Staff, Major General Sean MacKeown, and the Garda Commissioner, Michael Wymes. We could see the flames from my office window and were receiving reports from the scene. The Garda Commissioner urged caution, the Chief-of-Staff said he had 200 troops concealed across the square behind Leinster House but was reluctant to send them into the fray unless they had live ammunition and the authority to use it. I was not prepared to play into the hands of the Provisional IRA, authorising the opening of fire on our own people to protect a 'British building' after the outrage of what had occurred on Bloody Sunday. As soon as I heard it confirmed that everyone was safely out, along with their classified files, cypher equipment and other necessities, I let it go up. With the building aflame, the venting of passions was satisfied and the emotions were burned off along with the building. It demonstrated, however, that the Provos had the ability to cause serious trouble in the Republic too.

For the Irish Government, since August 1969 events in Northern Ireland had been one crisis after another. The outbreak of street violence and house burnings at the outset of the Troubles, the murder of Garda Richard Fallon, the 'Arms Trial', the emergence of the Provisional IRA, the blundering of the British army and now Bloody Sunday and the burning of the British Embassy in Dublin. The already shaky position of the Government was now extremely precarious and the threat posed by the Provisional IRA to the democratic institutions in the Republic was far more serious. Military operations were not the solution to the problems in Northern Ireland. Solutions needed to be found through political means based on the full equality of treatment for everyone.

The Political initiative was with the British, but they were not taking it, while the armed 'military' initiative was with the Provisional IRA, who *were* taking full advantage of the situation. The Irish Government was in the middle, frustrated and trying to persuade all sides, though no one was listening. The objective had to be to show that political activity was more beneficial than violence. In the South the public mood was fragile, and the Government was left with a situation full of difficulty and danger.

CHAPTER 6

Truckloads of Troops

The clamour, the uproar, the shouting and yelling was overwhelming and the large crowd was in a hostile mood. The commotion was confusing, the riot was supposed to be inside Mountjoy Prison, not outside it as well! When RTÉ (Radio Teilifís Éireann), the Irish State television channel, had announced on the news that the prison riot was taking place, it was like a rallying call and people from all over the country gathered outside in support of the prisoners protesting inside. The demonstrators had overturned cars and set them alight and were busy throwing stones and bottles at the Gardaí. Into this melée arrived truckloads of troops from the Defence Forces, having responded to an Aid to the Civil Power (ATCP) request to give assistance to the Gardaí to restore order inside the prison.

At 8 pm on 19 May 1972, a group of Provisional IRA prisoners had overpowered the prison officers, seized the keys to the cells and released upwards of thirty fellow prisoners; B Wing was taken over and three prison officers held hostage. The prisoners then went on a rampage, mindlessly wrecking the interior of the building. They sang songs, shouted slogans, and some who had clambered up onto the cell block roof were making demands and giving a running commentary to reporters outside the prison walls on what was happening inside. 'There is no prison left,' one prisoner told the assembled journalists, 'it is gone inside and there will be no walls left unless we get our conditions by tomorrow morning.' They claimed to be protesting against conditions inside the prison, the length of time being held on remand without trial and the refusal of release on parole in some instances for inmates. They had directed their ire in destroying the newly completed kitchen and dental facilities in the prison wing. The situation was beyond the control of the prison officers and Gardaí and so the army were called in:

It had been a day's leave for me and shortly after 8 pm I had arrived back to Collins Barracks, Dublin, and became aware of a lot of activity in the main square. A riot company, its equipment and transport was being assembled. Mountjoy Prison was in a state of riot and we, the 5th Battalion, were the lead company going in. Fifteen minutes later, with no orders other than [to] report to the Senior Garda Officer present in situ, we were ready to go. Before exiting the Barrack main gate proper, the main gate policeman stepped forward and informed me that there was a phone call for me. To my astonishment it was the Defence Forces Chief-of-Staff, Major General LL O'Carroll, to wish me good luck on my mission, and with that we headed out the gates of the barracks.

On approaching Mountjoy Prison there was a large unruly mob outside and a violent disturbance was ongoing around the exterior of the prison's perimeter. Our trucks pulled up and while our troops were 'shacking out' (getting organised into an orderly and appropriate formation with their equipment) I went forward towards the prison gate with my signaller/radioman accompanying me. Some of the disorderly mob were between the two of us and the prison gate and as I strode forward I was wondering to myself how I was going to navigate this situation. However, the small in stature signaller/radioman accompanying me had also taken in the scene and without any prompting from me he used a long baton in his possession to skilfully strike out at the knees of those blocking us and cleared a path to the main gate without losing a step.

We went into the prison, where I was met by a Garda Superintendent who briefed me to the effect that three hostages had been taken [and] the wing was in the control of the prisoners, some of whom were on the roof. The phone rang and it was the Minister for Justice, Mr Des O'Malley, who wished to speak with me. For some reason I declined to answer and instead had the conversation relayed through the Garda Superintendent. The Minister wished to know if I had CS gas with me and had I intended using it, I think in the sense of comfortingly encouraging me to do so. Surprising myself, I replied that the Mater Hospital was nearby and really it was an operational decision for me to make. The conversation ended there and I thought no more about it because a copy of the layout of the prison, which I had previously requested, was handed to me and I concentrated on this. My focus went to the block housing the 'political prisoners' and I asked, under the present circumstances was there any place possible to infiltrate, or otherwise to secretly and gradually make a covert point of entry. By now a platoon from Clancy Barracks had joined me and at a point identified we surreptitiously gained access.

Our sudden appearance inside the prison wing and that of the riot company outside now revealing themselves caught the prisoners off-guard, knocked their composure off-balance and threw them into complete confusion. I greeted them in Irish and continuing through this medium [told] them to return to their cells or resolute action would be taken. They were entirely bewildered and bemused by the appearance of the military, who had arrived in numbers, well equipped, orderly, disciplined and obviously purposefully determined. They realised they had bitten off more than they could chew and now in disarray at the point of confrontation decided they had made their point and that their protest was at an end. With order restored, the riot, having altogether lasted six hours, was over.

This show of physical force, weight of numbers, professional posture, discipline and cohesiveness, overtly and obviously held together by a system of command and control, was what the Defence Forces – if resourced and empowered – could contribute in response to the challenge.

The outbreak of large-scale violence in Northern Ireland caused deep unease that it could precipitate a worse tragedy across the entire island. The root causes of the conflict were difficult to get at and the Troubles lasted for far longer than anyone expected. From the beginnings of the conflict, the Irish Government's position was that there was no room for force or coercion in Irish policy towards Northern Ireland. Unity was only to be achieved through peaceful means, and significantly the rule of law must be maintained and made to prevail down south. To meet the ever-changing challenge of the Provisional IRA and other groups involved military intervention in civil affairs. This did not mean Irish soldiers acting as policemen, but rather in a role that was not quite military. To achieve this the Defence Forces had first to deploy then conduct necessary framework operations, followed intermittently by intelligence-led or reactive surge operations. However, throughout it all, the Gardaí Síochána took the lead and the Defence Forces aided them. In the prevailing circumstances, force may be used against those groups attempting to subvert the State. The Garda Síochána were essentially an unarmed service, a posture favoured by themselves, the government and the general public at large. Force had to be met by force and how it was applied was an all-important matter, too little and hesitancy would imply weakness, while being too heavy-handed would be counter-productive.

The swaying of public opinion for or against the State's institutions was an important consideration. Any approach regarding the use of force had to be measured, appropriate and proportionate. For their part, the Provisional IRA held the Irish Government in contempt, regarding the Dáil as an illegitimate institution, and operated well outside the law.

The Aid to Civil Power policy placed the Garda Síochána in the lead, with primacy over operations and the Defence Forces there to support them. It was a very wise policy and proved steadfast in such a difficult situation. There was a very close working relationship and regard for each other's role. There was an overall mutual respect but, it has to be said, without either force necessarily trusting the other wholeheartedly. The Defence Forces' reservations stemmed from the nature of the actual ATCP role itself and the active application of it by the Gardaí.

Although definitely a role for the military, operating in the arena of Internal Security – within the State's boundaries and among the people – is as often as not an undesired role. It may even be said it is one to which the military has an aversion as it fundamentally compromises the core principles under which armies operate, concentration of force chief amongst them. Dispersing units into many infinitesimal sub-units over a large area with an overly extended span of control and stretched lines of communication dilutes the sole chain of command. Armies fight armies in open conventional form on a battleground, operating within the rules of war. Aid the Civil Power meant the Defence Forces had to adapt and adhere to a totally different tempo and mind-set, and work to a completely different code of conduct and rules of engagement. It also required new standard operating procedures and operational guidelines. In the first instance, militaries operate against identified threats, determine what end state is required, apply capabilities to achieve effects and determine a 'troops to task' ratio to achieve the identified objectives. If you set a mission for the military and make operational demands of it, it is preferable in their eyes not to tell them how to do it, but instead to identify the effect you want to achieve and for how long, allocate the resources and let them get on with the task. Give a soldier a clear mission, adequate means and let them set themselves to the task, however difficult.

The specific reservations, reluctance and reticence of the Defence Forces in operating alongside the Garda Síochána arose from these fundamental differing views in relation to awareness and understanding of their respective comprehensions regarding a defined command and control structure, as importantly as the cultural gap between the forces; Gardaí normally operate as individuals in the course of their duty. A young Garda has the authority to arrest the Garda Commissioner himself if the latter is breaking the law. On the other hand, soldiers operate in units and sub-units under a very clearly defined chain of command and adhere to very strict discipline.

The Garda Síochána annual duty roster lists Garda for one of three inflexible 8-hour shifts within any 24-hour working day, extending for twelve months. This meant that manpower levels were not always readily available in response to putting sufficient Gardaí towards specific incidents. It was almost as if the occurrence would have to operate around their duty roster rather than the other way around, which it most certainly was for the military. Therefore, if the duty roster could not provide the manpower levels required for specific situations, the incentive of overtime allowances necessarily had to be offered and the costs incurred. This was all well and good in its own right, however, an 'overtime culture' was sometimes evident, which even in itself was not a difficulty *per se*, but it perhaps led, in turn, to an approach where the military sometimes felt the Gardaí were looking after the Gardaí, secure in the knowledge that the army were looking after the situation. Regardless of overtime being paid or not, this led to a feeling amongst the military that there was a tendency for the Gardaí to sit back and let the army worry about the operation.

These different approaches were evident also through the Defence Forces eyes of the Gardaí being more laid back, informal and casual – punctuality was not a priority – whereas the Defence Forces were generally attentive to time and place. In areas other than the border, where Gardaí were gathered for large-scale operations or reacting to incidents, it became obvious that they were not comfortable marshalling big numbers on large scale protracted operations. It took them a long time to understand 'crowd control' and the use of the riot drill. At the time it could not be expected to be their forte, as they operated differently, but it seemed that any push towards conforming to and with military codes was beyond them. The establishment of designated Garda along the border, consisting of a Superintendent or Inspector, and larger Garda stations, with four sergeants and twenty-eight Gardaí, helped to minimise the Command and Control difficulties as closer liaison and cooperation between them and the local Defence Forces battalions and companies developed.

The Defence Forces felt that the Provisional IRA Active Service Units (ASU) had worked out Garda weaknesses and were using them to their advantage; the by-the-clock shift changeover times and perhaps lesser attentiveness to areas where divisional boundaries intersected or were remote – each leaving it to the other, thereby no one paid too much attention as to what was taking place – hence it made a good location to work in. But the Gardaí were 'in the lead' and the Defence Forces there 'to support' – that is how it was and it worked. There were many dedicated, professional, skilful Gardaí and the Defence Forces loved to operate alongside those members hungry for the task.

For their part, the Gardaí had their perspective too – some members resented working alongside soldiers who they knew came from 'troublesome' families, or may even have had direct policing encounters with themselves. Many army officers were the sons of serving and former Gardaí. In the 35th Cadet Class alone (January 1961–July 1962) of the twenty-six members, five had fathers who were Gardaí. Members of the Defence Forces and Garda Síochána working together also often found that they came from the same counties and communities, clubs and parishes, or indeed sports clubs as each other, yet the different institutionalised cultures inherent within each organisation threatened to present a gap too wide to bridge.

Underpinning this, it was felt by the Defence Forces that there was resistance by the Garda Síochána to adopt management measures to foster a functioning cohesiveness into the Command and Control structure of the force. There was a sensed top-down reluctance to appreciate what this lacking Command, Control and Communication (militarily known as C3) structure could bring to them. Places were even offered to Garda Síochána personnel on its own Defence Forces Command and Staff Course but the offer was not taken up. The Defence Forces appreciated the value of what ongoing structured education meant for their management personnel, making them more open to, and adept at, managing change. This inter-organisational cooperation often only worked efficiently due to good but individual instances of person-to-person working relationships, which was enough to find, forge and fix the firmest of common ground. There was common cause and while this was mostly a good and solid basis on which to interact, it was in realty not without its reservations and remoteness.

The decision to deploy troops to support a state's police force is, in a sense, an easy one to make. It is this decision's reversal where matters become complicated, because if proved to be premature, whoever made the decision must face and take the responsibility for it. Faced with a spate of armed bank robberies, and murders of Gardaí once again becoming prevalent – there were twelve Troubles-related murders of Gardaí between 1970 and 1996 – the issue of arming the Gardaí was considered. Given that these events were happening in a wider overall security-related context, the threat not only confined to these occurrences, arming the Gardaí alone would simply not have been enough. The magnitude of the problem was too great for that measure on its own to address the situation and so the Defence Forces were called upon. However, putting 'state weapons' on the streets is more serious and complex than first imagined. Countering the threat, containing the violence, combating the fear and intimidation is important and the government must be being seen to take action, to reassure the public and make matters more difficult for the IRA.

Not so clearly seen and understood was the ever so gradual increase in the tasks assigned to the Defence Forces as inevitable 'mission creep' – the expansion of the roles required and the duties performed by the military – emerged. All this necessitated the proportionate allocation of resources, which all too often happened too slowly, inadequately or not at all. This 'security on a shoestring', if allowed to prevail, overburdened the military and could have debased the very quality of the security it was meant to provide in the first place. Sustaining the role over time, in many cases years, indeed decades, was another complication, the nature and conditions under which they performed were often difficult and demanding.

Irish Taoiseach Jack Lynch gave Des O'Malley, his newly appointed Minister for Justice, clear instructions to ensure that the IRA was curtailed. Des O'Malley pressed for the introduction of an effective legal response to the threat and one of his main concerns was to ensure the institutions of the State continued to work effectively – chief amongst them the legal system – and prevent the widespread intimidation of jurors. On 26 May 1972, the Irish Government brought Section 5 of the Offences of the State Act (1939) back into operation. This established the Special Criminal Court consisting of three judges sitting without a jury, which sat for the first time on 8 June 1972; ordinary criminal law would have been wholly inadequate if employed against the Provisional IRA.

Special Criminal Courts had been established previously in Ireland during the 'Emergency' years, when matters of defence, security and subversion had to be grappled with. Leading up to and during the Second World War, at the same time the Irish Government was combating the threat from the IRA they also had to deal with the very real possibility of a Nazi invasion. A bombing campaign in Britain was initiated by the IRA in January 1939, following the rejection by Lord Halifax, the British Foreign Secretary, of an Irish ultimatum demanding the withdrawal of all British forces and civilian representatives from Ireland, a campaign that continued for months. Nazi Germany wished to support the IRA in their creation of this havoc, so Oskar Pfaus, a member of the Abwehr, the German military intelligence organisation, was ordered to establish contact with them to act as agents for sabotage and innate insurgency in potential collaboration with the Nazis. Joachim von Ribbentrop, Hitler's Foreign Minister, appointed his coup d'état specialist, Edmund Veesenmayer, to ignite insurrection in Ireland. In May 1940, a radio link between Germany and the IRA broke down so a Nazi agent, Hermann Görtz, was parachuted into Ireland to promote an uprising and bring about a violent overthrow of the Irish Government. The Germans believed that the twenty-fifth anniversary of the 1916 Easter Rising could be an opportune moment for a landing, psychologically that is, if occasion and circumstance did not lead them to invade before then.

Following the German invasion of Europe, on 7 June 1940 a 'State of Emergency' was declared by the Irish Government. Ireland declared itself neutral, but the dilemma for de Valera's government was that they could not be seen to invite attacks from without if not being able to keep order within. His response to the IRA's British campaign was the introduction of the Offences against the State Act, which became law on 14 June 1939. This gave the Irish Government of the time the authority to establish a military tribunal and to order arrests and detention without trial. The bombing campaign continued and in December 1939 the IRA raided the Magazine Fort in Dublin's Phoenix Park and carried off thirteen lorry loads of ammunition, most of which was recovered quickly afterwards. De Valera acted quickly and harshly to ensure that his entire policy of neutrality was not jeopardised. During the Emergency, 550 members of the IRA were interned in military custody in the Curragh Camp. Six members were sentenced to death for the murder of six Gardaí, and were subsequently executed, while three others were allowed to die on hunger strike. Through this strong Government stand, backed up by the Garda Síochána and the Defence Forces, the IRA threat was averted.

The IRA was to engage in a further armed campaign, mounting 'Operation Harvest', mostly a border campaign, from December 1956 to February 1962. In all a total of twelve were killed; six IRA members and six RUC (four of the six IRA in a premature explosion), and overall nearly forty were wounded. The first year saw half of the overall total attacks on border custom posts and RUC barracks take place. In July 1957, the Irish Government's Taoiseach, Seán Lemass, reintroduced the Offences Against the State Act (1939) and military tribunals handed down lengthy sentences. Initially, some sixty IRA activists were rounded up by Gardaí and interned under Defence Forces guard in the Curragh camp, where Number 1 Internment Camp had been rapidly prepared for its new intake. Barbed wire entanglements were strengthened and the camp was surrounded by five sets of fences. Two fence lines were erected, outside of which was a 6-foot deep, 8-foot wide trench, complete with tripwires connected to flares to prevent tunnelling. Three more lines of fence were laid out beyond. Inside the camp there were four forty-man huts (at peak an occupancy of 131 was reached).

Escapes were attempted; the first from the internment camp medical hut when two inmates sawed through the bars of the window of a shower room to get onto unfenced open ground. A large search operation followed, with troops from the Curragh involved, and a number of nights later the two escapees were discovered sleeping in a ditch covered with sacks. A second attempt was thwarted by an alert guard who noticed some tunnel soil that had not been concealed properly. However, a third attempt on 27 September 1958 was successful. A playing field was available for the internees and when its grass was cut it was put into piles around the edge. Some of the grass was taken by a number of internees and glued to a groundsheet. On the selected day the groundsheet was smuggled to the edge of the playing field during a football match, placed in a corner and further grass was thrown onto it. Masked by onlookers, two internees, Dáithí Ó Conaill and Ruairí Ó Brádaigh, slipped under the groundsheet and later escaped. Improvised wire cutters were used in the next attempt on 2 December 1958, when twenty-six selected internees made a determined effort to escape. The attempt in progress was discovered by a guard, but not before the first four would-be escapees had succeeded in cutting through the first fence. This cleared the route for the others to follow and they all successfully negotiated the first two fences.

The trench obstacle, however, proved a more difficult impediment and the group was reduced to ten following the hindrance of aimed leg shots by the guards and the obstruction of the blinding flash effect of ammonia grenades. An immediate follow-up by troops saw furze bushes set alight to flush out escapees from likely hiding places. One such covered area, a field with a substantial ditch about a mile away, was where the remaining escaped prisoners regrouped. Two were unable to carry on because of their injuries, and with the troops closing in on them fast the group split into two and moved off in different directions. Two more escapees were subsequently picked up in further extensive searches. This was the last of the escape attempts and the internment camp was closed in March 1959. In February 1962, the IRA 'Border Campaign' ended.

Stern but necessary, the measures proved expedient and effective in countering the 1940s and 1950s IRA campaigns, respectively. Now, a decade and a half later under more fraught and difficult circumstances – causing far greater public unease – it was once more required of the Government of the day to gauge their usefulness. It had been only two weeks after the burning of the British Embassy that the prisoners in Dublin's Mountjoy Prison had rioted and severely damaged the new prison wing. The decision was taken by the Government to transfer some of the republican prisoners from Mountjoy to military custody in the Curragh Camp's 'Glasshouse' (military detention centre). The Curragh plains would shortly and subsequently become the scene of demonstrations as supporters of the inmates protested repeatedly, sometimes violently. The first such demonstration witnessed agitation more so than aggression as a tentative and uncertain – if not exactly faltering – defence was made by the troops when faced for the first time by a group of well-practised protestors from the North. Irish troops formed a line when confronted by members of the 'People's Democracy' and the 'Northern Resistance Movement' well versed in protest. The surging crowd pressed right up against the line of soldiers standing steady with their rifles 'at the ready' complete with fixed bayonets, but the demonstrators did not gain access beyond that point. Shouts and taunts, sarcasm and sneering insults were heaped upon the soldiers by the protestors, in response to which the megaphoned message by the officer-in-charge bluntly informed them that the troops would use their bayonets if necessary.

This rather bizarre and face-to-face civil–military stand-off could have become untidy except for the stoic, calm, uncomplaining and highly disciplined restraint against verbal provocation and the physically antagonising practice of throwing flour bombs and tins of paint over the soldiers; the arrival of riot-clad reinforcements held in reserve proving timely. This first event played itself out within the confines of the Curragh Camp about 100 yards from the Detention Centre itself. Both sides learned and both sides would return more determined the next time. This 'next time', the attending media were invited inside the military line, their images subsequently reflecting the reality of the demonstrators' unruly aggression and hostile behaviour, throwing stones and violently attempting to force their way through the line.

There was an unstated but succinct edge to this demonstration; the Defence Forces clear about the challenge before them because underlying it was a growing sense of an emergent real threat to the Republic from the newly materialised Provisional IRA and their political wing, Provisional Sinn Féin. They began to gain traction in the Republic from 1970 to 1971, and from early 1972 onwards, particularly after the emotive response in the Republic to the Bloody Sunday massacre in Derry. Recruitment, sympathy and support for PIRA increased. Bank robberies in the Republic became an almost weekly event in order to raise funds for the campaign in the North. Protest marches and demonstrations under a Provisional Sinn Féin banner increased as did protestors' demonstrations to the Curragh Camp, seeking the release of Provisional IRA prisoners in the Curragh Detention Centre.

With the battle lines drawn, facing down PIRA and Sinn Féin was now an issue and the military erected a basic barbed wire perimeter barricading access to the Curragh Camp's western (Detention Centre) end. They had themselves called in 'truckloads of troops' as reinforcements, specifically from the 4th Battalion Group, which consisted of one Company each from the 4th, 6th and 12th Battalions. This was the first tangible step towards developing a cohesive unit to assist in dealing with internal threats arising anywhere within the State. There were also fire tenders ready in reserve, and one or two other measures necessary to repel a breach in their defences. Another expedient step was to drown out the protestors with three loudspeakers mounted on a lorry, which kept up a continuous din. However, the noise angered the crowd giving rise to scuffles with the Gardaí, after which more violent exchanges erupted along the line.

Continuing to provocatively jeer at the soldiers, and subjecting them to a hail of bricks, branches and broken banners, the protestors attempted to tear away the coils of barbed wire, only to be met by a deliberate and dogged defence, the clashes going the way of the Curragh Camp defenders. Commandant Ray Stuart (Retd.), born and raised and at the time living in the Curragh Camp, was then a Corporal, Cavalry Corps, and stood amongst those defending the camp: 'The protestors were loud and aggressive, intent on trouble and forcing entry through the barbed wire, which was both a demarcation line and a deterrent, only it was not restraining them. However, we were determined to stand in defence of our post, the Detention Centre, and that we definitely did.' The Detention Centre defending force was also augmented by members of the FCÁ on 'summer camp' in Stephen's Barracks, Kilkenny. Acting Company Sergeant Barry Bowman (Retd.), 20th Battalion (Pearse Battalion) D Company, Griffith Barracks, Dublin, recalls:

> I remember being called into Plunkett Barracks in the Curragh early one Saturday morning while attending a formal (training) camp in Kilkenny; those below the rank of Corporal being allowed to go home for the weekend. On arrival, we were told that the protestors were expected at noon. We had three hours' notice; riot training began in earnest. We were equipped with batons, shields and CS Gas. We practised moving forward in unison, hitting the shields with the batons as our left foot hit the ground. It had a stirring, salutary effect on us, however the exertion, when repeated, became gradually exhausting, energy sapping and debilitating. However, there was a job to be done and the protestors duly arrived. There was much disturbance and I remember seeing uniformed Gardaí being flour bombed and those soldiers in the forward positions having paint thrown over them. The protestors, despite their best efforts, were denied entry to the camp and after an exhausting day and all the anticipation and excitement; I remember we all drank the NCO's mess dry that night.

Colonel Bill Egan (Retd.), a member of the 4th Battalion Group remembers:

> I was with the 4th Battalion Group when the provisional protestors attacked the Curragh Camp. We were equipped and we were eager for the fray. We were confident, well trained, had hardy lads with us and good NCOs as well. I remember we were not at all afraid of the situation in any way. You could say that we were certain of ourselves and did not look too kindly on their hostility. I recall we lined up facing westwards and they were kept out of the Curragh.

Some months later, on 29 October 1972, a number of prisoners succeeded in burrowing their way out of their cells, using spoons and chisels, in an 8-foot deep, 12-foot long U-shaped underground tunnel, exiting in the middle of the exercise yard. An alert guard spotted them, intervened and succeeded in apprehending four would-be escapees. However, seven others scaled the 20-foot perimeter by means of a rope ladder and fled into the darkness.

Not long after, then Provisional IRA Chief-of-Staff Seán Mac Stíofáin was arrested after a controversial radio interview and on 25 November 1972 he was sentenced to six months' imprisonment for membership of the IRA. Despite a ban, RTÉ had allowed an interview to be broadcast between Mac Stíofáin and one of the station's reporters, Kevin O'Kelly. The Government subsequently dismissed the entire RTÉ authority. Mac Stíofáin immediately declared that he was going on hunger strike and was transferred from Mountjoy to the Mater Hospital in Dublin. An escape attempt was mounted at the hospital when armed Provisional IRA activists disguised as priests tried unsuccessfully to spring him. Despite shots being fired, his would-be rescue party succeeded only in joining him in becoming incarcerated themselves. Mac Stíofáin was removed to the Curragh Military Hospital. In Ireland, many towns had military barracks; the Curragh was a unique opposite, it was a military camp with a town in it.

Barbed wire and barriers, military policemen and armed sentries, arc lights and blocked access, the Curragh Camp was suddenly barricaded and large areas of it out of bounds. Entry to the rest was restricted and the atmosphere of the Camp altered; its nature was never quite the same again. A wing of the Curragh Military Hospital was fortified and over the coming years was to host other high-security prisoners transferred for overnight medical treatment and for longer periods. A special Hospital Guard was mounted and hospital staff rostered for the entire duration of each treatment. As it happened, Mac Stíofáin's presence in the Curragh was cause for further protest. Commandant Brendan Rohan (Retd.), then a cadet, recalls:

> I remember our Cadet class being herded into the drill shed in the Cadet School and issued pick axe handles and dustbin lids and told that we were the reserve platoon for the front-line troops

being attacked on the barricade into the Curragh Camp. The reason was that Seán Mac Stíofáin, then on hunger strike, had been transferred to the Curragh Hospital. The troops on the front line initially found the rioters very reasonable, so it was a relatively peaceful stand-off until a bus of 'professional rioters' arrived from Northern Ireland. They attacked with ball bearings propelled from catapults and Molotov cocktails with petrol and paint mixed so that it stuck as well as burned. The officer in charge of the camp's defence had been assigned the camp's fire engine as a water cannon. The Northerners laughed because they were used to real water cannons, not a gentle sprinkle. In any event, at a point in time it had to [be refilled] only it is believed not from the water tower as expected, but from the camp's sewage farm. The demonstrators ran in every direction.

As it happened, Mac Stíofáin ended his hunger strike after fifty-seven days, losing influence within the Provisional IRA.

If the atmosphere in the Curragh had changed alarmingly as a consequence of the Troubles, so too did that throughout the Republic as well, not only around other Defence Forces barracks. This was to get all the more fraught as events unfolded, even before the year's end. Abhorrence was felt at the Provisional IRA's engagement in their campaign of violence, 'no warning' bombings in particular. Support withered and sympathy and camaraderie with the organisation declined. The movement's appeal was hurt badly and the Government's approach became more assured. An amendment to the Offences Against the State Act was sought by the Government whereby the word of a Chief Superintendent became sufficient evidence to convict a suspect of IRA membership.

Despite receiving the support of the leader of the opposition, Liam Cosgrave, his party members in Fine Gael were not as supportive and the vote on the measure was looking unlikely to succeed. Dramatically, on 1 December, when the amendment was being debated in the Dáil, two bombs exploded, one close to the CIÉ (Córas Iompair Éireann) bus depot at Sackville Place off O'Connell Street and another close to Liberty Hall. Two people were killed (George Bradshaw and Tommy Duffy) and 127 were injured. After hearing the reverberation from the actual explosions and news of the casualties, Fine Gael abstained from the vote and the measure passed. It was considered unlikely that the Provisional IRA was responsible for the bombings, as it was not in their best interests to do so, and the incident was indicative of the conflict morphing into the sinister and the covert.

PART 2

THE BORDER

CHAPTER 7

Soldiering on the FEBA

Someday you'll be on the border, and you'll have to make a decision. And you'll have to ask yourself – is it a decision the Taoiseach wants you to make?

(Irish Cadet School Instructor to Cadet Class, 1975.)

Heavy water-laden clouds hung in a low, slate coloured sky as a gusting, swirling wind drove continuous cold and cascading sheets of unrelenting rain downwards and sideways. Exposed for hours to the soaking wild, windy rawness of the winter squall, the soldiers at the border checkpoint huddled from the inclement weather and vainly attempted to seek warmth and protection against the elements. Within their already rain-sodden combat uniforms, their outer wet gear and heavy plastic ponchos were no match for the constant downpour.

Shivering involuntarily, the Defence Forces troops alternated between stamping their boots on the tarmac-surfaced road and extending their fingers within gloved hands, momentarily loosening the grip on their FN rifles, to aid blood circulation and regain some feeling in their extremities against the chilling numbness. Although they took turns to seek shelter – of sorts – behind their Land Rover, this was not where their duty required them to be so they maintained 'covering off' positions around the checkpoint by crouching in soggy ditches, lying on waterlogged ground or standing on the roadway, poised and postured to provide protection for the two Garda Síochána (policemen) with them – who for the most part sat inside their vehicle with the engine running and the heater on.

Sometimes that was just the way of it and a soldier's fatalistic acceptance of his lot was what sustained him. This was also true when an indiscreet Garda might occasionally make reference to the overtime rates and allowances. The muted reaction of the military – who did not share parity of such payments, but who shared the same risk and responsibility – suggested that perhaps the matter was better left unexplored. There was a job to be done and better to concentrate on it; the uncertainty of the task not allowing for complacency or distraction. For now, it was enough to stay vigilant while coping with the streams of water sweeping across the stormy landscape, the lashing rain splattering and surging headlong into them.

It was barely mid-afternoon and the premature wintry dullness blurred into darkness. The blustery wind and the incessant rain soon began to make the surrounding terrain indistinguishable, and the checkpoint party's eyes wandered along the roadway stretching out in front of them in the direction of any would-be oncoming northbound and southbound traffic from across or approaching the border. Their gaze took in the road's rough undulations and the wild swaying of the stunted trees and shrubbery on either side. Inevitably, their stare veered towards the nearby bungalows, farmhouses and dwellings, minds musing at the normality of the household rhythm within; the typical everyday functioning of comfortable family routines and their ordinary cosy commonplace reality.

In contrast, the Defence Forces' role was both physically and psychologically removed from normal life, the contrast cutting sharply. They wondered whether those inside were reassured, supportive and appreciative of the checkpoint's presence. They were not there to be admired, they knew that, they were there – and elsewhere – to monitor the northward movements of known and suspected Provisional IRA activists, to prevent them transporting weapons and bombs, to 'fly the flag' and demonstrate a presence against incursions southwards by the British army patrols and loyalist paramilitaries (the UVF Death Squads) and were otherwise placed on the ground to react as necessary or directed. This was the Border, often informally referred to as the 'FEBA' – Forward Edge of the Battle Area, a term taken from conventional warfare military manuals – all 301 meandering miles of it (485 km) with 285 border crossings. It could quickly become a very dangerous place – half of the total number of Royal Ulster Constabulary (RUC) and British army fatalities during the Troubles occurred along the Border.

A few months previously, at 0400 hours (4 am) on 31 July 1972, the British army launched Operation Motorman, seizing the initiative and opportunity afforded by the unpopular public reaction to the Provisional IRA's Bloody Friday bombing fiasco. The aim was to enter and occupy the firmly established no-go areas of Belfast and Derry, within which the Provisional IRA gunmen had held complete control, roaming the streets with total impunity. The communities within were held in the grip of the paramilitaries who were meting out their own justice: beating, knee-capping, tar and feathering and shooting. The RUC had dared not enter, wisely leaving the hornet's nest unprovoked. All roads into the no-go areas were barricaded, except the main ones, and checkpoints controlled who entered and left. Municipal services to these areas had ceased; refuse collection, road clearing and public lighting – most of the street lighting had been shot out anyway. Rents and utility bills (gas, electricity etc.) had not been paid and many cars were untaxed and uninsured, indeed many of the cars used there were stolen.

The British army had not underestimated the task in hand and had concentrated some 21,000 troops in Northern Ireland in advance of the operation, including British NATO troops stationed in West Germany brought in to swell the numbers. Considerable planning, 'war gaming' of options and possible outcomes, courses of action and other necessary preparations preceded the plan being put into action. Royal Engineer Centurion AVRE Bulldozer tanks, to remove the barricades in Derry, were landed off four landing craft from HMS *Fearless*, which had journeyed up the 25-mile Foyle estuary escorted by the minesweeper HMS *Gavington*. The landing craft arrived minutes before midnight, with the Bulldozer tanks coming ashore over pre-laid tracking. The Operation's intention had been broadcast in advance to give the Provisional IRA the opportunity to leave the areas so that bloodshed could be avoided.

However, if PIRA gunmen were prepared to stand and offer opposition – they were prepared both to take and accept casualties – then all this had to be taken into account. It was the biggest British army operation mounted since the Suez Canal crisis in 1956. Although not completely without fatalities, (two people were killed during the operation), there was little resistance encountered as eleven fully equipped British army battalions, complete with all necessary support, moved into the Belfast no-go areas. The Provisional IRA gunmen melted away in advance, as they did prior to internment, many crossing south over the border but staying within the confines of the 'War Zone' – the border counties.

Upon successfully entering the no-go areas, British army units took over previously identified potential 'strong point' buildings: schools, factories, mills and the like, fortified them against attack, made them habitable, then set about 'dominating' the area and building up an intelligence picture. Bloody Friday and Operation Motorman gave the initiative back to the British army. Previously they had struggled to get to grips with the proliferation, progress and success of the Provisional IRA's development and operational effectiveness; a problem compounded by the British army's mistakes which brought them into conflict with the Catholic nationalist community, who now viewed them as a force of occupation – the speed of which had been beyond the expectation of the Provisional IRA strategists. Heretofore the British army was without a Northern Ireland Operational Headquarters and possessed neither an Intelligence Organisation nor sources, and were not operating like the Irish Defence Forces were in Aid to the Civil Power.

The continued existence of the sectarian regime did immeasurable harm to politics in Northern Ireland and overall was very damaging, providing the Provisional IRA with domestic and international credibility. The Provisional IRA, despite the setbacks of Bloody Friday and Operation Motorman, knew they continued to gain from the polarisation of attitudes within the communities, and the British army remained obliged to react to events over which it had little control and were left on the defensive. Operation Motorman was an effort to move from being one step behind to get out in front and change the game. However, the former no-go areas remained dangerous places, with ambushes, firefights and the use of booby trap bombs continuing. Meanwhile, activity along the border areas began to increase.

Partition, history and geography, security jurisdiction and topography transformed terrain into territory, natural features into boundaries and countryside became characterised. Not to understand the border was to understate its hazard, underestimate its risk and underplay its peril. What made the border dangerous were armed men with deadly intent and local knowledge. You might not always see them but they were always there. For that matter, it was often very difficult to see the border itself. Meandering, haphazard and invisible, designated perhaps by a dried-up stream in the middle of a field or along a border road, the left-hand side ditch might be in the south and the right-hand ditch in the north. Or a house might have its front door in the south and its back door in the north, a church in the south and its adjoining cemetery in the north. All frequently set in hilly, undulating countryside where a warren of narrow roads with blackthorn hedgerows wound around lakes, rocky outcrops and boggy ground. Often there was nothing to suggest an actual border existed at all – indiscernible but not imaginary – and while it was imperceptible, it was also very real. Along its length, smuggling thrived. Colonel Harry Crowley (RIP) said of the situation:

> The Northern situation, the Troubles, seemed to blow up out of nowhere. Overnight we found ourselves on the border with little notion of what we were there to do. There were suppressed, economically starved rural communities with little employment and very few industries, the landscape dotted by tiny towns and villages surrounded by small farms with the occasional larger trading town spread along it. Some of these towns along the border were very republican. There was a lot of heat in the situation. The British tried to establish contact – army to army – but we rejected it. Our relationship with the British army was a non-relationship, and a good thing too. We did not want to appear to be in cahoots with them.

The British army stressed the importance of desirable and necessary co-operation with the Irish Defence Force. However, Lieutenant Colonel Louise Hogan, Officer Commanding 27th Infantry Battalion based in Dundalk and Castleblayney (later Chief-of-Staff of the Irish Defence Forces) stated when interviewed on a BBC TV *Panorama* programme:

> I don't see the point of it (co-operation with the British army); we have a mission to perform and presumably they have a mission to perform as well. I don't know what their mission is, nor do I wish to know. We have a job to do and we do it in our own way, and as far as I'm concerned, I am satisfied that we do it effectively.

The border was porous and highly penetrable and for the most part uncontrollable; the British and Irish armies had to respect the border, Provisional IRA active service units did not. Often, but far from exclusively, PIRA's modus operandi was to set up an ambush on the northern side then after springing the ambush flee southwards across the border back into the Republic. The 'war zone' for them was eleven counties, their 'area of operations' conveniently containing a border line delineating two separate jurisdictions. Many roads across the border were 'cratered' or blocked by the British army in an effort to control, manage and restrict cross-border vehicle movement, although in many instances the immediately adjoining fields were crossable anyway. On 28 October 1971, an early attempt by the British army to 'blow a cross-border bridge' at the village of Munnelly – connecting counties Monaghan and Fermanagh – resulted in a major stand-off between Irish and British troops. Explosive charges had been laid by the British to destroy the bridge and the issue centred on the claims that at least half the bridge was in the 'south'. The British disputed this but the Irish insisted and eventually the British withdrew.

Colonel Harry Crowley (RIP), when Officer Commanding 27th Battalion, stated that he was well served by adopting a relaxed but at the same time a considered approach in relation to this matter:

> Sometimes the best thing to do was to do nothing, to hang back [and] not intervene immediately [or] to jump into a situation prematurely. One day, I accompanied one of our Border Patrols and we came across a small group of local men filling in a recently cratered road. We halted our patrol [and] the group looked at us, unsure of our reaction. One came forward and asked, 'Well you can see what we are up to; are you going to do anything about it?'
>
> 'Why should I?' I replied. Relieved, the man explained – as he pointed at his house not more than 100 metres beyond the crater (in the north) – that he was a farmer with fields on both sides of the border and the crater meant a detour of six miles (9 km) out and six miles back to reach his fields not 200 metres from his house.

Another incident on a crossing point along the Cavan–Fermanagh border was described by an eyewitness:

We occupied key terrain, a hill with a vantage point overlooking the border crossing, arriving well before the British army did. We were responding to a formal request to secure our side of the border in advance of their operation. In situ well before the time requested, we observed the British army moving towards the border crossing post and then puzzlingly, past it, moving one hundred yards into the Republic. Controversial to begin with, and a Provisional IRA orchestrated demonstration of 'locals' and others was already expected, this [attempt] to block the border crossing forward of where it actually was could only contrive to add another level of ... contentiousness to an already disputed and fraught situation, and was foolhardy in the extreme.

The British army security party had arrived along with the Royal Engineer Officer and were busy establishing their checkpoints as he conducted his flawed reconnaissance, seemingly full sure of his surroundings. I decided to let the Engineer Officer know of his imminent miscalculation before it became an impending mistake and before they were confronted by an outraged onslaught of agitators and an ugly incident resulted. [Approaching] to inform him of the error he was about to make, his response was an insistence as to his correctness, whereupon I requested we first consult his impressive-looking map. The main body of his engineer company work party was now beginning to arrive proper and I did not want him to lose face in front of them.

Before I could suggest the situation as I knew it to be, he condescendingly made reference to his beautifully detailed large-scale map to prove his point. Without speaking, in a nonchalantly blasé manner as if totally unimpressed by my approach, he pointed to a spot on the map where the border was delineated. His unswerving self-confidence quickly unravelled, however, when I pointed out that the stream shown on his map, which he was reliant on as the unequivocal exact, correct border crossing location, had in fact long since been diverted on the ground by the local farmer for ease of access to ... his fields, and that where he now stood was in fact well inside the Republic. He had not thought of that, nor that he might ever be told such. They hurriedly relocated and left us to deal with the lively protesting mob.

The closing of many such border crossings on secondary roads and bridges used daily by villagers and farmers was hugely isolating, disruptive and inconvenient. Such attempts were enormously unpopular, resulting in tension towards the British and support for the Provisional IRA. The border became identified by the paramilitaries as a place to escalate the intensity of their campaign. Border customs posts and checkpoints were bombed constantly and British army patrols ambushed. Sealing the border in certain strategic places in order to stop, or at least contain, certain clandestine Provisional IRA movements was the British army response. These attempts to militarily fortify the border often stirred the locals into action and sometimes provoked a show of strength by nationalists, often orchestrated by the Provisional IRA. Other times, defiant farmers and villagers with legitimate grievances at the obstructions that were playing havoc with their daily routines, organised themselves to repair the blown-up bridges or fill in craters in order to restore access.

One 'organised' undertaking, or Action Day, occurred at Rosslea on the Monaghan–Fermanagh border on Sunday 19 March 1972, when locals were joined by others, who arrived in buses and cars, at Clones, Castleblayney and Monaghan, proceeding then to within half a mile of the cratered border crossing road. The group involved itself with a two-pronged activity, one group blocking an approach road from Rosslea to impede the arrival of British troops and hindering their advance to the border crossing point. Meanwhile, a larger group began filling in the large crater in the road with timber and rocks as the newly arrived British troops were kept at bay by others throwing stones at them. This situation continued for some time, the repair work and disturbance going on simultaneously, until finally a concerted effort by the troops with 'snatch squads' advancing in the wake of multiple CS gas canisters being discharged, forced the crowd to stop.

At other times, craters were successfully filled in only for deeper craters to be blown in the roads – these in turn filled in with hijacked cars covered with rubble and earth – and the Royal Engineers constructed concrete anti-tank 'dragons' teeth', which were also blown up by the Provisional IRA. The ongoing problems saw the placing of Braithwaite tanks, a series of modular panels bolted together, filled with concrete to create enormous concrete blocks, which were moved into place using cranes. And so on it went, the construction, the removal, and the re-construction of obstacles placed to block border roads.

Hampered but certainly not curtailed, inhibited, but definitely not discouraged, the Provisional IRA continued and intensified its campaign to 'liberate' sections of the border, drawing 'the Brits' into the dilemma of having to defend rural and remote border areas in terrain favourable to conducting small independent actions. With the increased sophistication and lethality of PIRA land mines and improvised explosive devices, hit-and-run tactics and sniping, this form of 'fighting' proved to be a 'force multiplier' for the IRA and activity along the border increased. The British army had thirteen separate battalions deployed across and throughout Northern Ireland. By their own estimates they would have needed fourteen battalions posted along the border to control it, one more than was posted in all of Northern Ireland. While they honed their skills and drills, learned lessons and allocated huge resources, the Provisional IRA's 'shoot-and-scoot' tactics caused a lot of problems for the British army units deployed there.

A British Army unit's tour of duty could be one of three types: a short-term 'roulement' battalion (four to six months), a 'resident' battalion (two years) or on 'emergency' tour of duty (for specific operations, threats or occasions). Their service in Northern Ireland and their many interventions thwarted numerous Provisional IRA incidents and caused some attrition. Security initiatives were regularly undertaken and this frequently involved cross-border 'straddle operations' requiring a Defence Force presence on the Republican (southern) side. A newly arrived young officer posted to Support Company 27th Infantry Battalion in Castleblayney, Co. Monaghan, describes his initiation to one such operation:

> During my first week, I was sent out with a body of troops among the countryside to occupy the hill tops with a physical presence to deny their use to any would-be IRA snipers firing across the border onto a large British army operation in progress in South Armagh's 'Bandit Country'. This deployment also involved my liaising with a British Army counterpart, but out of policy this necessary one-to-one conversation was conducted by four people, the two additions being a member of the Gardaí and RUC present, through which the conversation was channelled. For the new boy, i.e. me, the

whole situation itself was strange, the entire encounter surreal, but what was stranger still was the surprise I got, even knowing beforehand that I was going to meet the British officer, [that] when I actually did hitherto unregistered feelings at the sight of a British uniform on an 'Irish' road came rushing forth from my feet upwards, coursing through my veins with the message forcefully registering in my brain being: 'GET OUT OF MY COUNTRY, YOU BRITISH BASTARD!'

I was alarmed, completely taken aback at myself and could only hope my face was not betraying my thoughts. I was unsure where they originated from and am glad to say that there was no repeat. Indeed, not long afterwards, a similar type of operation occurred, but this time a PIRA active service unit managed to engage the British and a cross-border fight ensued. I, sent with a body of troops to reinforce what we had out there already, on arrival and deploying, came across three armed men running across [the] fields towards us. I and 'my little force' immediately took up fire positions and were ready to engage if we had to. Only I noticed that one was armed with an Uzi sub-machine gun, and while not necessarily meaning that he was a Garda plain-clothes detective, it could. So, I ordered 'safety catches on!' and breaking cover, called on those approaching to halt and identify themselves. They were three Gardaí 'Special Branch' men. A short report written by me resulted in an enquiry from the Battalion Intelligence Officer the next day and I was asked to confirm had there been a British army helicopter overhead throughout the incident and asked in detail about where exactly it had hovered – could it have hovered on our side of the border? It had! Whereupon I got a 'bollocking' for not reporting this, no mention of not shooting the three Special Branch men.

Another British Army helicopter incursion was described by a different officer:

We had set up a routine checkpoint with the Gardaí at Hackballscross (HBX) and in the course of conducting the checks on the passing traffic we noticed a British army helicopter landing on 'our' side of the border and British army troops 'de-bussing' (getting out) on the southern side. This happened in fields near a well-known farm complex near Ballybinaby, whose farmhouse and sheds straddle the border. Thinking it possible that an opportunistic search or snatch was being undertaken, we rushed to the scene and informed the British that they were on the southern side of the border and to return to the northern side, which they did. We had disrupted their raid on the farm complex.

A more completely innocent incident, but one infinitely more unbelievably blatant, was when one morning we were gathering for mid-morning coffee in the Officers' Mess of Monaghan Barracks and the sound of a helicopter approaching our helipad filled the air. Ours had returned to Baldonnel and its replacement was not due until much later in the day. Perhaps it had arrived early. Nonchalantly looking out the window, my calm casualness turned to confusion and alarm on realising the helicopter was not one of ours, rather one of 'theirs'. A British army helicopter was landing in an Irish army border base; this base (my base) and right now! What did this mean? A hell of a diplomatic row for starters, but were there more immediate implications, I wondered? So I had the 'alarm' sounded and the barrack stand-by party 'stood to', surrounding the much bemused helicopter crew. [...] their confusion and alarm even exceeded ours to find that they had landed not in the nearby British Border Base at Aughnacloy but in the Irish Border Base at Monaghan! These not too far distant Border Bases had, obviously, inflight from height, been mistaken by the crew one for the other and they had landed in the 'wrong' one on the 'wrong' side. Well the incident became the subject of some lengthy 'diplomatic discourse' [and] the helicopter and crew [were] allowed to lift off, embarrassed but unharmed.

The possibility of harm and hurt, however, was far more centrally at play when at border crossing H26 at Courtbane, an officer described a serious incident as follows:

I was part of a two vehicle military patrolling party out near the border and we decided to call into Hackballscross Garda Station to let them know that we were in the area. As we headed in the door the whole place shook. A bomb had exploded in the nearby Crossmaglen (XMG) area. Taking two separate approach roads, the two vehicles headed for the appropriate border crossing and on arrival took up positions along ditch lines, coming under fire as we did so. Each time we attempted to observe the scene by putting our heads above the ditch line, we were fired upon. Notwithstanding, we managed to detect where the fire was coming from and with our lives endangered we returned fire. It became apparent that our quick reaction and arrival had trapped a Provisional IRA active service unit and a firefight between us ensued.

To my utter horror and disbelief, a school bus arrived onto the scene and the driver, not comprehending the commotion, seemed prepared to drive right into the midst of the fray with what could have been dreadful consequences. I had to 'break cover', halt the bus and encourage the driver to reverse the bus away from the danger. It was then that wires were discovered stretching across the border, probably associated with the prior explosion. Reinforcements from 27th Infantry Barracks, Aiken Barracks, Dundalk, were called for, as was the Explosive Ordnance Disposal (EOD) Team. Next there was the sound of a British army helicopter arriving at speed. This was followed by further firing from our right.

I moved forward towards the source of the firing. Overhead, the British Puma helicopter flanked left, slid open its doors and a machine gun opened up, its fall of shot impacting all around me. Further total disbelief and plenty of indignation. The helicopter departs and full of anger and aroused infuriation I saw that our armoured personnel carrier's turret was still pointing southwards and I challenged the gunner as to why he had not opened fire with warning shots over the helicopter's flight path. I insisted he turn the turret northwards and skywards in case the Puma helicopter returned.

It became dark and the bus, 'command wires' and helicopter incidents had allowed the IRA active service unit slip away. Before we left the scene, statements were taken and full reporting followed. It was to give rise to a big diplomatic exchange subsequently and it transpired that some six hundred tracer rounds had been fired from the British army Puma helicopter.

The incursions were not always South to North, particularly in the early days of the border operations. A former senior non-commissioned officer, ex-CQMS Tom Brace, describes his first patrols:

I myself went to the border in the beginning of December 1969 to Tanagh House in Cootehill, an old monastery, as part of the 16 Infantry Group (16 INF GP) to relieve a married man in order to let him go home for Christmas. I will always remember my first patrol; when the officer in charge of the patrol issued his briefing orders, inclusive of 'if you come across an armed party (meaning RUC or British army) you are to escort them back across to the other side.' I cheekily asked the question, 'what if they are not from the other side?' to be promptly answered by, 'don't be smart.' As it happened, on our second patrol we bumped into an RUC patrol and told them: 'I think you need to go back to your own side of the border.' They replied, 'we were just about to tell you the same thing.' In fact, they were right.

On another occasion, during a requested border 'straddle operation' an officer explained a cross-border conversation one of his platoon members had with a British soldier: 'On taking up an all-round defence position, I become aware of a nearby British soldier similarly deployed who said to me, "I think you are on the wrong side," and I replied, "I think you are in the wrong country."'

Barry Bowman has distinct memories of time spent on the border:

I was a 20-year-old university student, a member of the 2nd line reserve (FCÁ), specifically D Company, 20th Infantry Battalion (known as Pearse Battalion), Griffith Barracks, Dublin. We were largely drawn from Belvedere College Secondary School. During the summer of 1970, we received a 'please report' notice as there was likely to be trouble along the border. I remember we went to Castleblayney Military Post in single-decker CIÉ buses. It was totally different from [our] normal routine. We had no prior training in operational and patrolling drills and when assigned onto a patrol we had no maps. Our orders included the phrase: 'if you see a red phone box, turn back!' We were, however, delighted to be of service, were very committed to the occasion and our duties involved being part of the checkpoints with the Gardaí on the southern side of the 'concession road' into Cullaville, motorised patrols at night to the Customs Post at Killeen and patrolling from Blaney (Castleblayney) to Monaghan town.

It was a singular approved peculiarity, unique to the Pearse Battalion, that our dress code allowed the wearing of a red-coloured strip of fabric worn around our neck and tucked inside our shirts; a red cravat. Some years later, this small concession to unit individuality was to cause an unexpected 'stir' when again on 'summer camp' along the border. One day in 1977, [we were] out patrolling near Monaghan town looking for the body of Captain Robert Nairac (a British Officer attached to the SAS, who when involved in undercover work, was rumbled by the Provisional IRA in the Three Steps Inn pub in South Armagh, abducted, taken south of the border and interrogated and shot). We received a radio report that British paratroopers had been seen south of the border and we were to proceed to the church in Monaghan town, take up an all-round defence position there and await further orders. After a while there, and with no further sightings of the red-bereted British Paratroopers reported, there was a realisation that it was us, the red-cravated Pearse Battalion patrol, that had been seen and mistakenly reported as 'Paras' and now here we were on the steps of the church in the centre of Monaghan town defending ourselves against ... ourselves!

We also performed 'static guard' on vital installations, one such being an ESB (Electrical Supply Board) sub-station which served Dundalk and Drogheda. One night during a previous 'winter camp', in the midst of a thunderstorm, one of the guard members became nervous about discernible movement he heard and saw in nearby bushes. Fearing it was a planned UVF attempt to sabotage or otherwise wilfully do damage to the ESB sub-station's machinery and equipment, he brought the matter to me as Guard Commander for my attention. Alerted to the possible intruder, I advanced towards where I too could see movement and called out: 'Halt; who goes there? Identify yourself or I will fire.' My verbal warning was ignored so I poured a blast of Gustav sub-machine gun fire into the bushes. Result? One dead donkey!

These incidents had humorous endings and are funny to relate, but underlining them was a fraught uncertainty, an anxiousness and nervousness; such was the prevailing edgy atmosphere of an understated unsettledness arising from the state of being that nobody could be completely sure of what would happen next. It was even difficult to fathom what was happening in the now. Because along the border, while everyday life continued – with children going to school, cows being milked, babies being born, hay being saved – a powerful undertow of menace was masked amid the norm. Attacks were being carefully planned, bombs prepared and placed, ambush sites were being selected, all of which displayed a cool, calculated callousness on behalf of the perpetrators. Scratch below the surface, even gently, and an apprehensiveness and unease was evident. A local doctor based in a border town had such a conversation with an Irish army officer friend to the effect that:

> Maybe some night or early morning somewhere out along the border area you might be on the side of the road with a checkpoint or patrol in an out of the way place and I might happen along and you would think it odd of me being there. Well I am telling you now before that ever happens, I might get a call in the middle of the night to take a bullet out of some fella and that is what I will do because that is what doctors with families in border towns have to do.

People living along the border, getting on with their everyday lives, were busy and preoccupied with life, but they were scared and fearful also, their view of the situation influenced by being frightened and intimidated.

How then were matters for the newly arriving members of the Defence Forces in the early 1970s? When sub-units were rotated up-country for two or three months before 'organic' border units became established, consolidated and integrated. Ex-CQMS Tom Brace remembers Dundalk:

> In the grip of the Provos, mostly northerners (on the run who fled internment and 'Motorman') and those activists from the area itself. The local people were intimidated and expected to be 'patriotic'. There were pubs you could go into and there were pubs it was better not to go into. I remember it was feeling almost like being a stranger in your own land, but that was the temper of the times.

Brigadier General Séamus Ó Giolláin (Retd.) was a young Lieutenant stationed in Monaghan town: 'I remember my initial border deployment. We were under canvas in tents while Monaghan Barracks was being built. To begin with there was poor integration with the townspeople and there were fights with the locals.' Confrontations with townspeople in pubs and discos was one matter; Captain Greg Kelly (Retd.) describes another level of contention:

> There was a narrow line between the nationalist support for the Provisional IRA and us, the Defence Forces. If the Provisional IRA held a march, it would be well supported. The situations we faced were very real but the Provisional IRA did not want to engage (with) us, so they would avoid us. However, we still did not know if they were going to have a go at us. You could not be certain about their reaction in volatile situations. A more specific direct threat was made one night in Monaghan town by a highly active and dangerous Provisional IRA man (subsequently killed in the Loughall ambush by the SAS) to an Irish army officer. The exchange was blunt and unambiguous and the antagonism obvious: 'We'll get you.' To which the Irish army officer replied, 'you will, if you're able.'

This animosity was further echoed by another officer's account of an incident in a Dundalk pub:

> In Dundalk, when out for a drink in a local pub with some fellow officers, we were approached by a group whom we believed were active Provisional IRA from across the border, who addressed us

aggressively: 'Are ye in the Free State Army, and are ye aware the RUC are involved in a shoot-to-kill policy; well what are ye going to do about it?' To which one of us replied, 'look we are just out for a drink, so let that be enough about that.' Unhappy with this reply, one of their group responded, 'We'll be shooting ye some day on the crossroads,' and he was totally startled when he [was] suddenly grabbed a hold of by the collar of his shirt by one of us and was told firmly: 'We won't be shooting ye on the crossroads, we'll be shooting ye in yer beds.' They backed off.

Nor were the Garda Special Branch any more amenable towards the IRA, the killings of Garda Dick Fallon (3 April 1970) and Inspector Sam Donegan (8 June 1972) being early watershed moments in this regard (there were to be further such killings). Kieran Conway, a former IRA Director of Intelligence, commented on the situation, explaining its stark reality: 'The Branch were a tough bunch ... and hated us with a vengeance.'

The Government, aware of the growing disenchantment amongst the public towards violence and of the huge concern as to where all this was going to end, were conscious of the public mood and support of their stance against the IRA, the building up of the Defence Forces, the strengthening of the Garda Síochána, and the introduction of legal initiatives. So when and where possible, active members of the Provisional IRA were pursued, prosecuted and penal sentences imposed in Irish prisons in Mountjoy, Curragh, Portlaoise and Limerick. The notion then being put forward, that the Republic was a safe haven for PIRA, was false and the allegations levelled against the Irish security forces, of inaction and non-apprehension of PIRA activists, were wrong. The idea that the Provisional IRA operated with an approving, even authorised, 'wink and a nod' was incorrect and the concept that a blind eye was turned to their activities was completely inaccurate. All members of the Irish security forces were prepared to place themselves in the line of fire, to hold the line against those who would subvert the State's stability, undermine the integrity of its institutions and contest its rule of law.

The suggestion that the Republic was a safe haven for the Provisional IRA came from British military personnel, who when interviewed consistent with an 'information operations' messaging campaign expressing a tactical frustration at not being able to pursue ASU members across the border, where in fact another jurisdiction – that of the Republic – held sway. In addition, some Unionist politicians concentrated on a security option to the Troubles rather than addressing its root cause, perhaps in denial of the fact that Northern Ireland was a 'haven of hostility' toward equality of opportunity for all, and so avoided asking fundamental and searching questions of themselves. The longer there was no fruitful political discourse, the further 'into the mire' everyone went. The border became a highly contested area of operations in itself, a place where 'the conflict' could be carried to the British. Where better to trigger the downfall of 'occupation' than on the artificially created British boundary separating the Six Counties from the rest of Ireland.

'The patient determination to kill' is the military definition of an ambush, and the Provisional IRA spent many hours, days and nights in preparation. There were many more ambushes abandoned than actually occurred, mainly because of the non-appearance of a target, detonation failure, or other happenstance. There were more misses than hits and the level of activity was far higher than a simple compilation of statistics would suggest. Often described by journalists, authors and academics as a 'series of small actions', their actuality was far more vivid, vicious and violent in effect. Both dramatic and traumatic, the sensation of the shock, stress and strain of these ambushes was more heightened in their harsh reality than imagined. A well-executed surprise attack by people lying in wait is a stark occurrence to experience. Raw, ugly and savage, it has a callous fierceness and a calculated ferociousness. Their intention was to kill, to extinguish an individual's existence on earth and to deliberately end precious life; they were vile acts and an enormous wrong.

The Provisional IRA's armed struggle was a campaign of combative aggressiveness conducted concurrently in Belfast, Derry and elsewhere, as well as along the border. The escalation of action along the 'second front' as it were, was a combined effort to tie down the British army in Northern Ireland and keep it engaged, on the alert and constantly harassed. The aim was to provoke a British army reaction into nationalist communities, pressurising them to perform house searches, personnel checks and raids that would create and maintain heightening alienation with the community, with the Provisional IRA feeding off the support created. Such support, whether it be provision of safe houses, scouts, transportation, information, the provision of locations to store weapons, ammunition and explosive material, all were necessary and without which PIRA could not have operated.

From the early 1970s, the beneficial effect of the training camps were kicking in and Provisional IRA losses through premature detonation of their bombs – so called 'own goals' – lessened considerably as their expertise advanced, both in the use of firearms and especially explosive devices. From lighting fuses, to command wires to remote control electronic detonation, progress in this regard was witnessed to devastating effect at the double bomb ambush at Warrenpoint on 27 August 1979, when eighteen British soldiers were killed on the same day that Lord Louis Mountbatten and his boating party were blown up in Sligo. Also well emerged by then was another deadly dimension to the conflict, a sickening series of sectarian murders in terms of cross-community killings, 'tit-for-tat' atrocities bringing fear to urban and rural neighbours.

There was an awfulness about the border; it was the boundary where the limits of civilised norms were edged out by primal outrages, and tragedy and grief visited on a lot of households. At 8.22 pm on a Sunday evening in March 1976 in Castleblayney, Co. Monaghan, the main street was suddenly lit up by a sudden blue and yellow flash followed instantaneously by a horrendous bang. A car bomb exploded without warning outside the Three Star Inn, killing 56-year-old farmer, Patrick Mone. A member of the Garda Síochána recalls: 'I remember picking up the man's leg – it was still warm – and being shocked by the sensation and then of course the fear that there might be a second bomb.'

Bombs along the border were nothing new, and a string of border towns in the Republic had echoed to the sounds of explosions; three in one day on 28 December 1972 detonating within thirty minutes of each other. The first on Fermanagh Street in Clones, Co. Monaghan just after 10 pm seriously injured two men, the second before 10.30 pm on Butler Street, Belturbet, Co. Cavan killed two teenagers, Geraldine O'Reilly (15) and Paddy Stanley (16) and the third car bomb destroyed the licenced premises of Hugh Britten in Mullnagoad, Pettigo, Co. Donegal. On 17

May 1974, a car bomb exploded in Monaghan town and ninety minutes beforehand, three bombs exploded in Dublin, killing thirty-three people and injuring 300 (the biggest loss of life in a single day of the Troubles). On 19 December 1975, a car bomb exploded without warning outside Kay's Tavern public house on Crowe Street, Dundalk, Co. Lough killing Jack Rooney (60) and Hughie Watters (51) and wounding twenty people. On 29 November 1975, a bomb exploded in a cubicle in the gents' toilet on the ground floor of Dublin Airport, killing John Hayes

Nor were bombs in Dublin unprecedented. On 5 August 1969, a bomb damaged the RTÉ Television centre in Donnybrook and on 27 December 1969, the Daniel O'Connell statue on O'Connell Street was damaged slightly in an explosion. The following day, 28 December 1969, another bomb exploded outside the Garda Central Detective Unit. The nearby telecommunications headquarters is believed to have been the target. On 26 March 1970, a bomb damaged an electricity sub-station in Tallaght. The tomb of Daniel O'Connell in Glasnevin Cemetery was damaged by a bomb on 17 January 1971 and the following month, on 8 February 1971, the Wolfe Tone statue at St Stephen's Green was destroyed. In December 1972, George Bradshaw and Tommy Duffy were killed and 130 people injured by a bomb planted at Sackville Place off O'Connell Street (likely planned to influence a positive vote on the second reading of the Amendment to the Offences Against the State Act) and early the following year, on 20 January 1973, 25-year-old Thomas Douglas was killed and seventeen injured in Sackville Place.

There were other incidents, such as the fatal stabbing of Christopher Phelan on 26 June 1975; it is believed that he came upon a group of men attempting to place a bomb on the railway line near Sallins, Co. Kildare (his actions likely to have delayed the explosion to let a train pass with 200 passengers on board, the majority considered to be heading to the republican commemorations at Bodenstown Cemetery). These bombings were suspected to have been undertaken by loyalist paramilitary groups, as were two earlier 'own goal' premature explosions, one on 19 October 1969, killing the man planting the bomb in an electricity sub-station near Ballyshannon, Co. Donegal and another who died on 17 March 1973 in Cloughfinn, Co. Donegal when his car bomb exploded prematurely.

Whatever attempts loyalist paramilitaries made to make the Troubles impact down south, in Dublin and elsewhere, the increasing tempo and intensity of the Provisional IRA's campaign to convert the conflict into a revolutionary situation commanded the attention and concentration of the security forces on both sides of the border.

There was a lot to be aware of along the border; loyalist paramilitaries heading south, inadvertent (and perhaps not so inadvertent) British military incursions and of course, mostly, the activities of the Provisional IRA. It was important to be out patrolling in order to see what was happening, and of course also to be seen in order to reassure the people and to disrupt and deter PIRA. Then there was the border itself. There was a lot to see there for those with an eye to see it and it was best observed by thinking like the IRA. When out conducting searches it was appropriate to carry out 'ground appreciation' in terms of its suitability for cover and concealment of weapons, explosives or people – specifically an ambush party or more precisely a 'firing point', the place from which to detonate a bomb. Such a position would need observation of the 'killing ground', be secluded and have access to an escape route. Typically, it was not infrequent for such ambush site selections to have the killing ground in the north and the firing point in the south. Prior to the use of electronic remote control, bombs were detonated by command wire, which could run for upwards of several hundred metres and were concealed as best as was possible. The bombs, typically a milk churn packed with fertiliser mix, was placed in a culvert (an underground cutting beneath a road to drain surface water) or dug into the side of a ditch, or otherwise concealed in the everyday natural features. Alternatively, it could be a claymore mine-like device or sticks of gelignite (an explosive containing nitro-glycerine) taped together with a primer and a detonator.

Garda-led searches of farms and farmland and sweeps of countryside along the border and its hinterland were conducted and finds of arms caches and hidden stores of materials resulted. Often the information that led to any particular place being searched was incorrect, outdated or otherwise inaccurate. Sometimes it was correct or partially so, or in other cases vague and requiring a thorough search. While ground appreciation was a military skill, the scrutiny and interpretation of search areas in Aid to the Civil Power situations required a different talent and mind-set. There were those who showed a proficiency for this task, and one such young Irish Defence Forces officer displayed a highly developed, almost uncanny, ability to understand what he was both looking at and for:

Somehow I found the task straightforward and obvious. When I looked at an area I automatically took in its vicinity in relation to its wider locality, and the search site's intrinsic natural arrangement, angles and undulations would be suggestive to me of an alignment suitable, or not, to further focus my attention. Thereafter, as it were, the ground would gradually give up its secrets, even though such materials may have been skilfully concealed. On one occasion, when requested to provide the 'southern side' covering party while the British army conducted its operation on the northern side, an area of ground took my interest and I went to investigate. Our presence (but mine in particular) must have disturbed the occupants of a 'firing point' location because on my arrival I could see matters were set up for immediate exploitation. Wire leads and a battery were ready to be connected, the presumed target the ongoing British army operation just across the border. The life-threatening exigencies of the situation – and it being the 'early days of the border' – allowed for the ... solution to the pressingly urgent ... circumstances to be addressed by [us] in the absence of bomb disposal teams (yet to be formally situated on main border posts) and with the bomb not found it was decided that the British would withdraw to what was regarded as a safe distance and I, rather unusually, would initiate the device's detonation. It blew with a deep, deafening, dumbfounding eruption, which shocked me. I was astonished and appalled to realise the point of detonation was not hundreds of metres away, but barely over fifty metres distant. This was to be a close-in attack; its ruthless audaciousness pointing to the cruel wickedness behind it. In all respects the incident was exceptional but nonetheless in the event, rendered redundant.

Increased sophistication, anti-handling devices and timer units would procedurally militate against any similar course of action in the future; the Provisional IRA set out to make the cost of remaining in Ireland prohibitive to the British, in military, economic and political terms. On the border this included the targeting of Customs Posts. A British Customs Post was symbolic of the division of the country and emblematic of empire, it was representative of repression and the power of an imposed Northern Ireland mini-state. Practically too, it was striking at the mini-state's administration, and their destruction had a monetary worth in terms of a financial loss to the British Exchequer.

The Provisional IRA had become robust and young, and the members were getting younger. Trained, well-armed and sophisticated, they used another valuable weapon, surprise, to good effect and wreaked psychological havoc. They were particularly strong in South Armagh, referred to by locals as God's Country, but labelled 'Bandit Country' in 1974 by then Northern Ireland Secretary, Merlyn Rees. Crossmaglen ('Cross' to the locals, XMG to the British and Irish militaries) was the major town in the area. The majority of the town's population were nationalists and pro-republican – one community where there were no warring factions to be kept apart – and hostility instead was heaped towards the British army, who were unwanted and regarded as alien. A tour of duty in South Armagh was one of the most dangerous postings for the British Army – 127 soldiers (twelve by sniper) and fifty-eight RUC men were killed there and many more injured. Their base was in constant threat of bomb and mortar attacks.

Along the low rugged heather-clad hills of Slieve Gullion on the South Armagh border, there was a chain of twelve 'Romeo' and 'Golf' security watch towers studded with the antennae of electronic gadgetry providing 'total security' protection. Cameras, observation, listening, jamming and other devices – more sophisticated, powerful and invasive than previously imagined – were mounted on these watch towers, greatly assisting the intelligence-led counter insurgency effort. Notwithstanding, South Armagh was a major heartland of Provisional IRA activity and freedom of movement was denied to the British army. It was too dangerous to use travel by road because of the high propensity for orchestrated and planned attacks. The use of helicopters became a vital means of supply and the main method to convey almost everything. Over the three decades of the Troubles, the clatter of Wessex, Sioux,

Scout, Gazelle, Lynx, Chinook and Puma helicopters were all heard over the rooftops of the villages, the bogs and the woodlands of South Armagh. It was only in strength, or in small specialised covert teams, that the British army dared to undertake on-the-ground movements. The everyday reality of normal life in the area appeared on the surface with almost disarming rural rustic charm.

Yet all was set to get worse; the sectarian murder rate began to escalate and a number of notable incidents caused major concern, among them the slaying of members of the Miami Showband as they headed south on their way back to Dublin after performing at the Castle Ballroom in Banbridge on 31 July 1975. Their murder was believed to have been carried out by the loyalist paramilitaries, the Ulster Volunteer Force (UVF). In an interview in Aaron Edwards' book *UVF: Behind the Mask* (Merrion Press, 2017), Billy Mitchell (1940–2006), a UVF Brigade Staff Officer in 1975 recalls:

> The UVF was not formed to deal with interfaces, it was formed because they believed there was a sell-out. There was a rebellion which had to be stopped; whether you were from the Shankill or East Antrim, you had the one enemy – the IRA. Indeed the Nationalist community, as most UVF volunteers did not distinguish between the IRA and those they fought for.

On 4 January 1976, Brian and John Martin Reavey were shot dead in their home a half mile from the village of White Cross. Earlier that day, three members of the O'Dowd family – two brothers Declan and Barry and their Uncle Joseph – were killed when men burst into their home near Gilford and shot them. The following day, masked men waved down a linen factory workers' mini bus at Kingsmill, lined up and shot dead ten Protestant workers in revenge. All this had been provoked by a prior series of killings and counter killings conducted by both Republican and Loyalist paramilitaries. Two months earlier, on 22 November 1975, three soldiers were ambushed and killed at Drummuckavall when their covert observation post (OP) 'hide' was discovered. 'Bad camouflage, wrong routine and incorrect OP layout' were the conclusions that the British army's follow up report established.

All this greatly unsettled the Loyalist population living in the area, heightened tensions and suggested that the conventional 'green army' and their tactics were inadequate and simply not working in South Armagh. The fatalities also starkly pointed to a large difference in the death toll of British army soldiers (45) in comparison to almost minimal number of Provisional IRA operatives. For reasons then of the suppression of violence, preventing a deterioration of the security situation in South Armagh, and the appeasement of outraged Loyalist opinion, D Squadron of the British army's elite Special Air Service (SAS) were drafted in, its members recruited from their regiments and used in the conventional military role for long-range patrolling and surveillance, raids, ambushes and assassinations. Highly trained, self-reliant and expert in many regular military skills, they also had a proficiency in irregular warfare.

After their insertion to the North of Ireland, some dubious deaths and abductions began to occur on both sides of the border. The possible involvement of the SAS and loyalist paramilitary squads in these activities became a concern for the Irish Government. Garda and Defence Forces' patrols were stepped up as well as increased checkpoints and presence along the southern side of the border. On the night of 5 May 1976, one such checkpoint, carefully positioned 700 yards inside the Republic near Cornamucklagh, Co. Lough, gave rise to what became known as 'The Flagstaff Incident'. A yellow South Armagh registered Triumph Toledo 2000 with two plain-clothes British military SAS occupants was stopped at the checkpoint at 10.40 pm. Claiming to have made a map reading error and otherwise ambiguous as to what they were doing, the Garda Sergeant arrested them under Section 30 of the Offences Against the State Act, 1939 and they were taken to Omeath Garda Station. When they failed to return to their base in Besbrook, six more armed SAS men in two cars, a white Hillman Avenger and a Vauxhall Victor, were dispatched to locate them, as it happened running into the same Defence Force/Garda checkpoint and somehow committing the same 'map reading' error.

There were four occupants in the first car, all armed, with two Browning automatic pistols, a Sterling sub-machine gun and a Remington short-barrelled pump action shotgun, and two in the second car, both with Sterling sub-machine guns. Ordered out of their cars and to hand over the weapons, they refused, until the army personnel emerged from the cover of darkness, one saying, with his FN rifle raised: 'Get out or I'll blow you out.' An additional weapon, a large bladed knife, was also found. The six SAS men were arrested and taken to Omeath Garda Station and all eight SAS troopers were then transferred to Dundalk Garda Station.

How then to proceed? To release them would be tantamount to condoning their activity, but not to release them would cause a diplomatic, political and legal furore. It was a hard decision and reaching a conclusion was proving anything but decisive. Meanwhile, out on the Coley Mountains, A Company, 27th Infantry Battalion were out on the ground and received an urgent radio message to return to Aiken Barracks, Dundalk:

> I received a radio message to return the Company to Barracks immediately. We broke off from our on-ground activity and returned to Barracks from where we took up positions inside Dundalk Garda Station to secure the SAS troopers and if necessary the Garda Station itself. All of this, the arrests, the transfer and the holding of the SAS troopers had been successfully conducted in secret until, that was, it was announced on the RTÉ lunchtime news. A crowd immediately gathered outside [the Garda Station] and continued to swell throughout the afternoon. But still no decision was made or direction offered. Meanwhile the crowd's mood was becoming one of public anger; there was excitement but also a very definite tension.
>
> 'Are we waiting for the pubs to close before we move?' was a comment from an exasperated Garda, thereby articulating what we were all thinking, fearful as we were of having to defend the station against a surging crowd. Finally, a decision [was made] to transfer the SAS troopers to the Special Criminal Court in Dublin's Green Street. Only now to negotiate the mob. Fortunately we had managed to secret an AML-90 Panhard armoured car into the rear of the Garda Station and this was placed in the vanguard of the convoy as the back gates of the Garda station's courtyard was suddenly sprung open and we emerged into the street. This vehicle took the brunt of the hail of bottles and stones as the convoy forced its way through the furious crowd, who had quickly recovered from the surprise, but it was enough to begin to get us through; the strength of the convoy maintained our momentum thereafter.

The matter did not end there, however, as we were followed down the road, a chasing convoy of some forty cars in pursuit, ensuring we were not swinging back northwards to let the SAS troops cross the border.

The fervour of the chasing convoy waned around Slane, as it became clear that our destination was southwards. I was hugely relieved because the AML-90 Panhard, having played its part in our initial surprise thrust through the besieging mob, was just not able to maintain the pace and was holding back the convoy's progress. Its lack of speed [was] a security issue, one fortunately that did not come to bear as I was able to return it to Dundalk escorted by an oncoming patrol. We continued to the Special Criminal Court and there I handed [the SAS men] over to the officer in charge of the Guard.

At a special sitting of the Special Criminal Court on 6 May, bail was fixed at £5,000 each. The trial hearing was held nine months later, on 2 March 1977, and the SAS members involved were flown into Casement Aerodrome, Baldonnel, and escorted across Dublin in a large army/ Garda escort. A charge of bringing weapons into the State with intent to endanger life (with a maximum penalty of twenty years imprisonment) was not pursued in favour of imposing a £100 fine each for taking weapons into the Republic without firearms certificates. The weapons, having been checked forensically for any matches with prior murders proving negative, were handed back.

The altercation outside Dundalk's Garda station was not the first such occurrence of its type, a far more threatening commotion having taken place there a number of years earlier on 21 September 1972. Commandant Eamon Kiely (Retd.) recalls:

I remember an off-duty Garda coming to the military barracks seeking immediate army assistance as the Garda Station was on fire and Sergeant Hugh Sreenan and his family were trapped within. I mustered the best part of a platoon (thirty men – mostly Kilkenny men) and headed out in a few Land Rovers with a couple of armoured vehicles. I learned from the Garda that a mob was attacking the station so I asked him to direct us to a position where we would meet the mob head on, coming in ideally from the Carrick side.

He did this very effectively and the appearance of armoured vehicles in front of the mob had a temporary shock effect. They fell back from their petrol bombing of the station and I deployed my platoon in riot gear at the double in front of the rioters and with our backs to the Garda Station. At this time a number of fire tenders had been turned on their side outside the station, and a wing of the Barracks was burning. Our intervention allowed other fire tenders in to quench the fire and rescue Garda Hugh Sreenan's family.

The mob then started taunting us, calling us 'yellow bastards' and to 'go back to the Curragh'. They then started throwing missiles, stones, petrol bombs, etc. I had a loud hailer and called on them to disperse, as was the drill at the time. After one of our lads was burned (not badly) by a petrol bomb, I decided to fire CS gas. I had to apply the rule of minimum force despite being strongly exhorted by some of my people to cock weapons and fire ball ammunition. I was very conscious of what had happened in Derry (Bloody Sunday) not long before and didn't want to repeat that mistake.

I appealed over the loud hailer to those who were merely bystanders to go to their homes as this would assist in dealing with the troublemakers. This has come down in army folklore as my having said: 'Good people of Dundalk, go to your homes!' A number of canisters of CS gas fired from the gas guns had the desired effect and moved the mob. We moved them right down the town. About £80,000 of damage was done to shop windows, etc. This I understood was levied on the taxpayers. Dundalk came 'on side' (stateside) from that day on.

There was one possible dimension to this incident, little known but intriguing, of the reported sighting of 'a blonde haired fellow with an English accent' who was allegedly acting as an 'agent provocateur' having rented the mob and set them on the Garda station, inciting and encouraging them from the side-lines – the thinking perhaps similar to that of the 3 December (1972) bombs in Dublin, providing encouragement to pass the Amendment to the Offences Against the State Act, 1939.

The following month after the Dundalk riot, in October 1972, the Allied Irish Bank in Dublin's Grafton Street was robbed of £67,000 – at the time the largest amount stolen in any bank raid. Kenneth Littlejohn and his brother Keith were arrested and it was subsequently alleged they were connected with British Intelligence (MI6), in whose employ they had supposedly been recruited to infiltrate the Official IRA. Notwithstanding, after some liaison at government level they were convicted. Kenneth escaped from Mountjoy Prison in March 1974, was recaptured in England in December 1974, and served a sentence until both brothers were released in 1981 on condition that they leave the Republic of Ireland.

But there was stranger to come, all with a connection in one guise or another to the border and the conflict which raged along it. Three weeks before the Flagstaff Incident, on 15 April 1976, an 'on the run' member of the Provisional IRA, Peter Cleary, went to see his girlfriend in her family home fifty yards on the northern side of the border in South Armagh. The house was raided by British soldiers and Peter Cleary, it was declared, was 'shot while trying to escape'. The SAS were newly arrived into the area at that time. Also newly arrived to Ireland was the British Ambassador, Christopher Ewart-Biggs, who took up his appointment on 9 July 1976. Twelve days later, on 21 July, he was assassinated when a bomb, believed to contain 200 pounds of gelignite placed in a culvert, blew up his car near his official residence at Glencairn, Sandyford in Dublin. A fellow passenger, civil servant Judith Cooke, was also killed. Prior to his arrival in Ireland, it was believed that Ewart-Biggs had been a Senior Foreign Office Liaison Officer to MI6. In 2006 it was reported in the British media that the Gardaí had matched a partial fingerprint found at the scene to a known and named member of the Provisional IRA. It has been intimated that he was targeted because of his intelligence connections but that the timing was because of the Peter Cleary killing and other questionable assassinations and abductions in the border area. A large manhunt for the assassins was undertaken across the Republic and there were arrests of Provisional IRA activists but no convictions. The event commanded global attention at the time and it could have dramatically damaged Anglo-Irish relations, the British wishing to exert pressure for greater security measures to be introduced, but in the end these were not realised.

There were killings and murders both in the north and south, though there were far more deaths in the north than the south. Sometimes these resulted in bodies being dumped on the border, specifically those of 'informers' shot in the head after days of brutal interrogation and terrible torture. Every so often these bodies were callously booby-trapped or used as 'come-ons' to lure British soldiers and the RUC into ambushes. Often it would take a large-scale security operation lasting days to 'make safe' the situation and retrieve the unfortunate deceased. They had died at the hands of the Provisional IRA's own internal security section, the infamous 'Nutting Squad' – occasionally called the 'Head-hunters' – formed to root out those amongst their own who had become compromised, 'turned' or otherwise as 'walk-ins' chosen to act as agents for the security forces. Living under a constant threat of discovery, or making an unconscious slip, they understood if they were 'outed' or otherwise self-incriminated themselves, that the consequences that awaited suspected informers, 'touts' and spies would first and foremost be unforgiving and then fatal. A number of surviving self-confessed informers have written books articulating their perspectives and the pressures they were under. At any stage they might have been abducted, horribly interrogated and admissions extracted, confessions recorded and then dispatched from this world. For those who were drawn into the IRA but had become disillusioned, they may have sought redemption in doing the State some service; it sometimes ended badly, a few even becoming bodies on the border.

Ironically, in a complete turnaround it was the lack of a body along the border that caused a commotion and concern. Captain Robert Nairac, Grenadier Guard, had a niche role as a liaison officer between the SAS, RUC Special Branch and 3 Brigade Headquarters. He operated from Bessbrook Mill and Lisburn and developed a *modus operandi* of working without back up. On one such occasion, at the Three Steps Inn pub in Drumintee, South Armagh, it appears his cover story as an ex-Official IRA member from Belfast called Danny McErlaine failed to stand up to scrutiny and he was 'rumbled' by the South Armagh IRA, abducted and taken south across the border to Ravensdale, near Dundalk, where he was beaten and shot dead. His body has been missing ever since, a massive search on both sides proving inconclusive.

However, his killer was arrested by Gardaí, convicted and served a sentence in Portlaoise Jail.

This liaison and communication role, if extended to co-operation with loyalist paramilitaries, became 'collusion' and following a number of murders over time this was strongly suspected to be the case; enough to arouse allegations of British intelligence collusion. Deputy Chief Constable of the Cambridgeshire Constabulary, John Stevens, was requested by the RUC Chief Constable, Hugh Annesley, to conduct an inquiry into collusion between the security forces and loyalist paramilitaries. It was discovered that sensitive intelligence documents and information did find their way into the hands of loyalist paramilitaries, but whether it was a deliberate policy or the work of a range of disaffected RUC and UDR men was less clear. This elusive 'hidden hand' of direction for a deadly and deceitful purpose, suspected of stretching at times across the border, has always been part of the narrative of the Troubles. It will remain part of the hidden truths, half-truths, mistruths, paranoia, fear and tribalism of those times for some time to come, those actually responsible hopeful that the real truth will become lost in the maze of time and shifting memory. Meanwhile, incursions continued, both inadvertent and intended:

> Do you still have those noisy Panhard APCs? We could hear them miles away. In fact one time we did hear them miles away, so, happy ye were miles away, we crossed over to occupy an area of interest to us. Only of course, not thinking that ye, the actual occupants of the APCs, had been dropped off prior, and were now in fact in behind us, between us and the border, and we were caught. Fair dues. We were 'geographically embarrassed – ye caught us.'
>
> (An exchange between a British and an Irish Officer on a foreign military course.)

Thirty years ago, British officials raised the prospect of erecting a physical border along the entire length of the 'frontier' between Northern Ireland and the Republic, the main issue that of incursions. The British argued that their best efforts might not be sufficient to reduce significantly the occurrence of incursions, given the nature of the threat, the intensive security operation required to meet it and the lack of clear physical delineation along the border. The British toyed with two ideas that might affect the number of incursions. The first was for more extensive communication between the British army and the Garda Síochána (they had correctly identified that the Secretary of the Department of Justice was the centre of gravity of Irish Security policy in relation to the Troubles, and that army to army co-operation was far from where they wished it to be). The second was physically delineating the border along its full length. They cited the frontier between East and West Germany, then in vogue, which was delineated by posts set in the ground at intervals of five metres or so to support a fence with watch towers along it. The Irish response argued in very strong terms that it was unthinkable that the proposal should ever seriously have been put forward.

Again, it was incursion incoming from the Republic that caused difficulties; this time in the form of a radio signal triggering a simple switch in an Improvised Explosive Device (IED) exploding a 700-pound fertiliser bomb hidden in milk churns surrounded by petrol cans. Parked in a lay-by and hidden on a flatbed trailer piled high with bales of hay, the bomb was detonated by a radio signal that travelled across the lough at Narrow Water separating Omeath in the Republic and Warrenpoint in the North, and the bombers' target was the rear truck of a British army convoy. After the detonation there was a bright flash, a rumble, then a ball of flame and a blast wave. Eardrums were perforated, lungs collapsed and bodies were ruptured. Heads, limbs and flesh were ripped apart, leaving burning body parts and pieces of clothing strewn along the road. Seven members of the 2nd Battalion Parachute Regiment were blown asunder. It was 4.40 pm on 27 August 1979, but the deadly drama was not over yet. For the first time, the Provisional IRA had planted a secondary device, correctly anticipating both the location and timing of where and when the arriving reinforcements would be most concentrated and vulnerable. Thirty-two minutes after the initial explosion, a 1,000-pound bomb exploded in milk churns mounted inside the front wall of the gatehouse of Narrow Water Castle, killing ten more soldiers from the Parachute Regiment and two from the Queen's Own Highlanders. In all, eighteen British soldiers were killed, sixteen of them from the Parachute Regiment, their biggest number of fatalities since the Battle of Arnhem in 1944. Nor was this the end of the incident's fatalities because the Paras, believing they had come under fire from woodland on the southern side of the border, fired across the water killing an innocent Englishman, Michael Hudson, and wounding his cousin, Barry Hudson. Both had been birdwatching in the wrong place at the wrong time.

The country was not finished with the reverberations of the South Armagh-made bombs, as shockingly, in Mullaghmore, Co. Sligo, Lord Louis Mountbatten, a prominent member of the British royal family, was killed when a radio-controlled bomb exploded on his boat, the *Shadow V*. Three others were killed alongside him; his daughter's mother-in-law, the Dowager Lady Brabourne, his grandson, Nicholas Knatchbull and a local boy, 15-year-old Paul Maxwell. This was a high-profile assassination and the Warrenpoint ambush a massive propaganda coup for the Provisional IRA. Significantly, both sets of bombers were arrested by the Gardaí, though evidence, or the lack of it, played its part in subsequent proceedings.

Meanwhile, the awful sequence of sectarian slayings became regularised and an appalling pattern of tit-for-tat revenge killings continued to play itself out. This grim situation gave rise to fear throughout the north but along the border also. It was this fearfulness, combined with the presence of guns, that led to the 1974 murder of Senator Billy Fox in the Republic, a respected member of the Irish Parliament (the Oireachtas), who had previously been a Fine Gael TD for Monaghan. Senator Billy Fox was a Protestant, and on the night of 11 March 1974 he was visiting his girlfriend's family farmhouse, that of the Protestant Coulson family near Scotstown, when he interrupted a raid and was shot dead. The raiders were operating in the completely incorrect and mistaken belief that a delivery of guns for the loyalist paramilitary group the Ulster Volunteer Force (UVF) had arrived to the house, and decided to raid it. When the robbery was in progress, Senator Fox arrived on the scene, alarming the raiders and in the resulting struggle and confusion he was shot dead. A decision was then made to burn the farmhouse in an effort to destroy any forensic trace evidence and the raiders fled into the night. Five men were subsequently arrested, charged and found guilty of murder, setting fire to the farmhouse and possession of firearms without a certificate.

Before the facts of the case became known there was fear that the killing might be the start of attacks on public representatives. The Minister for Justice, Des O'Malley, had previously been targeted by the Provisional IRA and for six years carried a weapon, changed his accommodation weekly and had continuous Garda protection. One such 'live situation' occurred early one morning at the start of 1972 when staying with a friend in a flat on Waterloo Road. Des O'Malley recalls:

> Early one morning the Gardaí arrived at the front door and ordered the two of us to lie on the floor. We, the host, myself and his cat, the three of us lay there for three hours, and I eventually exited the flat in the middle of a huddle of surrounding Gardaí as we rushed to a car and sped off. It became known that a rifle with a telescopic sight had been discovered in a flat directly across from my friend's flat. The landlord told the Gardaí that the flat had been rented a few weeks previously. The name given was not correct and he appeared to be from the north.

Nor was this an end of the threats to Government ministers. The next was to a different Irish Government and the source of the threat from a different origin. Fine Gael Minister for Foreign Affairs, Peter Barry TD, needed Garda protection for himself and his family home on the Blackrock Road in Cork city after a direct threat from Protestant paramilitaries because of their dislike of proposals for the Irish Government's involvement in Northern Ireland affairs contained in the Sunningdale Agreement.

The Defence Forces and the Gardaí had to hold the line 'on the ground' along the border. Troops acting under Aid to the Civil Power had to be capable of performing a multitude of tasks in very different conditions. Army/Garda co-operation was always very good to excellent. This was mainly down to the regular meetings at which information was passed by both sides, and where difficulties arose they were resolved at a local level. There was overall mutual trust and a realisation of the capabilities of both organisations. Day and night patrols were conducted as well as the establishment of spontaneous random checkpoints 365 days per year; the provision of security escorts and guards for Gardaí when people were arrested; responding to shooting incidents; involvements in large-scale searches and cordons; arranging and maintaining security for VIP visits to the border as well as the everyday but hugely necessary vital installation patrols and static guards (at RTÉ masts and ESB sub-stations); and the escort of explosives from Enfield and Cash-in-Transit security were all necessary involvements. These routine framework operations were everyday common practice and therein lay the danger of the possibility of being caught napping; the challenge to maintain vigilance and the necessary heightened alertness while performing the ordinary routine duties. It was too easy to become comfortable and complacent because the one day you relaxed was the day you'd get 'hit'.

One who did not allow this to happen was Lieutenant David Gunning (Retd.) when in charge of the escort of a particularly large shipment of explosives, the collection of a consignment of gelignite from the Irish Industrial Explosive facility at Enfield, Co. Meath, and its transfer for handover to Northern Ireland security forces at the border crossing at Killeen, Co. Louth. These escorts were a necessary security measure to securely manage commercially used explosives in Ireland to prevent them falling into the hands of the paramilitaries. On the route southwards from Dundalk to Enfield to pick up his load for conveyance northwards, the occupants of a North-registered car were spotted by escort personnel taking a more than casual interest. Made aware of this unwarranted attention, Lieutenant Gunning took the executive decision to alert the escort's return route northwards and in the event ensured its safe arrival to the handover point. The follow-up investigation of the car's registration details revealed it to belong to 'people of interest'.

Lieutenant Colonel Noel Byrne (Retd.), then operating out of Headquarters 4th Cavalry Squadron in Longford, recalls another border incident, when one night:

A speeding car in the dark of night approached an Army/Garda checkpoint and on realising what it was they crashed the car into the ditch and the occupants took to the fields. Gardaí discovered a victim of a kidnapping in Dublin in the car and recovered him to the local Garda station. In the meantime, reinforcements were called for and deployed around the area, as well as with patrols throughout the area. By dawn, additional troops had been drafted in from as far away as Athlone as well as an Air Corps helicopter. The terrain was very difficult with bog and marsh predominating. A major search of the area was carried out by troops and Gardaí. Air–ground communications were mostly non-existent, so when a person in a very remote area was spotted waving at the helicopter it was necessary to land close to the nearest Army/Garda unit and get them to follow the helicopter. It transpired that 'visitors' had been around his cottage but were now gone. A number of persons were later arrested. Subsequently air–ground communications were substantially improved.

He spoke of a later involvement:

In May 1992, information [was] received from the Gardaí that a major operation would be taking place along the border between Swanlinbar, Co. Cavan and Ballyconnell. The purpose being to provide security to Northern Ireland forces who would be operating for a period just north of the border. This information caused a flurry of activity, not only in the unit, but also at Brigade and Command level and possibly General Headquarters. It was necessary to establish what the Gardaí would require under Aid to the Civil Power. Then it was necessary to source resources to meet the request. Initial reconnaissance was completed, including by helicopter. In essence, what was agreed was a series of observation posts (OPs) giving adjacent inter-visibility as well as [a] view of the border. Engineers were then tasked with constructing shelters at selected locations where troops and Gardaí could remain and operate 24/7. It was also necessary to have Department of Defence Lands Branch involved so as to be prepared for possible claims by land owners, even though all had agreed to the use of their land. One contractor even provided an access over particularly difficult terrain.

Planning and co-ordination continued with support units being tasked, plans for deployment and rotations, logistics including feeding, medical facilities, communications, night vision equipment, standard operating procedures, command and control, legal, toilet facilities, etc. 'Operation Hedgehog' commenced in mid-May under command from Headquarters 4th Cavalry Squadron in Longford, when all positions were occupied, and was to last until early July. The units supporting the operation were the 6th and 28th Battalions, 4th Field Artillery Regiment as well as the support units of the Command. The Army Ranger Wing (ARW) were also used on specific tasks. During the operation there were reports of a roadside bomb and some shooting north of the border, but it was easy to establish that none of these emanated from the south. Throughout the operation there were very frequent visits and reconnaissance by incoming platoons, briefings for higher formations as well as logistic replenishments. Following the completion of the Operation, a debriefing was held and all agreed the success of the Operation was due to the detailed planning and the level of co-ordination and communication during the Operation.

The main areas of activity along the border were North Louth/South Armagh, Monaghan/Fermanagh (into East Tyrone) and Donegal/Derry. These were called 'military zones', a fourth being West Belfast. An array of conventional and unconventional (highly specialised) units were deployed in these. An SAS-trained RUC Special Branch unit, E4A, which had backup from three Headquarters Mobile Support Unit (HMSU) groups were based in Armagh, Belfast and Derry; the SAS itself and the 14th Intelligence Company ('The Det') as well as MI5 and MI6. These along with the various British army units and regular RUC, all populated the security forces deployment, a total of 20,000–25,000 troops throughout the north.

There were differences in the approach, culture and thrust in the manner, means and *modus operandi* between security forces in the north and those in the south. Their respective perspectives on the nature of how they went about what they were trying to achieve was derived from dissimilar degrees of direct threat, in turn giving rise to different on-ground realities in their response. Fear of the destabilisation of the entire island was the grim reality to be grappled with down South, memory of the Civil War not too far distant, whereas the Troubles were more of a 'security focus' for the British. So the 'here not there' problem saw specifically separate responses to the conduct of the security forces to the internal security situation. The Irish version a more highly politicised security, ironically one no less intrusive or effective against the Provisional IRA than the more securitised approach of the British. The Irish Government had to be seen to be tough with the Provisional IRA while at the same time not seen as adopting a stance of pro-British co-operation.

As a result there was no Irish army/British army communication along the border; an antagonism existed between the Irish security forces and the Provisional IRA; the south was not a safe haven for PIRA (the simple fact was there were more PIRA activists in the north than in the south and also in the north there were areas in which movement was denied to the British army); and, finally the Defence Forces worked exceptionally hard and very professionally. They were armed without being aggressive, they were 'military' without being domineering and performed a very necessary role.

The Cork Examiner

NO. 47,306   SATURDAY MORNING, APRIL 4, 1970   PRICE SIXPENCE

Father of five shot dead as bank raiders escape

MASSIVE HUNT FOR KILLERS OF GARDA

AN intensive full-scale Garda manhunt was still in full swing last night for the killers of Garda Richard Fallon, who was shot dead when he tried to arrest raiders at the Smithfield Dublin branch of the Royal Bank of Ireland yesterday morning. All available Gardaí were switched to the hunt.

Garda Richard Fallon, the father of five, fell dead, shot through the head as he tried to catch the raiders.

Up to early this morning no arrests had been made.

£5,000 REWARD

The Minister for Justice, Mr. O'Morain has offered a reward of £5,000 for any information supplied to the gardai which leads to the apprehension of the murderers. Proportionate rewards will be paid for any information of value that is supplied to the gardai in the investigation of the murders.

DIED IN COURSE OF DUTY

Garda Fallon is the 11th member of the Force to have been killed in the course of duty since 1922.

A Garda checks cars and buses leaving Dublin after the bank raid

'A credit to great force'

Troops will 'shoot to kill,' bombers warned

PETROL bombers in Northern Ireland were warned last

Cork Examiner front-page article describing the killing of Garda Richard Fallon during a bank robbery in Dublin, April 1970. Courtesy of *Irish Examiner*, Cork.

PIRA arms shipment on MV *Claudia* intercepted off Helvic Harbour, Co. Waterford. Five tonnes of weapons were seized in March 1973. Courtesy of Military Archives, Dublin.

Irish Army officer and radioman giving an oral situation report ('sit rep') to their HQ while conducting a patrol along the border, June 1975. Courtesy of *An Cosantóir*.

Irish soldier maintains observation of a border crossing point while taking cover behind a blackthorn ditch, January 1976. Courtesy of *An Cosantóir*.

Shocked shopkeepers and residents observe the wreckage of one of three car bombs which exploded within 90 seconds of each other in Dublin, May 1974, while a fourth bomb exploded in Monaghan – 33 people were killed and over 300 injured. Courtesy of *Irish Examiner*, Cork.

An attempted breakout from Portlaoise Prison in March 1975 is prevented by the Defence Forces. An improvised and modified steel-plated truck – nicknamed 'the Mary Rose' – is used to batter down gates during the unsuccessful attempt. Courtesy of Collins Barracks, Cork.

An Irish Army mobile patrol passes through Glaslough, 'showing the flag' to reassure residents of the town whose garda station had closed that there was a reliable security forces presence in the area. Courtesy of Military Archives, Dublin.

Irish Army soldier in position along a ditch line secures an outer cordon while a tractor passes by, during one of many Cordon and Search Operations conducted by the Irish Security Forces during the Troubles. Courtesy of Captain Tony Doonan, retired.

With their outer cordon line set in place, Irish Army soldiers prepare to conduct a search of a wood as part of a Cordon and Search Operation during one of many such operations conducted by the Irish Security Forces during the Troubles. Courtesy of Captain Tony Doonan, retired.

A PIRA arms shipment on the *Marita Ann* was successfully intercepted off the Skellig Islands, Co. Kerry, September 1984. Courtesy of *Irish Examiner*, Cork.

Following the successful interception of MV *Eksund* in October 1987, it was realised that four similar (but smaller) shipments had got through undetected and a huge search (Operation Mallard) for these PIRA arms was conducted in the border areas. Here a 4th Infantry Battalion convoy from Cork prepares to depart northwards to assist in the search. Courtesy of Captain Tony Doonan, retired.

An Army/Garda checkpoint monitoring road movements during Operation Mallard, November 1987, while Irish Security Forces conduct searches for illegally imported PIRA arms along the border area. Courtesy of Captain Tony Doonan, retired.

An Irish Army soldier, helmeted and with a Steyr rifle, became a familiar sight throughout the Republic during the Troubles as the Defence Forces assisted the Gardaí. Courtesy of Military Archives, Dublin.

PART 3

'THE BOG'

CHAPTER 8

Break-Out

The alarm screamed, its shrill sound splitting the air. The standard routine of the duty shift was splintered, the tension heightened as the atmosphere instantly changed to one of alert with the high-pitched wailing. It was not a rehearsal, the alarm's sharp sound brought a vital urgency. As the prison's military guard were shocked into a sudden awareness, an instant reaction was demanded and there was an electrifying imperative to get parts of the reserve into motion – a critical race against time and circumstance. The guard moved into position, and a different mind-set became engaged. As the frightening and frenzied situation unfolded there was anticipation and excitement, apprehension and uncertainty. It was a moment of operational intensity and reaction time had to be pared to an absolute minimum. Why had the alarm sounded, what was the nature of the problem? A riot? An escape attempt? A siege? Where exactly was the danger and how might it all end – what needed to be done to prevent it finishing badly?

The guards' hearts pounded and pulses raced as everyone around the Portlaoise Prison perimeter and on the military posts experienced different degrees of a heady dizziness. Spines tingled and adrenaline flowed as they tried to come to terms with what was happening. Pre-rehearsed drills were activated, laid-down procedures were brought into play and emergency positions were taken. The reaction had to be right – perfect in fact – there was no margin for error and there were no second chances. The prevention of a breach of the prison boundary was at stake. The butts of weapons were settled into shoulders and safety catches clicked off. Weapons were cocked and the soldiers struggled to control their breathing. Their minds were clear, however, uppermost in their minds was one thought: no one was escaping today.

Duty in Portlaoise Prison, formerly Marlborough Jail adapted to twentieth-century use, was an onerous task and the military involvement there was critical, as described below:

> Soldiers did not join the army to end up guarding prisons, so duty there was neither looked forward to, nor enjoyed. But they knew that the subversive inmates had to be kept in, and were keenly aware that only their presence could hope to ensure that. It was always considered a place without colour, without atmosphere, without soul.
>
> Strangely, however, it had a taste, an unsavoury dry residual sensation [that] clung to the inside roof of your mouth and stayed with you. Once you entered inside the prison's perimeter, a distinct dehumanising aura enveloped you; it was like a spirit clung to you, [and] a demented absence of all hope descended.
>
> An operational priority, the tasking there was taken very seriously and it was interesting to find oneself on the roof of E Block looking down into the exercise yards at the inmates, whose exploits which had earned them incarceration we were all too familiar with. At the dead of night it was quite strange to hear the birds singing heartily, confused by the glare of the arc lighting into thinking that it was daytime. For us, day and night, rain or sunshine, our firm focus was in meticulously maintaining the detail of our routine designed to keep the inmates in, knowing that they were all the time thinking about black spots, weaknesses and getting out.

✦✦✦

The Squadron Commander, 1st Armoured Car Squadron, was the commander of the operation. As well as his Squadron, under his command was a Company from 3 Infantry Battalion and the 1st anti-Aircraft Regiment. These were 'army troops', the Defence Forces Reserve, and as such came under Operational control of the Chief-of-Staff through the Director of Operations, even though they were units from the Curragh Training Camp.

Planned with the greatest secrecy, the Operation was so 'need to know' that the Commander was not in a position to fully brief the officer commanding Curragh Training Command beforehand, and he kept knowledge of the full truth, detail and nature of the mission between himself and the planning cell of officers at General Headquarters, Director of Operations Section. Instead, a cover story was given that the Operation's objective was the escort of a major ammunition consignment from Dublin Port to the ammunition depot in the Curragh.

Three Air Corps Alouette III helicopters provided observation from the sky and parallel road routes were controlled as the large Army/Garda convoy and a fleet of CIÉ buses pulled up outside Mountjoy Prison at 6 am on 9 November 1979. The Operation was to move all IRA prisoners from Mountjoy Prison (and the Curragh Military Detention Centre) to what the IRA would come to refer to as 'The Bog' (Portlaoise Jail). Prisoners there were being moved to other prisons to make room for them. The low-profile, high-security, strictly secret Operation was being conducted as a measure to better contain Provisional IRA prisoners, which involved their transfer and segregation onto E Wing in Portlaoise Prison. With a population of high-risk prisoners, the Irish army was also deployed to guard the prison.

The Operation was a direct consequence of the spectacular escape by helicopter nine days beforehand, on 31 October 1973, of three high-ranking PIRA men from Mountjoy Prison. The escape of JB O'Hagan, Seamus Twomey and Kevin Mallon, known as the 'Birdmen of Mountjoy' was a great propaganda coup for the IRA and a serious embarrassment for the Government. It was a blow to the new Coalition Government led by Liam Cosgrave of Fine Gael, who knew that he needed to curb the activities of the Provisional IRA, who were in danger of becoming dangerously powerful as the organisation strengthened as a result of the Troubles. While they did not pose a direct armed threat to the south, Cosgrave knew that he needed to provide the strong leadership that the previous Taoiseach, Jack Lynch, had shown in 1969–70 to prevent the Republic of Ireland being drawn into a civil war.

A raft of new legislation had been introduced, and old legislation reintroduced, and the Government had gained significant powers at its disposal in their fight against the IRA. In August 1969, a public appeal on RTÉ Television by IRA veteran Joe Cahill exhorted the Irish army to disregard the orders of their political masters and support the nationalist people of Northern Ireland. Section 31 of the Broadcasting

Act censored the paramilitaries and cut off their access to the airwaves. The non-jury Special Criminal Court, set up in 1972, was achieving convictions at a steady rate and the Gardaí were getting tough on PIRA. The Provisional IRA's policy of not recognising the courts left them open to being almost automatically found guilty of membership, once arrested and accused of being so by a superintendent of the Gardaí, and offering no defence – just a statement of non-recognition of the court – they were subject to a mandatory 12–24-month sentence. Ongoing internment in the North was also having its effect and the combination of these security measures was beginning to seriously inhibit their momentum. As a result, the ranks of important leading and other Provisional IRA men were thinning while within the prisons the population was increasing proportionately.

The daring plan to snatch O'Hagan, Twomey and Mallon involved the hijacking of a commercial helicopter from the Irish Helicopter Company, piloted by Captain Thompson Boyes out of the company's Westpoint hangars in Dublin Airport. On 20 October, some eleven days before the attempt, a man posing as 'Mr Leonard' – supposedly an American – hired the helicopter for an aerial photographic shoot of Dunmore in Co. Laois. On the day, 31 October, as the helicopter arrived at Stradbally, Co. Laois, 'Mr Leonard', having got on board in Dublin, jumped out and a gunman jumped in and hijacked the helicopter, instructing the pilot to head for Mountjoy Prison and land in the exercise yard. Once the three prisoners were on board, the pilot was instructed to fly to Baldoyle Racecourse where a waiting getaway car drove the occupants away at speed. Audacious, straightforward and effective, the plan worked. The Mountjoy prison officers were initially confused by the unannounced approach of the helicopter, some thinking it might be the Minister for Defence, Paddy Donegan, on an inspection visit or the medical airlift of a sick patient. Others were just surprised. As the prison officers in D Wing's exercise yard were overpowered, amid the scuffle and confusion O'Hagan, Mallon and Twomey clambered into the helicopter. Ten minutes later they disembarked at Baldoyle Racecourse into a waiting car and sped off, leaving utter disbelief behind them in Mountjoy. It was a great victory for PIRA, a bold escape that attracted worldwide attention and was later emulated in other attempted and successful escapes around the world.

Kevin Mallon was recaptured one month later on 10 December 1973 at a GAA dance in the Montague Hotel near Portlaoise. JB O'Hagan was taken back into custody fifteen months later in Glasnevin. It took longer to apprehend Seamus Twomey, but he was eventually rearrested on 2 December 1977 after a high-speed car chase from Sandycove into Dublin city centre, where he was intercepted. It was believed that among the papers recovered there was documentation which demonstrated his input into the Provisional IRA's 'Green Book', the manual of regulations governing the conduct by which its members were to abide. It set out the structure, Army Council, Executive, etc., outlined their claim to be the rightful government, having supposedly inherited the right from the 1918 Dáil. Other documentation suggested the reorganisation of the Provisional IRA along cellular lines and a supposed manual on counter interrogation techniques; all to make PIRA secure from penetration by British agents and informers and all of the ingredients for their 'long war' strategy.

For now, the aim of the newly arrived inmates to Portlaoise Prison was to be the newly escaped ex-inmates of Portlaoise Prison, and an escape committee was immediately formed. Although not accorded political status, the Provisional IRA prisoners were not prevented from maintaining their own paramilitary structure inside the prison; they were allowed to wear their own clothes and had control over who to nominate to conduct communications with the prison authorities. They endeavoured to be regarded as political prisoners, which Minister for Justice Paddy Donegan, along with Taoiseach Liam Cosgrave and his Government, steadfastly refused to grant. Indeed, if anyone in the media stepped over the line and called them political prisoners, they were sternly rebuked by the Government.

Meanwhile, matters along the border and north of it continued apace. There were Provisional IRA bombs in Britain and Loyalist bombs in Dublin. Throughout the republic there were bank and factory payroll robberies, training camps, weapons imports and bomb factories. All were responded to by security forces with searches, raids and arrests and a significant number of convictions were the result. One such incident near Portlaoise was the discovery of bomb and mortar-making equipment on 13 May 1974 in Athy, Co. Kildare, when nearly two tonnes of explosive materials were found. The haul also included home-made mortar bombs and improvised mortar parts. As a result, six more PIRA members joined the list of inmates in Portlaoise prison. At the end of the following month there was another discovery, this time outside the prison – but only just – of an 80-foot escape tunnel prepared in an adjacent house leading towards the prison. The IRA first bid for freedom was thwarted but their enthusiasm was not and they had certainly given notice of their intent to escape from Portlaoise. The paramilitaries tweaked their plans and another mass break-out attempt was prepared. Less than two months later, on Sunday 18 August 1974, their revised, carefully prepared and well-executed escape plan was put into effect. This time they were not going under, they were going through, breaking out by blowing up the gates with smuggled explosives. It has been suggested the explosives were smuggled into the prison in a box of Lucky Numbers sweets; there were over 100 visits to the prison the day before.

Everything was taken into account in planning their escape: time and space, opportunity and layout. A vulnerable area was identified to which access was achieved by overpowering a handful of prison officers and stealing their keys and uniform (caps and tunics). From the adjoining flat roof of the laundry, the escapees were able to descend to ground floor level and quickly sprint to a locked interior gate in the wall surrounding the Governor's house. Although they had achieved surprise, speed and confusion, the alarm was nonetheless sounded by alert sentries. The guards hesitated to open fire when they saw some of the escapees were wearing what appeared to be genuine prison officers' uniforms, and may have been such. Those among the escapees experienced in the use of explosives used their smuggled-in gelignite to blast open the gate leading to the area surrounding the Governor's residence and then with a second charge, precisely and quickly blew open the gate in the exterior wall. Nineteen prisoners made it outside the prison perimeter and haphazardly ran for the road to hijack passing cars to take them to freedom. There was a gap between this first group of escapees and a second, far larger group of hopeful prisoners, only now the armed sentries were pouring 'a wall of gunfire' in between the advance line of the group and the hole in the wall. For them to reach the gap the escapees would have to run into this deliberately aimed rain of gunfire and risk being hit and they halted. Only the first group of nineteen got out; many more did not. There were 120 inmates in the prison at the time.

Two of the hijacked cars were reported later found abandoned at Mountmellick and another was discovered crashed at Portarlington. A massive manhunt for the escaped Provisionals ensued. Checkpoints were set up in every town and village around counties Laois and Offaly; fields and outhouses, farmyards and farmland, bog land and forests were scoured and searched. Helicopters flew overhead, but the nineteen were gone. The search area was widened and all over the Republic there were road blocks mounted by combined army and Gardaí members. The security breach at the prison was debated in the Dáil and the Minister for Justice was called upon by the Opposition to resign. Official unionists commented that 'the jail-break demonstrated the total failure of the Dublin authorities to come to grips with terrorism, refusing to face up to the IRA, first along the border and then through not extraditing (the formal handing over of the accused Provisional IRA men to face trials in Northern Ireland's jurisdiction where the crimes were allegedly committed) and thirdly in the lack of security in southern jails'.

High Court Judge, Mr Justice Finlay, was appointed to inquire into the escape and make recommendations to improve the security system at Portlaoise prison. As a result there was an increased Garda and military presence at the prison and restrictions on food parcels and free association among the prisoners were implemented. These measures and stricter supervision were to cause restrictions which the prisoners disliked, and there were protests inside and outside the prison. These, however, were as much an effort to solicit overall support for the Provisional IRA's campaign, as 1974 had begun with the new Power Sharing Executive Assembly in Northern Ireland following on from the Sunningdale Agreement between London and Dublin. Unionists were wholeheartedly opposed to it as it meant power sharing with the nationalist minority and the Provisional IRA, having rejoiced in the fall of the Stormont Parliament, viewed this as its replacement. Neither did Unionists approve of the 'Council of Ireland' component, feeling that this could all lead to a United Ireland.

In May 1974, an Ulster Workers Council (UWC) all-out strike backed by UDA paramilitaries paralysed the process and the initiative collapsed. Stalemate followed and unremitting violence continued. There was also a change of government in Britain – the Labour Party was once more in power. The Nationalists had brought Stormont down and the Unionists had brought the New Power Sharing Executive Assembly down. There was no new beginning and the struggle went on.

In the south, the tacit support for PIRA was waning and their initial support decreasing. However, in 1973 Britain and Ireland had joined the EEC and the Provisional IRA's viciousness had become apparent. Violence on the island was not leading anywhere, only wasting precious life, causing heartbreak and overwhelming grief. The threat of spill over initially contained, it still had to be dealt with and facing down protests outside or inside Portlaoise Prison was all a necessary part of this. Colonel Harry Crowley (RIP) recalled:

> I was Officer Commanding the 3rd Infantry Battalion stationed in the Curragh Camp and we were tasked to support the Gardaí at an upcoming protest outside Portlaoise Prison. There was an evident tension apparent in the atmosphere of the time and it was felt that the protest had the potential to descend into violence. So, a number of days in advance, we conducted a thorough reconnaissance of the general area – the proximity nearest the prison and of all the adjacent roads – with a view to coordinating our effort with that of the Gardaí. We reached an early decision that we wanted to present a show of force while at the same time not being static and so avoiding the occasion of attracting confrontation, not being a focus for it. Instead [we wanted] to be able to move in any direction, responding as necessary and we made our plans accordingly.
>
> We positioned liaison officers with the Gardaí alongside the protest and at a temporarily established Crowd Control Headquarters at the gates of the prison. A slight confrontation occurred that could easily have sparked off disorder when a truck was, it appeared, about to be driven into a line of Gardaí. The quick-thinking reaction of a Garda present, however, by smashing the windscreen of the truck's cab and discouraging the driver from his intent, settled the issue before it became a concern. A Company of ours, one third of our strength, held in reserve on the outskirts of the town in a hotel car park on the cessation of the protest march

had to deploy, however, when two passing busloads of protestors stopped their buses, got out and squared up to them. In response they formed up, marched forward banging their riot shields with their batons and the crowd got back on the buses.

At 8.11 pm on the evening of 21 November 1974, the Newsroom of the *Birmingham Mail* newspaper received a bomb warning from a male caller with an Irish accent using the recognised PIRA code word 'Double X'. Six minutes later a bomb exploded in a city centre pub, followed ten minutes later by a second bomb in a separate pub. Twenty-one people died and over 180 were injured; it was the biggest death toll to date on English soil. The horror, anger and revulsion were huge, carnage and chaos had reigned throughout 1974 and it was ending on a very grim note. Before it did so, however, there was another notable incident in Portlaoise Prison.

During the afternoon of Sunday 29 December, the prisoners in the recreational room after the midday meal staged a riot and took six prison staff as hostages. They barricaded themselves in E Block and gave the kidnapped staff a good beating – one had a noose put around his neck. They ripped the heavy iron radiators off the walls and forcibly tore out the wrought iron stairs on the ground floor to prevent access to the landings. They also fashioned spears from tubular bed frames and cut up and used the sponge mattresses as protection – like American football players – and removed a number of heavy steel-backed cell doors from their frames. The rioters also prepared bottles and glass jars filled with paint, urine and faeces and other substances as missiles – in general they wrecked the prison wing.

The general alarm was sounded in the prison and back in the Curragh Camp unit recall plans were implemented and personnel reported to guard rooms in the various barracks there. The guard officer in the prison, a Lieutenant in charge of a platoon, turned out his platoon in the armed 'military' role (not in the 'police crowd/riot control' mode) and they secured the prison internally and from any additional external action. Garda reinforcements were summoned to the prison and the platoon on immediate standby in Magee Barracks in Kildare town rushed to the prison equipped for crowd/riot control. Troops from the Depot Cavalry at Plunkett Barracks in the Curragh were the first to assemble in reasonable numbers before deploying to the prison, and these two platoons brought equipment for both the 'military' and 'police' roles. They were equipped with Gustav sub-machine guns, FN rifles, batons, shields, riot guns, CS and CN gas canisters, baton rounds (rubber bullets) and respirators – everything but rations. One of the platoon commanders from the Curragh Camp takes up the story:

> The two Plunkett Barracks platoons, having travelled to the prison in two packed Mercedes trucks, arrived around 4.30 pm and were met by press photographers already assembled outside the perimeter walls. We were briefed on arrival inside by the platoon commander of the platoon on immediate standby. As he spoke he stood there with his combat tunic and full length riot shield splashed in sky blue paint from missiles thrown by the prisoners. The Operations Officer from the Curragh Training Camp, of Lieutenant Colonel rank, on arrival took charge. A number of other platoons from the 3rd Infantry Battalion, and a composite platoon from other Curragh Camp units, remained on standby outside the prison and at the FCÁ training centre adjacent to the Portlaoise Garda station.
>
> I think the prisoners refused to have any negotiations with the Governor, and so following discussions between the military operations officer, the Governor and the senior Garda, it was decided that as the lives of the prison staff hostages were in danger, the military would deal with the rioters using force as necessary. The two Plunkett Barracks platoons were instructed to secure their weapons and to prepare for intervention with batons and shields. A senior prison officer briefed the three platoon commanders (the two from Plunkett Barracks and the one from Magee Barracks on immediate standby) on the layout of the ground floor and landings. We questioned him on the likely ringleaders and weapons, possibly tools from the workshop available to them. I remember he was very on edge and obviously much shaken by events. The other Plunkett Barracks platoon commander was a trained crowd control techniques instructor and so he briefed each of the platoons individually, emphasising striking on joints, knees and elbows, no blows aimed at the head.

The Curragh Command Operations Officer emphasised that the action had to succeed. At this stage I had completed a few tours as platoon officer in the prison myself and I had been inside E Block after lock up time on one occasion so I had a good idea of the layout. I knew that the riot control drills taught on courses would not work in the tight confines of the prison so I divided my platoon in half; an assault group and a group to secure and ferry back the incapacitated detained prisoners and hand them over to the Gardaí. The assault group was divided into teams of three; one baton man and two to protect the baton man. I laid down one ground rule; the prisoners encountered had to be taken out and rendered incapable of attacking or acting against us from behind as we progressed from the ground floor through the landings. I selected two large NCOs as my team and I demonstrated how to put down the opposition so they could not present a threat to the platoon.

While we were waiting for the order to go into what would have been vicious hand to hand combat, we heard a number of bangs from inside the prison. It transpired that the Prison Guard Platoon Commander and a Section of his platoon had managed to saw through a metal barred gate on the laundry roof and had entered the prison wing on the first floor. They fired baton rounds, ricocheting them off the interior walls, and these warning shots ended the incident. I was directed to join those who had gained access and they were jubilant that they had saved the prison staff and ended the stand-off. The electricity was off and I could see with the help of a number of hand torches used by the Gardaí that the prisoners were lined up in four rows, all standing at ease. Two or three of their leaders were speaking with the Governor and a senior Garda Officer. After a few minutes the leaders re-joined the rest and on one of them giving a shouted order, the first rank went up the ladder to the landings while the other rows marked time in about eight inches of water from the smashed radiators. It seemed the Guard Platoon Commander acted on his own initiative and created an opportunity to end the stalemate. A few days later he was in the office of the Minister for Defence being commended for his actions.

After a second attempt at peace talks involving a seven-month extended ceasefire (10 February–22 September 1975) petered out, the Provisional IRA found itself heavily infiltrated by the British security services and was seriously demoralised and worryingly weakened. A new policy of 'Ulsterisation, criminalisation and normalisation' was introduced in the North and the task of controlling security was handed to the RUC, taking the lead in the responsibility for the fight against PIRA. Also, with internment gone any political status for prisoners was ended. Roy Mason was made Secretary of State for Northern Ireland and oversaw a tough regime against the Provisional IRA. In response, PIRA reorganised itself, the 'northerners' took control and the 'Long War' phase began.

Throughout this period there were shocks, upsets, surprises and sometimes stunning 'spectaculars'. There was a steady and sickening continuation of attrition and atrocities, death and destruction, and all the while the shameful litany of sectarian attacks were sustained. The perpetuation of this level of action took enormous effort, planning and preparation – and of course personnel – to execute, and such levels of activities led to the arrests of activists; these necessarily prosecuted in the Special Criminal Court in Dublin's Green Street.

On the establishment of the Special Criminal Court in 1972, then Minister for Justice, Des O'Malley, favoured the use of civilian judges to replace the three military officers who had previously presided over such cases. He found, however, great difficulty in getting civilian judges to serve on the new court. Many reportedly refused because it was 'too dangerous' to do so, fearful of the Provisional IRA and other republican groups. Threats against judges and the possibility of pickets on their homes were also put forward as a reason for their reluctance. Eventually, three judges said they would take the positions and special protection was provided for them. A subsequent Government plan to construct court facilities for the Special Criminal Court (SCC) in the grounds of Portlaoise Prison came to nothing because the judiciary and legal fraternity objected to it. So if the court would not come to the prisoners in the then existing special circumstances, then the prisoners had to go to the court.

The 1st Armoured Car Squadron was the main Defence Forces unit tasked with escorting Provisional IRA prisoners to and from the Special

Criminal Court in Dublin's Green Street. A normal escort consisted of a Section commanded by a Sergeant, and prisoners were transported in two Land Rovers; a 'special escort' for high-profile Provisional IRA members was commanded by a Lieutenant or a Captain with four Land Rover crews. Normally the Gardaí used two mini buses, or four if more than one prisoner was scheduled for an appearance at the SCC. Armed detectives travelled in an unmarked car in the centre of the convoy. The military escort Commander travelled in a Fitted for Radio (FFR) Land Rover with a Pye HF radio for communications with the Gardaí. The escorts were timed to arrive at the SCC around 10 am and a number of Garda motorcyclists would meet the escort on the Naas Road before Newlands Cross and 'blue light' the convoy through traffic. In the early months, 1st Armoured Car Squadron personnel remained as guards at the SCC on Green Street and Halson Street for the entire day and were fed at midday from Collins Barracks cook house. Later, Eastern Command units were detailed as Court guards and they would be in position before the escort arrived. The 1st Armoured Car Squadron Escort Commander would check with the Court guard commander and then report to Operations Eastern Command in Collins Barracks. Normally the escort commander prepared to return to the SCC by 4 pm, unless Eastern Command Operations turned out the escort earlier if the court adjourned before the end of normal sitting times.

As the years passed, the predictability of prisoner escorts was recognised as a weakness, as one direct route to Naas dual carriageway was used and court sitting times were set by an inflexible judiciary and court system. Two other routes were used and this did not always go down well with the Gardaí. In addition, 'shadow military escorts' (a separate additional escort, sometimes with armoured military vehicles) were employed on flanking routes or to the rear of the main escort as a reserve. This introduced a variable element that would have to be factored in by any would-be attackers of the prisoner escort convoy.

CHAPTER 9

Break-In

M easures to prevent the escape of prisoners from the convoys transporting them to and from the SCC proved sufficient to the circumstances, so if that prisoners sought freedom it was back to seeking escape from Portlaoise Prison itself. So it was that at 8.22 pm on Monday 17 March 1975, a carefully prepared and elaborate attempt to effect a break out from Portlaoise Prison was made by a large group of prisoners. At the time the prisoners were in the recreation hall where a film was being shown. Suddenly the lights went out and at a given word of command the prisoners threw themselves to the floor. Explosives were used to blow open a doorway from the recreation hall to the exercise yard and a second explosive charge blasted a gate in the wire enclosure around the exercise yard. A group of 40–50 escapees prepared to surge towards a large gate in the prison rear wall which gave access to an outside farm complex but was still within the prison perimeter. Here, however, was where a cunningly designed plan came into play. A specially prepared lorry had been fitted with sheet metal and customised into a mobile armoured battering ram for use against the farmyard gate in the prison's perimeter. It successfully crashed through the gate and was now heading for the back gate in the interior wall to effect a similarly destructive outcome, resulting in a foolproof escape route.

By coincidence, the military guard Commander on the night was the same officer who was in charge during the previous break out seven months beforehand:

> I remember the prison lights suddenly went out and the emergency lighting kicking in. As it happened, a new sentry post had been built to cover the back gate and this had been occupied

by us the previous Friday, three days beforehand. Once the break out attempt commenced, the sentry on the post reacted well. Confronted by the prisoners, having blasted their way out of the recreation hall and in turn the exercise yard, he fired a warning shot, called out (alerted) the Guard, cleared a stoppage in his rifle (removed a jammed cartridge from his rifle breach) and called on the prisoners to halt.

The alarm reverberated around the prison, the military turned out (reacted) and so newly installed was the emergency lighting that the trenches for the wiring of the emergency lighting had yet to be filled in; these were occupied by the troops. I got between the back gate and the prisoners. With me was an NCO [and] we were covered by troops in overhead sentry posts. I told the prisoners to go back into the recreation room; this order was met by a stream of abuse. Three leaders of the would-be prison escapees came forward. I told them I'd only speak to one. The three continued forward. I fired a round from my Browning Automatic Pistol as a warning shot. The Corporal with me fired a burst of Gustav sub-machine gun containing shots into the ground. It was then I heard one of the prison leaders say to the others: 'I told you they would open fire.' They returned to the exercise yard and from there to the recreation hall.

On the exterior side of the back gate the improvised armoured battering ram vehicle had run into difficulties; it had overheated and broken down just short of its objective. The two occupants were arrested by the Gardaí. During the escape bid one prisoner, Thomas Smyth, had been killed and there were two injured. At the time it was unclear if it was shrapnel from the explosives or as a result of ricocheting warning shots fired by the soldiers (the State Pathologist, Dr John Harbison, conducted a post-mortem on site the following day and an inquest was subsequently held). Reviewing what had happened with colleagues, specifically as to the feasibility of the improvised armoured battering ram vehicle, we wondered if it could actually have burst through the back gate and there was a heated debate as to its feasibility or not. Three days later the argument was settled when strong winds caused the back gate to come crashing down.

Over the years, such violent escape attempts staged by prisoners placed the most serious risk of death or injury onto very many people: innocent civilians, prison staff, Gardaí and Defence Forces personnel. The Minister for Justice, Mr Paddy Cooney, said in the Dáil a few days after this incident that 'the responsibility for any such deaths or injuries rested squarely on the shoulders of those who planned and those who helped in this attempt'.

CHAPTER 10

Blocked

S worn-in members of the Provisional IRA were involved in a deadly enterprise and the organisation depended on them, more so after the pointless 1975 ceasefire, and as 1976 progressed it proved to be the second bloodiest year of the Troubles (with 308 deaths) and they were relied on more than ever as the movement struggled. This was also the year of the announced arrival of the SAS to the North and the murder of the British Ambassador to Ireland, Christopher Ewart-Biggs, in the South on 21 July. A week beforehand there was another escape attempt, not from Portlaoise Prison but from the Special Criminal Court itself, and again it involved the use of smuggled-in explosives. The door was blown off the holding cell and the four escapees ran along a corridor out to a yard when a second explosion blew a hole in a perimeter wall. Running onto the street they were confronted by an armed soldier and Special Branch men who did not open fire because there were people on the street and the circumstances did not allow them to. The 'getaway' part of the plan had been left open and the prisoners desperately sought means to escape from the area, alternatively jumping into a taxi, attempting to hijack a car and then a van and finally onto the number 16 bus. All but one, who made it to the United States but was extradited back to Ireland eight years later, were recaptured and arrested.

However, the Provisional IRA were failing to attract the widespread public support they had hoped for. The no-nonsense upholding of law and order by the two successive determined Irish governments had garnered the backing of the people, who were happy they were exercising their duty to rule. They had faced up to some of the most testing problems and upheld confidence in doing so. The strong, sensitive and balanced handling of the tense security situation was vital, and more especially so in the wake of the murder of the British Ambassador to Ireland. A State of Emergency was announced in the aftermath of the assassination and additional security measures were introduced; the Criminal Law Act increased the penalty for IRA membership from two to seven years and a range of new offences were provided. A second piece of legislation, one which was to prove controversial, was the Emergency Powers Bill, a measure which allowed the Gardaí to hold suspects for up to seven days without charge. The Provisional IRA reacted by deciding when charged to now recognise the court.

The President of Ireland, Cearbhall Ó Dálaigh, a former Chief Justice, referred the Emergency Powers Bill to the Supreme Court to validate its constitutionality prior to signing it into law. The Supreme Court upheld the Bill's constitutionality and on Saturday 16 October the President signed it into law. The same night, Gardaí were lured to an isolated unoccupied two-storey house up a lane off a side road at Garryhinch, near the main Portarlington to Mountmellick road, five miles from Portlaoise, and 24-year-old Garda Michael Clerkin was killed in a booby-trap explosion and Garda Thomas Peters blinded. This was a premeditated murder and the three other Gardaí present were extremely fortunate to escape with their lives. The Provisional IRA had given their response to the signing into law of the Emergency Powers Act.

Two days after the fatal bomb explosion at Mountmellick, the Minister for Defence, Paddy Donegan, annoyed at the President's referral of the Emergency Powers Bill to the Supreme Court, called the President a 'thundering disgrace' when attending a Defence Forces function at Columb Barracks in Mullingar, Co. Westmeath, and a Presidential crisis soon developed. Cearbhall Ó Dálaigh construed the insult as a slight on the office of the President, and when the Government failed to censure the Minister for his outburst the President resigned. Under the Criminal Law Jurisdiction Act 1976, the Defence Forces were legally permitted to set up and conduct checkpoints without members of the Garda Síochána. Lieutenant Colonel Eamonn Fogarty (retd.) recalls: 'I found myself as a Second Lieutenant setting up checkpoints in Garryhinch Portarlington after the murder of Garda Michael Clerkin.'

The Provisional IRA campaign continued and then broadened, taking on both a military and a political strategy. They persevered in seeking support based on emotive publicity and empathy for some Portlaoise prison inmates on hunger strikes, but with little success.

This was in contrast to the later Hunger Strike of 1981 in the Maze Prison, which was an initiative originating from inside the prison by the prisoners themselves – only reluctantly embraced by the Provisional IRA leadership – resulting in a huge international propaganda coup and the subsequent election to public office of three of the Maze prisoners, two of whom subsequently died on hunger strike. New recruits swelled the paramilitary group's ranks and the significant strategy of continuing the armed struggle 'with an ArmaLite (rifle) in one hand and a ballot box in the other' had begun.

The early 1980s saw a re-energised Provisional IRA step up their campaign, fought now both militarily and politically, and on 15 November 1985 at Hillsborough Castle outside Belfast, the British Prime Minister Margaret Thatcher countersigned the Anglo-Irish Agreement with Dr Garret FitzGerald, the Irish Taoiseach. At the political level the Irish Government had to demonstrate they were not afraid of the responsibility to govern, while on the ground the Irish security forces – not under direct threat from the Provisional IRA – had to interface with a degree of menace. This was to manifest itself in Portlaoise Prison, where they again had to stand firm. The Provisional IRA were inspired and determined to make another break-out attempt from Portlaoise Prison. Spurred on by the success of the escape from Long Kesh Prison of thirty-eight IRA paramilitaries on 25 September 1983, they resolved not to let anything stand in their way – up to and including murder.

The escape of the thirty-eight Provisional IRA men from H-Block compound (H7), Long Kesh Prison was the biggest prison escape in British history. There had been a number of prior escape attempts from jails in the north; in November 1971, nine men climbed rope ladders over the wall of Crumlin Road Jail to freedom, two months later, in January 1972, the 'Magnificent Seven' escaped from the Prison Ship HMS *Maidstone*, and two years on, in November 1974, thirty-three prisoners attempted to tunnel their way out of Long Kesh but were immediately recaptured. A few months later, in March 1975, some of those on trial for that escape attempt ironically escaped from the courthouse in Newry. Finally, in June 1981, a further eight prisoners escaped from Crumlin Road Jail.

Important as these escapes were, they could not compare to the massive propaganda coup and morale boost of the escape from the

Maze Prison in September 1983. It was a complicated escape plan to execute and a patient strategy was pursued. Under the supposed guise of co-operation, inmates undertaking prison work slowly built up trust with the prison officers, eventually gaining access to the whole of the block. In the meantime, six handguns were smuggled in over time, allowing them at 2.30 pm one September afternoon to seize control of the block with a simultaneously co-ordinated hostage-taking of prison guards and taking over command of the control centre. In the attack, two prison officers were shot, four were stabbed and fourteen beaten. Of those stabbed, one subsequently died of a heart attack. An hour later they hijacked a food delivery van bringing supplies to the prison and hid inside it to make their escape. Fifteen prisoners were recaptured on the day and a further four over the following two days. Nineteen got clear away, the majority of them via South Armagh.

Encouraged and energised by the Maze break out, escape was on the minds of the Portlaoise Prison inmates too, and aroused with new innovative thinking, patient preparations began for a carefully planned prelude to an attempted break out. On 25 March 1983, Chief Prison Officer Brian Stack was shot as he attended a boxing match on Dublin's South Circular Road. He was left paralysed and brain damaged after the shooting and died eighteen months later. It has been suggested that under Brian Stack's direction, prison officers carried out frequent searches of E Block looking for any hidden escape paraphernalia, hoping to deny its use to the prisoners and at least disrupt any intentions to escape. Sometimes quarrels or disturbances on the block resulted with a fracas breaking out and it is believed that Chief Officer Stack would not shirk from dealing directly with prisoners on such occasions and took no nonsense. In 2013, after a long campaign by Oliver Stack, Chief Prison Officer Stack's eldest son, the IRA admitted that they had committed the shooting but that it was not sanctioned by the leadership. 'In Portlaoise a brutal prison regime saw prisoners and their families suffer greatly,' the IRA said in a written statement, 'This is the context in which IRA volunteers shot your father.'

The Provisional IRA had tried tunnelling out of Portlaoise, blasting the walls with explosives and breaking in with an improvised armoured battering ram; what methodology would they attempt next? In the event it was the simplest, most straightforward and surprising method yet. The Guard Platoon Commander explains:

It was a Sunday morning; the prisoners were drilling as they normally did on a Sunday and with the Platoon settling into their posts I returned to the Governor's House. The alarm suddenly went off. I went to the window and saw a stream of prison officers emerge from E Block, opening gates, then turning left towards the main gate. I ran to the Guard Room where the Platoon Sergeant was busy urgently deploying the 'Reserve' from the Guard Room reacting to the alarm, taking up the positions to be occupied in the event of just such an alert, including covering positions outside the perimeter wall. Suddenly there was a 'bang!' the sound of an explosion, in reaction to which I drew my pistol and together with the Platoon Sergeant we let ourselves into a sentry position over the main gate itself. We found a private soldier there having adopted a firing position and questioned him as to what his intentions were. He stated that he had selected a fixed point and if it became necessary would fire into that (and if the escapees ran into that wall of fire that was their choice).

I remember thinking there was 'no comms', as if the radios were blocked, but I did not dwell on this because what struck me most in the instance was that the older private soldiers had done instinctively what they were supposed to do – get into firing positions as soon as possible – only they managed to do it even quicker! On the sounding of the alarm they grabbed their rifles and brought with them their helmets and flak jackets, putting these on after they arrived to their 'stand to' positions, as opposed to what the younger private soldiers did, i.e. put them on first in the guard room and then move. The older soldiers' experience and subconscious impulse gained vital seconds in getting to where they needed to be. We waited.

Almost as quickly as it had begun, the main action subsided. It was over, no one was going anywhere. In the event of a breach in the perimeter I was happy that the platoon were, prior to the explosion, already in place – ready – and the 'old soldiers' had their minds made up: they were opening fire! The old experienced soldiers reacted well, knowing the right thing to do. An incident room was set up; the prison was searched and an array of stuff was found. Prison officer uniforms had been fashioned out of tracksuit material – the correct blue in colour – the belts were leather belts covered with the same material and buttons were from Aran cardigans covered with tin foil. There were two small .22 calibre pistols and an array of keys, one of which had stamped on it 'Main Gate Tested'. There was an inquiry and I sat in with the soldiers as they were making their statements. I got a sense that there was a feeling from higher headquarters that we somehow ought to have opened fire, but I was happy that on the occasion the circumstances did not meet the criteria for opening fire, the occasion's on-ground actuality for doing so did not fit into our orders.

Three days after the failed escape bid, the Minister for Justice, Michael Noonan, during a Dáil debate on the issue, stated:

While the single most important fact is that the attempt failed, as I have already indicated publicly, [it is] deeply disturbing that prisoners were able to get from the main cell block of the prison as far as the main gate using duplicate keys. In the past, the prisoners have used explosives and so on during escape attempts, but this is the first occasion on which prisoners have used keys in this fashion or have had firearms in their possession.

The circumstances are under investigation by both the Gardaí and the prison authorities and the House can be assured that every effort will be made to bring to justice those involved in this incident.

I have already commended the security forces of the prison for the manner in which they reacted to this incident and I would now like to say that the foresight demonstrated by those responsible for security at the prison is illustrated by the replacement last year of a wooden gate by a steel gate which led to the failure of this escape bid.

Incidentally, I understand that RTÉ, in the course of a purported reconstruction of the escape bid broadcast on Monday evening last, said that prisoners could have taken keys from an officer and opened the gate which they attempted to blow up. If that was true there would indeed be cause for public anxiety, but it is not the case as the gate in question required two keys, to be opened simultaneously from either side of the gate.

As I have said, the principal feature of this incident was the failure of the escape attempt and I am confident that the prisoners, even if they had succeeded in blowing the gate, would have been dealt with by the army, because the army, alerted by the general alarm, were, by the time the prisoners reached the main gate, deployed outside the gate in anticipation of the prisoners succeeding in breaching the gate. This aspect of the incident demonstrates again the degree of planning and thought given to all sorts of possibilities by those in charge of security.

The escape plan was reliant on surprise, speed and a supply of duplicate keys, and adding some confusion by the use of convincing-looking prison officer uniforms. The extra contingency of explosives was held in reserve in the event of having to blast open the main gate, which when it came to it only blew it further closed and stymied the escape plan. The prospective prison escapees had targeted the Governor's gate, the back gate and now the main gate itself. On occasions, E Block inmates were transferred for treatment at the local hospital and a military guard had to be put in place, much to the concern and inconvenience of the hospital staff, patients and visitors. These hospital guards became routine, as were the prisoner escorts to and from the Special Criminal Court and on occasions to courthouses elsewhere in the country.

In September 1979, during the visit to Ireland by Pope John Paul II, intelligence indicated that a loyalist paramilitary group had planned to mount a mortar attack against the prison in a bid to kill republicans. August 1979 had seen the Warrenpoint massacre, when eighteen British soldiers were blown up in a double explosion and Lord Louis Mountbatten and his boating party suffered a similar fate in Mullaghmore, Co. Sligo. The 1st Armoured Car Squadron deployed constant mobile patrols with the Gardaí on the road network around the prison over a forty-eight-hour period. It was an ironic situation to have had the 'enemies of the State being protected by the 'soldiers of the State benefitting from the defenders of a democracy that they themselves were doing their best to undermine.

A decade on from the eruption of the Troubles, a reinvented Provisional IRA reignited a campaign of violence for which an initial ambivalence amongst the Irish public turned to antipathy, the vast majority in the Republic becoming completely repulsed by their viciousness. Neither did they favour the paramilitaries' fervour for their political aim of replacing the existing body politic in both the South and North by an All-Ireland Socialist Republican State ruled by the Provisional IRA. Any early feelings of enthusiasm and positive sentiment they may have enjoyed had evaporated as it became apparent that PIRA's supported propensity for the use of violence was largely what defined them – and they were also seen as prone to use it against the Irish State security forces. The callous and deliberate murders of Garda Michael Clerkin and Chief Prison Officer Brian Stack amply demonstrated this. For their part, the Defence Forces proved their worth in keeping PIRA prisoners in Portlaoise Prison. It was not a job for soldiers but only soldiers could do it.

PART 4

BEYOND THE BORDER
AND 'THE BOG'

CHAPTER 11

The Battle of Ballsbridge

The presentation and manifestation of events and incidents in the Republic of Ireland during the Troubles were not neatly linear in occurrence. Instead of proceeding from one involvement to another, the demands on the Defence Forces were overlapping and concurrent. This placed a heavy workload on the Forces, the nature of which was different, difficult and dangerous, and the span of three decades meant an unceasing commitment to defend democracy was required of its soldiers. Times were grim and they daily placed their lives on the line in an increasingly violent society. If you were to ask an Irish soldier what his first thoughts were that automatically come to mind whenever the Troubles are mentioned, inevitably it is almost always duty on 'the border' or in 'the prison' (Portlaoise Prison) or both. If pushed further, the next mention is that of 'poor pay and conditions', thereafter if pressed yet further again, mention is made of involvements in individual incidents and happenings as a result of many deployments and operations resulting from riots, arms seizures and kidnappings.

'There is a crowd gathering in the town preparing to march on your post. I'll keep you updated. Oh, and the mood is angry.' The Garda sergeant at Castleblayney Garda Station hung up the phone, leaving the young Irish army Lieutenant in Castleblayney Military Post to take in the significance of the call he had just received. A potentially riotous demonstration was assembling in advance of heading towards the small border outpost. Castleblayney, Co. Monaghan, was not a large border town, so once the assembled throng began heading from the town's centre in the direction of the military post they would not be long in arriving. It was after normal duty hours so the Lieutenant immediately ordered the camp's personnel recall plan be put into effect, and while waiting for those notified to respond he exited the Operations Room, went outside onto the post's square and took a fresh look at his surroundings, making a mental appreciation of 'the ground' in a whole new light – that of maybe having to defend it. Now August 1981, the Post Commander, Commandant Eoghan Allen, then away on leave, had arrived there exactly twelve years beforehand in August 1969 and described the Post as follows:

> We had moved to Dundalk and then on to Castleblayney. We developed a post centred on the existing 'Slua Hall' purpose built for the part-time Local Defence Force (LDF) during the Emergency in the early 1940s. We lived under canvas (in tents) from August to October, thereafter moving into the Hall itself. Officers lived on the Hall's stage, the NCOs and Privates in the Hall itself, (army nurses in the town's 'Central Hotel') and meals were cooked in an adjacent lean-to (a simple structure next to an existing building with the rafters 'leaning' against another wall) and served in the 'miniature range'.

An imposing, heavily fortified solid stone barracks 'Camp Muckno' was not. Sufficient at the time of its inception, the Post had not been sited with defence in mind. Except the reality was even worse than that; located on the town's periphery, one perimeter side was edged against the back gardens of modest properties, the others fringed with fields and, unbelievably, it was actually overlooked by a neighbouring drumlin (hill). The camp functioned really as a patrol hub, a location with some space for troops and equipment rather than a 'military' base. Hastily fashioned around the old Slua Hall, in the intervening years a number of eclectic timber huts had been added. It had a wire fence surround, more to demarcate its boundary than for any defensive purpose. Far from ideal, it was nonetheless made to work. Its garrison, Support Company of the 27th Infantry Battalion, were fully occupied, positive and purposeful troops and the demanding tempo of border operations had forced their attention and functional focus onto the main mission out along the border. The priority had always been to get the patrols out, maintain soldiering standards and otherwise respond to border incidents – of which there was seldom a shortage in their area of responsibility. They were a close-knit, proud, loyal, hardworking border unit, whose personnel were from the area or integrated into the town. Of course, not everyone liked them but that was part and parcel of 'soldiering' on the border.

Right now the 'safety of the post to be protected' was possibly in jeopardy; the serious destruction of Government property at issue, and in its defence they now had to be prepared to face the danger and risk harm. Hostility and trouble was coming their way and they had to use what time was available to best effect. A difficult defence against disorder and disturbance had to be organised and it was a worrisome situation for the Lieutenant. Among his suddenly many worries, as the clamour, commotion and confusion of troops hastily preparing for the challenge ahead surrounded him, was of how to effectively defend against petrol bombs (because if it was he that was orchestrating the mayhem against the camp that is what he would use). A recent image from the television news – from recent rioting in the North – kept flashing into his mind; footage of a British soldier behind a vehicle during a street disturbance in Belfast as a petrol bomb exploded in flames at his feet, his leg quickly set alight, his torso soon engulfed in flames. A quick-thinking Corporal had reached into the Land Rover the soldier was sheltering behind, taken out a fire extinguisher and doused the burning soldier in foam, saving him from terrible injury. Grabbing a passing Sergeant by the arm, the Lieutenant confided his concern and quietly ordered him to collect all of the fire extinguishers from around the camp and centralise them so that they were to hand in an easily identified and conveniently reached location. 'Good idea, Sir,' responded the Sergeant and he went off in search of the fire extinguishers.

The Lieutenant decided to seek reinforcements from his Battalion Headquarters in Aiken Barracks, Dundalk, Co. Louth. 'Fuck off, we've problems of our own over here!' was the response he received. So, he picked up the phone again and rang directly across Battalion boundaries, not going through Eastern Command Infantry Force (ECIF) HQ based in Gormanstown Camp, Co. Meath, and instead rang HQ 28th Infantry Battalion in Monaghan Town. 'No can help, we've problems brewing here too,' was the reply. The Post were on their own. Discouraged, he had little time to dwell on the matter because the fire-extinguisher seeking Sergeant returned and gave him a status report on the situation. 'Good news and bad news, Sir. I found fifteen fire extinguishers but only seven of them work.'

'OK,' responded the Lieutenant, 'go to the outside of the dining hall, empty the swill barrels, half fill them with water and place blankets next to them.'

'Good idea sir,' responded the Sergeant and dutifully went about the task. The Lieutenant rang the Garda Station for an update on the gathering crowd, to be told it was 'getting bigger and angrier'. Nothing for it but to settle the defence, set a determined tone, remain resilient and face up to whatever was about to confront them. How it was all going to go, he had no idea. They waited … and waited … and waited.

The next thing he was aware of, a Corporal from the Company Operations Room was beside him: 'Word from the Guards sir, the crowd down town have got into buses and cars and gone to join the riot in Monaghan.' Relief, absolute deliverance, tinged with a slight sense of anti-climax too, but overall an almighty alleviation of anxiety and tension. The following day the Lieutenant's duty replacement arrived and he was able to take three days off. Returning to resume duty a few days later, on arrival at the camp's entrance gate the Military Policeman told him to report directly and immediately to the Company Commander, who had himself arrived back from leave the day before. The Lieutenant knocked on the Company Commander's office door. 'Come in!' was the rather abrupt reply. Not at all daunted, the Lieutenant surmised the Company Commander probably wanted a first-hand account of the incident.

The Lieutenant opened the door and hadn't placed one foot inside the office before he heard the Company Commander snap: 'Why shouldn't I bill you for the cost of eleven blankets destroyed at the weekend?' The Sergeant must have put the blankets into, not next to, the swill barrels full of water. A look of total astonishment crossed the Lieutenant's face; next he heard the Commander chuckling: 'Only joking, well done – that can't have been an easy situation!' Humour in such dire situations was one way to temper the dark mood of the times, keep intact an *esprit de corps*, and maintain morale. This was especially important to counter the hysteria from the hurt, horror and hate of the H-Block Hunger Strikes.

Since 1976 onwards, the republican movement had recognised it was seriously struggling, and by 1980 – despite its reorganisation and the emergence of a young, hard, pragmatic 'Northern' leadership, its switch to a more tightly organised cellular structure and its possession of high calibre weapons – they knew they could not force a British withdrawal from the North by purely military means. Sinn Féin was being side-lined the armed struggle was stagnant, and then, like a surprise gift, along came the Hunger Strike in the Maze Prison over a dispute with the prison authorities. Eventually, ten prisoners (seven PIRA and three INLA) were to die, including Bobby Sands who had been elected to Westminster as MP for Fermanagh and South Tyrone. Sands died on 5 May 1981 after refusing food for sixty-six days. Now, in early August 1981, it was the occasion of the eighth Hunger Striker to die, Kieran Doherty after seventy-three days refusing food, which sparked disturbances along the border on the night of 2 August 1981. Doherty, along with Paddy Agnew, an IRA volunteer who was not on hunger strike, had been elected TDs for Cavan–Monaghan and Louth, respectively, in the General Election in June. Their election and inroads elsewhere were sufficient to damage the Fianna Fáil vote, denying them power, and leading to a change of government in the Republic.

The Hunger Strike campaign evolved from within the Maze Prison, it was not a planned PIRA strategy. Less imagined still was the contesting and winning of the elections. The campaign witnessed the orchestration of a huge upsurge in emotion, bringing an enormous groundswell of support nationally and internationally, especially from the USA and, ominously, from Libya. In the North, street disturbances and violence escalated, the separate communities re-entrenched and the Provisional IRA increased its operations. The number of deaths rose (to sixty-one, thirty of them security forces), and back in the Maze Prison, the staggered start times of the individuals commencing their hunger strikes ensured that there were ongoing intervals between those near death, dying, actual deaths and their funerals. It was a highly charged conveyor belt of dramatic, raw emotion which had a continued impetus – the impact momentous – one forcefully favourable towards the Provisional IRA. Its leadership had not been positively disposed towards a hunger strike campaign, believing it distracted from the main effort, the military campaign; also should a hunger strike not go 'all the way' there was the potential for a loss of face, which was felt detrimental to morale.

Its initiation came from an ongoing campaign of protest against the loss of political status in 1976 within the Maze Prison and the Women's Jail in Armagh; instead they were classified as criminal prisoners. Refusing to wear prison uniforms, the prisoners were naked except for blankets draped over their shoulders, a form of action known as 'on the blanket'. The blanket protest escalated to a 'dirty protest' following a disturbance in 1978, when the prison authorities removed the furniture from prisoners' cells, whereby prisoners covered their cell walls with their own excrement.

By 1980 there were some 400 protestors 'on the blanket' between both prisons. The Hunger Strike began on 1 March 1981 and by mid-July six prisoners had died from self-starvation. The campaign was centred around the 'Five Demands': the right to wear their own clothes; to refrain from prison work; to have free association and organise their own leisure activities; the right to one visit, one letter and one parcel per week; and the restoration of remission lost during the protest. Down south in Portlaoise Prison, a pragmatic common-sense compromise had been reached whereby these conditions were largely the case but without it actually being termed 'political status'. The same situation in the North was not achievable because of the trenchant position taken by the British Prime Minister, Margaret Thatcher, preferring to stick to the 'criminalisation' policy.

There was a certain degree of admiration amongst republicans for the hunger strikers, and this martyrdom tactic had a preferential place in Irish Republican history going back to the War of Independence (1919–21) – when Terence McSwiney, the Lord Mayor of Cork, had died after seventy-four days without food – and its use became greatly revered. It was a respect de Valera gave no notion to during the Emergency (1939–46), allowing three IRA men to die on hunger strike; others were executed and the IRA put down. It had no part in the IRA's 1956–62 border campaign, but was used by OC Belfast PIRA, Billy McKee, in 1972, first gaining the concession of political

(Special Category) status. The Provisional IRA member, Sean Mac Stíofáin, then Chief-of-Staff, when arrested in the Republic in 1973, went on hunger strike and was transferred to the Curragh Military Hospital, coming off it after fifty-seven days. The 1981 Hunger Strike in the Maze Prison, however, was a crisis to be exploited for the full propaganda effect it could yield.

It was 0400 hours when the standby company (120 men) of the 12th Infantry Battalion was summoned from their beds and within two hours they were formed up, equipped, made ready and leaving Sarsfield Barracks, Limerick, heading for Shannon Airport in a strong convoy of armoured personnel carriers. During the course of the flight from Britain, an Aer Lingus cargo plane with the remains of Frank Stagg on board was diverted to Shannon Airport instead of its original intended destination of Dublin Airport. Directed to do so by the Irish Government, there was initially some resistance by Aer Lingus who felt they were being dragged into a highly conflicted situation. Kept overnight in Shannon airport, the remains were taken by road under heavy escort from Clare to South Mayo via West Galway. Frank Stagg's body was buried in Ballina town's cemetery in new ground and not in the Republican plot and without republican ceremony. A layer of concrete was laid over his grave to prevent disinterment.

Deprived of their own military funeral, over 5,000 republican supporters arrived in busloads from Belfast, Derry and Dublin the next day. Bars and businesses closed as the parade wound its way through the town watched by hundreds of blue-helmeted Gardaí and platoons of Irish soldiers in riot gear. Gardaí were also positioned in the cemetery at the grave but much more so 100-yards away around the republican plot. There were small clusters of individual platoons along the upper edge of the graveyard but most of the 600 or so troops (two battalions, the 6th and 12th Infantry Battalions from the Western and Southern Commands, respectively) were kept in neighbouring fields, out of sight, in reserve. Among the military presence that day, firstly deployed in the town, then forming part of the graveyard reserve, was Brigadier General Séamus Ó Giolláin, then a Lieutenant:

I was a platoon commander of a 12th Infantry Platoon which had been involved with the Frank Stagg funeral for a three day period, firstly at Shannon Airport and then onto Ballina, Co. Mayo, where mine and a second platoon were deployed at a remove in a field along a roadside. At one stage during the Republican ceremony, after they had marched into the graveyard and headed for the republican plot, we heard a muffled volley of shots being fired. I looked in alarm at my platoon Sergeant, thinking the Gardaí had opened fire. He, Sergeant John Power, later to win a Distinguished Service Medal (DSM) for his steadfast defence of OP Ras in South Lebanon in April 1980, assuredly and correctly said: 'A salute to the fallen, sir.'

We could see scuffles, and some hand-to-hand fighting had broken out in a somewhat confused struggle for a brief duration between those present and the Gardaí, but it did not sustain itself for long. We did come into action ourselves towards the end of proceedings when a section of the crowd, those from Northern Ireland, tried to outflank us, the two platoons (sixty men). They were fairly hostile and insulting, calling us, amongst other things, 'collaborators with the British' and then began hurling rocks at us. I ordered my platoon to adopt the kneeling position and we intertwined our riot shields like a roman phalanx to defend against the hail of rocks. Both platoons took casualties; that is one per platoon – in both cases the medical orderlies as they had no riot shields, so I eventually ordered baton rounds to be fired as did the other platoon and the crowd retreated.

The republican demonstrators seemed satisfied they had been allowed to conduct their commemoration and the authorities were happy that by force of numbers they had prevented serious violence taking place. The Government was also happy, as it had been seen to face down those who would otherwise make others fearful or feel intimidated and prevented the town of Ballina from being taken over by militant-minded republicans. The episode earned Mr Paddy Cooney, the Minister for Justice, the nickname 'Concrete Cooney' for a while. Six months later, secretly at night, the body of Frank Stagg was dug up and reburied alongside that of Michael Gaughan. Both men were unsuccessful in their bid for the right to be transferred to Ireland to complete their sentences and died on hunger strike because of it.

More successful were the Price sisters, Dolours and Marian, who were repatriated to Armagh Jail after over 200 days on hunger strike during which they were force fed by means of forcing open the mouth with a metal device and the insertion of a tube into the stomach. Such was the abhorrence surrounding this brutal practice that in June 1974 the British Home Secretary, Roy Jenkins, had the practice banned and thereafter any prisoner who went on hunger strike would not be force fed. Seven years later, in 1981 during the H-Block Hunger Strikes, none were force fed and ten died. At the height of the Hunger Strikes, on Saturday 18 July 1981, an H-Block demonstration to the British Embassy in Dublin was organised. After the death of six hunger strikers in the H-Blocks, feelings were running high. The organisers tapped into a wave of anger which had swept across people from all walks of life, many gripped by a political hysteria, some almost radicalised by the campaign. There were those amongst the protestors who wanted the occasion to become a flashpoint of aggression in a fraught time for Anglo-Irish relations. They came prepared for trouble and hoped to cause havoc.

The organisers of the demonstration were made aware in advance that an approach to the British Embassy building would not be permitted – there was to be no repeat of the scenes nine years beforehand of a British Embassy in flames, an angry crowd protesting against the fourteen fatal Bloody Sunday shootings in Derry – though there were some who were determined to bring about and purposefully orchestrate a repeat of the assault. The duty of the Gardaí and Defence Forces was to afford protection to the properties of the representatives of other countries accredited to the Irish State as expected in any civilised country. Some amongst the protestors hoped to capitalise on the prevailing sense of outrage and shape its expression beyond mere attendance at the march – to mobilise it for harmful purposes – borne out in the savage scenes which followed. This premeditated preparedness to clash with the Gardaí and army was amply evidenced by the amount and variety of weapons of all descriptions which were gathered at the conclusion of the event, used in sustained and unprovoked attacks of the most vicious character.

The idea that the British Embassy could be sacked a second time would have been to allow the reputation of the State to be gravely damaged internationally. In 1972, the Embassy's destruction gave vent to the outrage felt after Bloody Sunday; once the building was aflame tensions were released and passions dampened. Similarly stirred about the non-resolution of the hunger strikers' strife and the resultant deaths, it gave a powerful impulse to protest. The circumstances of the situation were ready to play out as occurred nine years earlier, only with one big difference: the posture of the security forces. They were prepared, present in sufficient numbers and single-mindedly persistent about affecting a dissimilar outcome. This determination would be severely tested:

> As acting Officer Commanding 2 Infantry Battalion, based in Cathal Brugha Barracks, Rathmines, Dublin, I received orders on the 17 July 1981 from 2nd Brigade Headquarters that the Defence Forces was to give assistance to the Gardaí in defence of the British Embassy at Ballsbridge, Dublin, during the up-coming H-Block protest scheduled for the following day. The plan was for the Gardaí to establish, using interlinked metal fencing chained together and secured at respective ends by chains attached to the Royal Dublin Society (RDS) show ground railings and the base of a lamp post, a barrier in order to close off Merrion Road at the Simmonscourt junction. This was to halt the protestors short of their objective, the British Embassy.
>
> The Defence Forces' contingent of a Company-plus strength with a Battalion Headquarters element was to take up position, out of sight, initially at the rear of the Embassy itself, with the Battalion Headquarters in the Simmonscourt building. Another Infantry company was placed in Government Buildings (a large building on Merrion Street in which several key offices of the Irish government are located) as the marchers' intended route was to take them past it. Once this had happened and all was well, they would then be available as a Reserve to me.
>
> On the day, I took the executive decision to co-locate them with me in the grounds of the British Embassy itself instead, to concentrate the forces available to me in defence of the 'main effort'. Out in front, at the fence barrier, in full view was the Gardaí, in strength of about 500 men. It had been emphasised at the prior briefing that there was to be no repeat of the British Embassy burning on this occasion, that as far as the Government

was concerned it simply was not going to happen. On the day, we deployed as planned and waited for the protestors to arrive.

We waited, and as we were deployed in the 'military' role and not the 'police' role, and equipped accordingly, armed with weapons and not riot gear, I decided that we would organise ourselves to act appropriate to the situation. We had CS gas available, so in the event of the Garda line being breached and confronted with an angry mob I would first use CS gas and selected 'snatch squads' to take out the ringleaders. Along with the Company we selected two officers, formidable in both physique and psyche, and allowed them [to] select from the NCOs and men those with similar characteristics. The 'Rifle Company Commander' requested of me if there were any specific considerations for opening fire and I replied to him to apply the criteria normally abided by, and emphasised that he could not allow any one of his troops to become forcibly disarmed. All that done, we settled and in due course could monitor the arrival of the protestors, some 10,000–15,000 strong by the ever increasing din. Not long afterwards a deputation from the demonstrators were allowed behind the Garda line to confer with the main Garda officer involved and the location chosen for this granted them line of sight onto us – as I remember the look of astonishment on their faces when they caught sight of our presence drawn up in orderly ranks.

As the deputation re-joined the demonstrators, the trouble makers among them began to throw stones, bricks and bottles and this soon became a sustained barrage. The Garda started taking casualties. This situation maintained itself for a good duration and the number of Gardaí injured mounted. At one point, the same Garda Inspector approached me as had before and requested I fire CS gas at the crowd. As whatever light wind was blowing on the fine summer's day was doing so into the faces of the Gardaí, and they did not have respirators, I declined to do so.

Meanwhile, the patient, restrained and admirable discipline of the Gardaí only served to embolden the rioters and they became ever more violent. There was an evident violent intent, as the rioters began an onslaught on the Garda line using bricks, bottles, petrol bombs, golf balls, pick-axe handles and a variety of poles, some with steel-pointed tips. The bricks were obtained from nearby garden walls, and sledge hammers that had been used to break down the walls were subsequently found by the Garda. Two cars were also removed from the gardens of houses and set on fire and six other cars were severely damaged. The one redeeming feature was the restraint, forbearance and courage shown by the Gardaí in the face of sustained and unprovoked attacks of the most vicious character.

All the while the attackers were being urged to 'burn the Embassy' and to 'move forward' as they threw everything they could at the Gardaí and hit them with everything they had to hand – all the while the Gardaí casualties mounted, to the point where there was no longer any merit in just standing there anymore, because to do so would mean there would soon not be anyone left standing. The only form of defence remaining was a baton charge against the onslaught, and clambering over the beaten-down, battered, bedraggled barrier they brought the confrontation full-square to the rioters themselves. The riot had reached its crescendo and the rioters were overrun in the baton charge. The British Embassy did not burn.

Nearly 200 people were hospitalised, 75 per cent of them Gardaí. The then Taoiseach, Dr Garret FitzGerald, accompanied by high-ranking Gardaí, inspected the rubble-strewn scene the next morning and afterwards he and his wife went to visit injured Gardaí in various hospitals around Dublin. The Irish public supported the Government action and historian Professor JJ Lee praised the then Minister for Justice, Jim Mitchell TD, for 'a striking sureness of touch in handling an ugly situation.'

A week later there was a repeat demonstration and the security forces took measures accordingly, including supporting the Gardaí tasked specifically with the protection of certain key and symbolic buildings. Lieutenant Colonel Sean Scanlon (Retd.) then a Commandant, was appointed Commander of a Company from the 4th Infantry Battalion Cork, sent to Dublin to secure Government Buildings, namely the Dáil (Irish Parliament):

> During the week after the Ballsbridge Riot I was called into 4th
> Battalion Headquarters and told I was to take a Company to Dublin

to secure the Dáil. We immediately commenced riot training and a day or so later moved to Cathal Brugha Barracks, Rathmines, Dublin. I attended a large briefing session and distinctly remember being informed of a curious constraint in relation to the fulfilment of our mission, namely that a lot of money had recently been spent on refurbishing the Dáil which included the procurement of paintings, carpets and furnishings and that in the event of trouble erupting, CS gas was not to be used. As this could seriously limit my responsiveness regarding degrees of escalation of reactive measures to a possible riot situation, I calmly requested to have this edict given to me in writing, and got on with our preparations.

Captain Jim Rea (Retd.) was then a Lieutenant and one of three Platoon Commanders with the 4th Battalion Company:

We moved to Dublin, staying in Cathal Brugha Barracks where we rehearsed anti-riot drills. During our time there we conducted a recce (reconnaissance) in the Dáil, met the Chief Superintendent involved, toured the Dáil to familiarise ourselves with our positions [and] any vulnerable points and the overall layout. The memory I had of the actual day of the demonstration was we rehearsed, were fired up and then escorted by the Gardaí to the Dáil. Our Platoon took up its position, a Sergeant and a radioman took up appropriate vantage points as an Observation Post, and the radio frequency allowed us know of the progress of the protest. They approached, we heard them passing, shouting, and we were unseen, our presence unknown. Nothing happened, however. Yet in protecting the Dáil we felt that we were literally defending democracy.

Within a month four more hunger strikers would be dead and the families of those still dying persuaded the influencers to bring an end to the protest. The stand-off ended with both nationalists in the North and the British Government claiming victory. The potential for arousal of public sympathy in the South, it could be argued, had reached its peak. However, during its 217 days, 71 people died (including 10 hunger strikers), and the situation was poised to escalate out of control.

The Provisional IRA had manipulated the situation to maximum effort, gaining huge international media coverage, worldwide sympathy and new respect, new recruits, more funds and weapons. Most significantly of all, however, was that they discovered a new political sense of direction.

CHAPTER 12

Balaclava Bandits

At the height of the Hunger Strike, an unconnected death occurred that unbeknown to anyone at the time was to have great significance on subsequent events. The death, through natural causes, was that of Frank Maguire, the independent MP for Tyrone, thereby creating the necessity for a by-election. The Provisional republican movement, with its long-established abstention policy, had traditionally always avoided electoral politics, but on this occasion, in a spectacularly dramatic U-turn, Sinn Féin contested the election with a candidate: the leader of the Hunger Strike, Bobby Sands. It was a risky strategy for the IRA because failure to become elected – even narrowly – would allow it to be said that even the nationalist community would not vote for them. On 9 April 1981, Bobby Sands was elected MP for South Tyrone.

This was an early opportunity to halt the Hunger Strike, because by his election Sands had actually achieved 'political status', no matter what Margaret Thatcher said. However, this was something quite different to concessions on the 'Five Demands'. The Hunger Strike continued and nine more hunger strikers died; there were sixty-one other associated deaths and two other protestors (Kieran Doherty, who was on hunger strike, and Paddy Agnew, who was not) were elected TDs. The Provisional republican movement was, almost despite itself, drawn to politics. On 5 May 1981, Bobby Sands died. The opportunity was identified as a launching pad into electoral politics and a Provisional IRA strategy to broaden the support base for its campaign. Politics was now to co-exist, albeit uneasily, with the 'Long War', and the two-pronged strategy of 'the ArmaLite in one hand and the ballot box in the other' was born. The IRA convention of 1986 subsequently cleared the way for Republicans to attend the Dáil.

But back in the eighties, the Provisional IRA was grappling with conducting its campaign of violence and simultaneously looking for votes. It was costing PIRA in the region of between one and two million pounds annually to conduct its 'war' and some believed that it divided the movement's energies at a crucial time. It also greatly increased the financial demands on its financial stream. These twin campaigns relied on cash and there was not enough money to back both horses; the Provisional IRA was hovering on the brink of bankruptcy. An extraordinary intervention was needed and sums far in excess of the combination of proceeds from bank robberies and other criminal sources were required. The PIRA Southern Command's role was to support the activities in the Northern Command's 'War Zone' by the provision of finance, training and bomb-making facilities. The Southern Command was deemed to be falling well short in the provision of sufficient amounts of money and was given responsibility to make up the deficit.

Tasked to find funding, they decided to raise it from the ransom paid for the release of a kidnap victim, only they selected not a person but a horse; the greatest racehorse of the day, 'Shergar' from Ballymany Stud near the Curragh, Co. Kildare. Winner of the 1981 (British) Epsom Derby, the Irish Derby and King George VI and Queen Elizabeth Stakes, all in one year, Shergar was a special horse – a sporting legend – and was now out to stud. The 5-year-old Shergar, Irish-bred and British-trained, was now back in Ireland commanding huge stud fees. The kidnappers, a Provisional IRA 'special operations' gang, got a number of factors right in their planning and execution. Security at Ballymany Stud was not strict; there was a horse sale at nearby Goffs the following day, so movement of horse boxes and horse trailers across the country would not necessarily stand out anywhere; and the stud season had just begun, so this would increase the pressure for a quick and safe return of Shergar so as not to lose out on stud fees.

On the night of 8 February 1983, Shergar was kidnapped from Ballymany Stud, and was never seen again. Various real, diversionary and bogus negotiations were undertaken but failed. The main reason being that Shergar was not, as was thought, owned solely by one owner, the Aga Khan – who as it happened was not prepared to pay anything for the safe return of the racehorse – but by a syndicate of thirty-four people living in six countries. Getting a consensus on whether to pay a ransom or not proved difficult, which was not what the Provisional IRA kidnap gang had planned on. Neither was the interest aroused beyond Ireland, as the international media descended on Newbridge Garda Station eager for news of any clues in relation to the progress of the hunt for the horse and its kidnappers. The general public too turned out to be far more concerned about Shergar than the IRA had imagined; it seemed that Ireland is a greater horse racing nation than the Provisional IRA had first thought. It was not simply sentiment either that they had underestimated; there was also a very serious and pragmatic matter of the effect of the kidnapping on the horse-breeding business in Ireland and the possible adverse potential the kidnap might have on it, an industry where 20,000 jobs might be put at risk, prompting the Irish Thoroughbred Breeders Association to offer a £100,000 reward for information leading to Shergar's safe return.

Conspiracy theories as to who abducted Shergar abounded: it was the Mafia in revenge for an earlier deal with the Aga Khan that went bad; it was religion related – the Aga Khan, as well as being a businessman was the spiritual leader for millions of Muslims; it was ordinary decent criminals who took Shergar. A further theory suggested Shergar was in Libya in exchange for weapons. All the while the real kidnappers, the Provisional IRA, were conducting secret negotiations via Paris for a £2 million ransom which eventually came to nothing. There was agreement across the Irish and British security services and governments that under no circumstances would a ransom be paid. Negotiations faltered, communications ceased and whatever happened to Shergar became a mystery. His initial disappearance, however, prompted a nationwide search, the hunt taking in stables, known 'safe houses' were raided and there were sweeps of many suspect areas by troops and Gardaí. As a result Provisional IRA activities were disrupted, operations interfered with and it led to the seizures of several arms caches. In the end Shergar was never found, but neither did the episode realise the fear that it might lead to a flood of racehorse departures from Irish stables.

The Shergar kidnapping attracted far more attention than the Provisional IRA had anticipated. It was, however, during its early planning stages that information about another kidnapping came to the notice of the security forces. Subsequently, six months later on 7 August 1983, there was a failed kidnap attempt of Galen Weston, a millionaire supermarket executive, at his Roundwood, Co. Wicklow home.

Following a tip-off, armed Gardaí lay in wait and in the subsequent shoot out four of the would-be kidnap gang were wounded. In all, five were captured and two escaped.

The attempted kidnapping was over before it entered the public domain. However, played out in the full national and international media glare had been the kidnap some years earlier of Dr Tiede Herrema, a Dutch industrialist and Chief Executive of the Ferenka plant at Ballyvarra, Co. Limerick. On his way to work from his home in Monaleen Road near Castletroy, Dr Herrema was stopped at a false Garda checkpoint and taken. Among the kidnap gang was Eddie Gallagher, from Ballybofey, Co. Donegal, and Marion Coyle, from Derry City. Shortly after the seizure of the industrialist, the Provisional IRA kidnappers telephoned the media and the Dutch Embassy and demanded the release of the PIRA prisoners Kevin Mallon, Jim Hyland and Rose Dugdale. The nature of the ransom demand betrayed a certain personal element, as one of those whose release was demanded was romantically connected to Eddie Gallagher, one of the kidnap gang.

Rose Dugdale was an English-born heiress who had been jailed for nine years for her part in the Beit art heist at Russborough House in Co. Wicklow. Dugdale gave birth to Eddie Gallagher's child in Limerick Prison on 12 December 1974. Kevin Mallon was a noted Provisional IRA activist, one of the 'Birdmen of Mountjoy' who had escaped with two others from Mountjoy Prison in October 1973 in a helicopter. Recaptured after a few weeks, he was also among the nineteen prisoners, which also included Gallagher, who blasted their way out of Portlaoise Prison with explosives on 18 August 1974. Gallagher and Dugdale had previously been involved in a spectacular bombing attempt on an RUC station in Strabane. They had hijacked a helicopter and directed it to fly over the RUC station, whereby they dropped two milk churns filled with explosives, which failed to explode. Gallagher was a bit of a maverick operator, reckless and resolute. However, when Tiede Herrema was kidnapped, a country-wide search was mounted with large-scale operations involving Gardaí supported by the Defence Forces. Colonel George Kerton (Retd.), then a Lieutenant, remembers:

> On the day after the kidnapping, I was sent with a Troop (minus) with four Land Rovers (Fitted for Radio – FFR) to Portlaoise Garda

Station to support the Garda search operations. We were equipped with sleeping bags and camp beds and were fed from The Curragh and from Portlaoise Prison. We spent the following days, up to the late Monday night, working out of the 9th Infantry Battalion FCÁ Training Centre adjacent to Portlaoise Garda Station. We started on the Heath (on the old National Primary Road N7 between Ballybrittas and Portlaoise) and worked across a lot of Co. Laois and Co. Offaly, through Mountmellick, Rosenallis and Clonaslee to Kinnitty and into the foothills of the Slieve Bloom Mountains. The Garda party was led by Inspector Peter Fitzpatrick and included a number of armed detectives as well as uniformed Gardaí. They were calling to houses of known subversives who had dropped off the radar and also checked derelict houses and remote farm buildings. Books written after the event claim that Dr Herrema was held initially at Kinnitty, Mountmellick and at Kildangan.

For eighteen days the Defence Forces supported the Gardaí in a huge search operation across the whole country, and on Tuesday 21 October, Dr Herrema and two of his kidnappers, Eddie Gallagher and Marion Coyle, were located at number 1410 St Evin's Park in Monasterevin, Co. Kildare. Sometime after 5 am that morning, the Camp Stand-To in the Curragh Camp, commanded by a Cavalry officer of the rank of Captain, was dispatched to Monasterevin to assist the Gardaí in a raid on the house. As the armed party and Gardaí approached, shots were fired, narrowly missing the Cavalry officer. This started a siege that lasted for another seventeen days under the gaze of the world's media:

> I received my orders in the Guardroom in McDonagh Barracks from the Operations Officer, Curragh Training Command, and on arrival at Monasterevin, we went to the Garda Station from where we travelled to St Evin's Park in unmarked Garda cars. We pulled up outside the house and one detective took off from the car, went straight through the closed front door without stopping and up the stairs. He came down even faster when shots were fired. At this stage I was behind a car outside the front door. Herrema was screaming at us to stay back. I saw his arm raised and a shot was fired from under his arm which hit the road close

to me. I was afraid to move in case they would shoot him. When I finally extricated myself I went around the group surrounding the house.

I had two snipers with me in addition to the Stand-To party, one of whom was a marksman and an All-Army rifle shot. The orders I had been given if they came out (firing or otherwise in a life-threatening manner) was for him to shoot the one holding a gun to Herrema and the rest of us would take out the other or others. We were not sure how many there were. I said to the marksman he would have only one shot. His reply was, 'Sir, I won't miss,' and I know he would not have. I eventually extricated myself. We were duly relieved and went back to the Curragh. I was debriefed by Command HQ Officers who were not impressed by the fact that we had no radio contact as we were in an area with poor coverage; that was their main concern.

Three of the bigger barracks in the Curragh Camp – McDonagh (General Training Depot), Connolly (3rd Infantry Battalion) and Plunkett (Depot Cavalry and 1st Armoured Car Squadron) – each supplied a reinforced platoon in rotation for a 24-hour period as an outer perimeter while armed Gardaí manned the inner perimeter. The 3rd Infantry Battalion and 1st Armoured Car Squadron also supplied armoured fighting vehicles (AFVs) while a team of snipers supervised by a Captain were deployed at vantage points near the house and operated under special rules of engagement for the operation.

On Friday 31 October, the first weekend of the siege, two Garda detectives climbed ladders at the back of the house and were attempting to remove a window pane in the bathroom when a shot rang out and a bullet shattered the index finger of one of them. There had also been a prior attempt to gain entry a few days beforehand, when tiles were removed from the roof of the house and two Gardaí gained admission to the attic only for a shot to be fired in response, which travelled through the overhead bedroom ceiling and up into the attic, causing that attempt to cease.

Meanwhile, back in the Curragh Camp, tactical options were being investigated. A series of trials were conducted as to how best to successfully effect a house assault. At the commencement of the siege, a team of Corps of Engineers had successfully and speedily constructed a room on the second floor of a derelict building near the Detention Barracks, known as the Western Expanses, that was the same dimensions and layout with similar furniture and fittings as 1410 St Evin's Park. Three officers were assigned to play the role of Gallagher, Coyle and Herrema. They were told that an attempt would be made over the following seventy-two hours to free the hostage. The officer playing Herrema was told not to assist the other two in any way and they experimented with using the furniture to jam the door. They were fed with sandwiches and flasks of tea hoisted up in a bucket to replicate the situation on the ground in Monasterevin. Experimental procedures were made and they soon fell into a routine. Every hour, on the half hour, an APC (armoured personnel carrier) would run its engine for five minutes and slowly circle the area. This was to represent the changing of sentries on the perimeter. Those within concluded that the rescue attempt would be on the half hour. One of those involved takes up the story:

> In the early afternoon we heard squeaking on the stairs and a stone crashed through the window. I grabbed the 'hostage' by the hair and shoved his face up to the broken window with the pistol to his head. After about four or five attempts to batter in the door the hinges gave way and the door seesawed over the head of the bed. Two strong officers with three large NCOs from the 3rd Battalion fell into the room spraying blanks from Gustav sub-machine guns. The rescue attempt would have been an absolute massacre! For the rest of the day we had similar attacks. They used blankets, canvas sacking and tentage (the canvas from tents) to muffle the noise of the stairs but it was impossible to achieve a silent approach.
>
> On the second day there was a change in direction and we [were] subjected to gassing from CS and CN gas fired from the anti-riot gun and hand canisters. We secured a blanket over the window as concealment. At this stage we were in overalls and we were allowed to have showers. Day three dragged on for a bit, we could hear a lot of talk from the ground floor – there was a very high level conference that lasted most of the morning with staff cars coming and going. I think some Gardaí in civilian attire were

present at this stage. After lunch we were told that the exercise/experiment was finished.

At the debrief we were told that the plan for Day Three involved the Ordnance Corps Adviser; he was to rig the ceiling of the ground floor with explosives and drop the bedroom into the kitchen. We received quick thanks for our work and we were never told if the plan included the three guinea pigs being in residence for the detonation. We were glad that 'end ex' (exercise over) was announced before the Ordnance were given the go ahead for a 'firing now'. The pros and cons of each trial assault was sent for assessment and decision and a preferred best entry method was selected.

The kidnappers surrendered on the night of 6 November after negotiations with Garda Commissioner Edmund Garvey and Chief Superintendent Lawrence Wren. Dr Herrema was given a medical examination and taken to the Embassy of the Netherlands. In March 1976, the Special Criminal Court sentenced Gallagher to twenty years in prison. He served fourteen. Coyle was given fifteen years and served nine. The kidnap of Dr Tiede Herrema had ended well but this was not always going to be the case.

Eight years later, the 1983 kidnap attempts of Shergar and Galen Weston having failed, the Provisional IRA tried again. On 24th November, Don Tidey, Chief Executive of the Quinnsworth supermarket chain, was kidnapped by a PIRA gang as he was driving his daughter Susan to school before making his way to work. His son, Alistair, was driving a separate car directly behind them. Using the ruse of a false Garda checkpoint in Rathfarnam, Dublin, both their cars were intercepted and Don Tidey was snatched at gunpoint, bundled into one of the kidnappers' cars, and driven away at high speed, leaving Susan and Alistair to raise the alarm by running to a nearby house. On its report, the Garda Special Branch immediately suspected the kidnap was the work of the IRA. The Defence Forces were called and one of the biggest manhunts the State has ever witnessed had begun.

Initially, the operation to seek and secure the safe return of Don Tidey concentrated around Tralee, Co. Kerry, then shifted to Ballinamore, Co. Leitrim, only to swing toward the Celbridge and Maynooth areas of

Co. Kildare before again moving back to Ballinamore. All throughout that three-week period there were searches, raids, arrests, cordons, checkpoints and a widening of the net of suspects and their supporters. Despite the security forces' activity not yielding any results, the focus of the hunt remained fixed on finding and freeing Don Tidey. A ransom of £5 million pounds had been demanded.

A mixture of detective work, thorough elimination of suspects and intelligence tip-offs suggested the immediate area in and around Ballinamore could prove fruitful in the hunt. 'Operation Santa Claus' was mounted on Tuesday, 13 December 1983 with hundreds of extra Gardaí and soldiers drafted into the area. It needed to be a large-scale operation to cover the ground in any amount of detail to have any hope of uncovering the hide inside which Don Tidey was held captive. A poor area of a thinly populated county – emigration had taken its toll – the landscape was rough terrain that offered little in the way of making a living. It was lonely, isolated countryside covered in forest, bogs and bushy scrubland – deemed by many to be a desolate and demoralising place. It was also an area in which the Provisional IRA had been known to operate from, trained, made bombs and engaged in a level of passive and active support and where some of the people who lived there were regarded as 'unhelpful' towards the Gardaí.

The next stage of the Operation was to determine the extent of the area to be searched and to place a cordon around it, with checkpoints positioned on the access road junctions and crossroads. With the perimeter sealed, the terrain within could then be searched systematically. To achieve this, the targeted terrain was subdivided amongst the available manpower. These were organised into mixed teams of Gardaí and army, referred to by radio call signs, 'Rudolph 1' to 'Rudolph 10'. Each 'Rudolph' team was comprised of a Garda Inspector, two Sergeants (one detective and one uniformed), five or six Gardaí (a mixed group of detectives and uniformed), five to ten recruit Gardaí and six soldiers. These ten teams reported back to Echo Base at Ballinamore Garda Station. Separate to these, operating independently in and about the area, were members of the Garda Special Branch.

On Saturday, 16 December, Rudolph 5 team, led by Detective Inspector Bill Somers, began its sweep across its designated area, 4-km directly north of Ballinamore town moving into Derrada Wood. The going was slow and difficult; a barrier of head-high briars and gorse bushes presented a thick undergrowth which had to be beaten through to effect progress; the two acres or so of wood itself consisting of 15-foot high fir trees. Unlike walking across open ground, it can be difficult to maintain a cohesive alignment and synchronisation suffered in such circumstances. Even line of sight of the person only a few yards away on either side can be lost, with one able to progress along their line of advance and others struggling to maintain forward momentum, one encountering more dense thickets of shrubs than another. Meanwhile, in and around the greater Ballinamore area, separately but concurrently, Garda Special Branch detectives were conducting investigations which included arrests and 'lifts' of people they considered of interest, perhaps potentially linked to the kidnap or otherwise associated to suspiciously connected activity.

As security forces swept across the terrain, setting up static checkpoints surrounding the search area, and Garda Special Branch men moved around the territory, there was a lot of on-going activity and the vicinity was swamped with personnel. The mixing and merging of so many forces saw an assortment of uniforms: A hybrid concoction of combat-type clothing with very little to distinguish Garda detectives and Special Branch men from the garb likely to be worn by the kidnappers. Weapons were also a necessary part of the scenario, the soldiers of 'Rudolph 5' with blackened faces in full combat gear carrying FN rifles, the Garda detectives wearing paramilitary style clothing, carrying Uzi sub-machine guns, and the unarmed uniformed Gardaí and Garda recruits all moving together more or less in line towards Derrada Woods. On reaching it they began to battle against the thick undergrowth. What happened next is described by one of 'the reserves':

> The Garda intelligence was very good; we knew or at least felt that there was a high degree of probability that Don Tidey was being kept against his will somewhere in the greater Ballinamore area. It was a large operation, necessitated by the extent of the ground to be covered in the level of detail required to find a possible 'hide'. The situation demanded a lot of manpower and teams of Garda and army personnel were organised, worked together, and were systematically searching the terrain. Separate to that there was also

groups of Garda Special Branch men operating independently; some dressed in paramilitary-type kit, making it difficult to distinguish them from Provo paramilitaries.

As the search team were going over the terrain of the forest's open ground and bogs, I was part of a team acting as an immediate response military reserve to the Cordon and Search operation, based back in Ballinamore itself, and we had one armoured personnel carrier (APC) and two Land Rovers. All of a sudden we heard shots going off in the distance (two-and-a-half kilometres north). After a while there was a radio message to say that Rudolph 5 had come across the kidnappers' hide in Derrada Woods. So we got into the Land Rovers and APC and sped off ... Some minutes later, as we were proceeding, there was a further audio message to say that those who had escaped out of the shelter were coming our way and shooting out of a blue Opel car.

We pulled the Land Rover across the road and as we were dismounting from our vehicles the blue car came around the bend ahead of us and began braking hard. We saw hands emerge out of the windows and in response a number of shots were fired by our party. The blue car stopped, only it was not 'the' blue Opel car, would you imagine it; it was a second blue car, unluckily in the wrong place at the wrong time (one driven by Special Branch detectives who had concurrently but separately arrested a local man whom they wished to question). All was happening quickly; there were shots being fired and confusion resulted. We 'mounted up' again and on arrival scrambled out of our vehicles at the bottom of Derrada Wood. Having dismounted we speedily swept up through the wood and about 150–200 metres in we found Private Patrick Kelly slumped across an earthen bank and recruit Garda Gary Sheehan slumped on the other side. Both were dead.

Amid the confusion, the story of what happened became clear. With the security forces closing in on the Derrada Wood dugout, screened with a black polythene sheet camouflaged with vegetation to disguise and conceal its existence and visible only from within a few feet, there was a sudden burst of gunfire – then more gunfire – followed by a grenade exploding and then a lot more gunfire. Private Patrick Kelly (35) and

Recruit Garda Gary Sheehan (23) were fatally wounded in this hail of bullets. Once gunfire had broken out, Don Tidey, seizing the moment, hit the ground, rolled down an incline into bracken, paused and took in his circumstances. When he looked up it was into the muzzle of a weapon just a short distance from his forehead. The situation was momentarily frozen as he looked down the length of the barrel and saw a soldier. Dressed as he was, he was unidentifiable and despite his insistence that he was in fact the hostage, the rescuers took no chances. They searched him, removed his boots and he was taken from the scene through the wood towards the road.

Taking full advantage of the shock and confusion of the situation, the kidnap gang made their bid for freedom. Grabbing those nearest, two Gardaí and a soldier who were fleetingly distracted, they held them in front of them as human shields and pushed through the scrub towards the top of the wood. Emerging from the wood, having disarmed and released their hostages, they succeeded in overpowering two soldiers and headed for the open fields. From there they made it to the road, where they managed to commandeer the blue Opel car. As they sped along the road, as chance would happen they encountered the group securing the hostage and the rescue party had to dive for cover as fire was opened on them from the passing car, those within spraying bullets widely. Don Tidey, his identity finally established, was shielded by his new protectors, primarily Detective Inspector Bill Somers.

Further down the road, a Garda pulled his patrol car across the road and the kidnap gang once more took to the fields. Here they displayed military-style discipline and field craft, leap-frogging in bounds, using cover and manoeuvre to affect an escape from view. It was considered likely that cars with full tanks of petrol and keys in the ignition were made available throughout the area by sympathisers, and the gang probably made use of these for their successful escape from the area in all the confusion.

The main mission was achieved; after twenty-three days Don Tidey had been successfully rescued and returned safely to his family. However, this came at a high cost: Private Patrick Kelly and Garda Recruit Gary Sheehan had been killed. Furthermore, the kidnap gang had escaped. Dismissing any false suggestions that the security forces had opened fire first, Lieutenant Colonel Pat Dixon, Military Commander of the search, was firm in his rebuttal of this notion: 'The first shots were definitely not fired by us. Our men were shot down in cold blood.' Another participant described the operation as follows:

> There were massive amounts of troops there from all over the Defence Forces, even from as far away as Cork. We took over the local school and operated from there. The weather was terrible throughout. Our function was to act as a reserve back up to the operation. The shooting incident had passed by the time we got to hear of it; there is a delayed response in such instances, a reporting, communication, decision and reaction time delay, so with real time events continuing to happen quickly there can be confusion accurately matching current occurrences with reported occurrences, the pace of the situation moving on all the time.
>
> We were then deployed in the search for the escaped kidnap gang in the so-called 'Ring of Steel' around the area; a phrase which appeared in the media reports of the events, but we felt ourselves that the 'Provo gang' were most likely long gone from the area. We later were involved in the Claremorris area to assist Gardaí there with an associated required search, in the event one which yielded no result. We had based ourselves in the local Dance Hall overnight, conducted a reconnaissance, and at first light the next morning had moved into the search area proper, but if there had been anyone there, they were long gone. It was a long trip back to our home station.

And it is the arrival back into one such station of one group that is described now:

> I was Orderly Officer for Collins Barracks, Cork, [and] the Officer-in-Charge of the Barrack security party for a 24-hour duration. I received a message to say that the Infantry Battalion Group involved in the Ballinamore, Co. Leitrim, search would be arriving back into Barracks in the early hours and to be aware, to be available to open the Barrack Armoury Building for them on their arrival. It was a wet, cold night, well into the early hours past midnight when the convoy returned into Barracks. They were

a weary, weather beaten, worn out lot; drained, exhausted, and spent. In sombre mood, their disposition and spirit was solemn and serious. I thought it best not to converse nor seek too much detail of the operation. As well as being a long haul back from the Co. Leitrim border it had been eventful as one of their trucks had caught fire.

As they returned their equipment, ammunition and weapons into the designated sub-unit cages within the armoury's interior, I overheard the Company Commander order the junior officers, the Platoon Commanders and the stores staff to be available to conduct a 100 per cent stock check of stores (ordnance check) later that morning after some hours sleep. I looked at this group admiringly, for being part of an operation that had successfully found and freed Don Tidey, allowing him to return safely home to his family, but was conscious also that Private Patrick Kelly and Recruit Garda Gary Sheehan were not returning alive to theirs.

As it happened, the same officer was Orderly Officer a month previously on the last Saturday in November when just before midday he received word that the Gardaí in Cork required six Land Rovers to be available outside the barracks at 2 pm as focus for the hunt for the then INLA leader, 'Mad Dog' Dominic McGlinchey was now concentrating in Cork City. The orderly officer stated:

> I was both lucky and unlucky. Unlucky insofar as it was a Saturday, a weekend, and troops were not in Barracks. Lucky insofar as a small party were due in for a ceremonial event and these together with the Stand-To party on immediate standby would form the bulk of the requirement, the residue to be filled by requesting some soldiers living locally to come in. This done, anticipating a continuation of this requirement for mobile checkpoint groups to be ongoing together with the Stand-To officer, we worked on getting this ready for the following day – Sunday – so that day's duty personnel would not encounter a difficulty in having a timely response available. The 4th Infantry Battalion would take up the tasking thereafter from Monday.

The Irish National Liberation Army (INLA) had first been the National Liberation Army, before which it was the People's Liberation Army, all the armed wing of the Irish Republican Socialist Party, a more radically left-wing faction of the Official IRA which had split from them in 1974 under Seamus Costello. The INLA dominated its political wing, the IRSP. A feud erupted between the Official IRA and the INLA and killings resulted, including Seamus Costello who was shot dead in 1977. In March 1979, the INLA managed to explode a car bomb in the vehicle driven by Airey Neave MP, a close confidant of Margaret Thatcher, as he exited the underground car park at the House of Commons. There was a raw recklessness associated with the INLA and more than a whiff of criminality. Penetrated by the security forces, informers being recruited by the RUC, chaos and paranoia resulted. In its early years, the group established links with extreme leftist groups in Europe, including the Red Army Faction (the Baader-Meinhof Group) in Germany and a similar group in France, Action directe (AD), who supplied the INLA with arms.

The INLA was to become characterised by deadly internal discord, a savage strife with bad-blooded vendettas and various factions engaged in feverish infighting, with fifteen of its own members killed in tit-for-tat assassinations. Dominic McGlinchey was to emerge as its leader, earning a reputation as being notorious amongst them and bearing the nickname 'Mad Dog'. Under his reign (July 1983–March 1984) one-man rule dominated; there was no collective leadership, notwithstanding the movement was badly fragmented, even out of control. McGlinchey himself was on the run, both in the North and the Republic. An ex-Provisional IRA man from the village of Bellaghy in South Derry, he switched his allegiance to the INLA while in Portlaoise Jail. They had gained a certain notoriety on both sides of the border in late 1982, when on 20 September the INLA blew up the radar tracking station at Mount Gabriel near Schull, Co. Cork, claiming that it was a high-tech tracking station working for NATO. On 6 December, the INLA was held responsible for a bomb explosion at the Droppin' Well bar in Ballykelly, Derry, where seventeen people were killed; eleven British soldiers and six civilians. Thereafter, the INLA became involved in sectarian revenge reprisals and attacks before becoming embroiled in an internal self-destructive vortex of violence. Meanwhile, the manhunt for its leader, Mad Dog McGlinchey, continued. As this was ongoing the Provisional IRA kidnapped Don Tidey, so between the two concurrent manhunts the occasion witnessed weeks of pursuit as the Irish security forces attempted to track down and pinpoint their prey.

On 2 December, with the hunt for the Don Tidey kidnap gang yet to settle on Ballinamore, Co. Leitrim, the focus of the hunt for Dominic McGlinchey was firmly set around Cork city, with a multitude of mobile army/Garda checkpoints in evidence. Meanwhile, in nearby Carrigtwohill in East Cork, two uniformed Gardaí called to a house and were confronted by McGlinchey and his gang who stripped them of their uniforms and tied them up before making their escape. The Don Tidey kidnapping was to come to its successful yet tragic conclusion in mid-December. However, it would be mid-March of the following year, on St Patrick's Day, before the army/Garda dragnet succeeded in cornering Mad Dog McGlinchey at a house in Ralahine South, Newmarket-on-Fergus, Co. Clare, with a team of Garda Security Task Force detectives engaged in a shoot-out with the gang. One detective was hit in the shoulder and the gang was forced to surrender. McGlinchey was extradited to the North on a murder charge, taken to the Border crossing at Killeen and handed over to the RUC. He was the first republican paramilitary to be extradited from the Republic to the North. Interestingly, he was re-extradited some time later, on 11 October the following year, due to a legal technicality involved with the murder case. He was then arrested on charges in relation to the shoot-out in Newmarket-on-Fergus, convicted and sent to Portlaoise Prison. After his release, on 10 February 1994 McGlinchey was gunned down in front of his son outside a telephone booth in Drogheda.

If the rampaging antics of 'Mad Dog' were to excite and enthral the nation's media, the escapades of the 'Border Fox', Dessie O'Hare, were to enthuse them even more – and their accounts of the gang's actions were to cause no little amount of fear among the Irish public. Previously in the Provisional IRA and originally from Keady, Co. Armagh, Dessie O'Hare served an eight-year term in Portlaoise Prison, having been found in possession of arms and ammunition. Released in 1987, he was to become associated with INLA feud-related activity and allegedly earned his nickname the 'Border Fox' for his elusiveness from capture for suspected involvement in armed bank robberies along the border counties of Armagh, Louth and Monaghan. From the incessant feuding within the INLA, a breakaway group led by Dessie O'Hare emerged called the Irish Republican Brigade, based around the border region. Others in the INLA gave this gang the nickname 'The Castleblayney Zulus'. Undoubtedly a dangerous individual, O'Hare was for a while to become the most wanted man in Ireland when on 13 October 1987 he and his gang kidnapped Dublin dentist John O'Grady from his Cabinteely home in South County Dublin. The real intended target was O'Grady's father-in-law, Austin Darragh, a wealthy medical entrepreneur who was the radio doctor on the Gay Byrne Radio Show on RTÉ Radio 1 during the 1980s.

Overall, the kidnap saga and nationwide hunt for the kidnappers was to last a total of forty days which saw a number of rescue attempts, shoot-outs, chases, narrow escapes and a viciously villainous twist or two. Having taken John O'Grady from his Cabinteely home, it was to be two weeks after the kidnap before Dessie O'Hare made any effort for a ransom demand. At one stage, in a demonstration of earnestness, the kidnappers, cut off the tips of the kidnap victim John O'Grady's two little fingers using a hammer and chisel, cauterising the wounds with a hot knife. The two mutilated fingers were sent with a ransom demand for one-and-a-half million pounds to Carlow Cathedral for collection. Experienced professional Gardaí have always regarded kidnapping as difficult crimes to become involved in as they are not usually straightforward affairs; the issues surrounding them being much more conflicted and the time factor crucial, having to find and free the hostage before the kidnapping becomes a murder. This particular kidnapping was to see shoot-outs in Cork, Dublin, Tipperary and Kilkenny.

Held initially in Dublin, John O'Grady was then moved to Cork to the gang's new hideout in an old yellow Tayto container in a field in the Ballymacsliney area near Midleton, Co. Cork. A report of suspicious sightings aroused Garda interest and a team of armed detectives rushed to the scene. A shoot-out resulted, and the kidnappers and their victim escaped by hijacking passing vehicles. The kidnap gang made their way back to Dublin and went to ground again in a house in Carnlough Road in Cabra West. Two days later, Dessie O'Hare made his first contact with the O'Grady family, three days later phoning the *Sunday Tribune* to reiterate his ransom demands. Feeling the need to impress his serious intent in relation to the urgency of his ransom demand, Dessie O'Hare severed John O'Grady's two little fingers, which were left for collection – with a ransom demand and a Polaroid photograph of O'Grady holding up his mutilated hands – behind a statue in Carlow Cathedral. A taped ransom message was sent to the family. Two days later, on 5 November, with arrangements for a ransom payment being actioned and with a high-profile priest, Fr Brian D'Arcy, acting as intermediary, the handover of cash was about to be finalised to the kidnappers' associates in the Silver Springs Hotel in Cork. Gardaí in Dublin, pursuing solid detective work, made inquiries at the Carnlough Road house in Cabra West and disturbed the kidnappers. Detective Garda Martin O'Connor was fired upon but survived gunshot wounds to the abdomen and shoulder and John O'Grady was freed. All but one of the gang made their escape by hijacking cars to Tipperary via Limerick.

Kidnappings were also very difficult for journalists to cover as the life of the hostage was at stake. Tom McCaughren, the RTÉ Security Correspondent, explains:

> A particular problem for me was that, whatever [was in] the newspapers, listeners, including the kidnappers, believed what was being broadcast on RTÉ. At least that's what the Gardaí told me. So I gave [out] as much as I could, bearing in mind that a life was at stake. Then, when the hostage was released, I was able to give the full background and any information I had held back. When dentist John O'Grady was rescued by Gardaí, I was able to give the shocking information that the kidnappers, in a very brutal act, had chopped off his two small fingers. Gardaí, I later learned, had intercepted a number of phone calls, including the ransom demands, made by the gang leader Dessie O'Hare, known as the Border Fox. I managed to get a copy of the tapes. This was a great exclusive, but the difficulty was that RTÉ was prohibited by Section 31 of the Broadcasting Act from broadcasting the voices of members of certain paramilitary organisations, including the INLA.
>
> However, a window of opportunity presented itself in that the INLA HQ in Belfast had issued a statement saying that the

individual, who went by the fanciful name of the Border Fox, and his associates, were NOT a faction of the organisation. In effect it said that he had been expelled for carrying out robberies not sanctioned by the movement. Furthermore, my inquiries yielded from unofficial sources in the Department of Justice and the Gardaí [were of] the opinion that O'Hare was no longer listed as a paramilitary. As a result I got clearance from Wesley Boyd, the then Head of News, to go ahead and use the tapes in my report.

When it hit the air, there was consternation in certain sections of the newsroom. I was called in by another senior member of news management and told in no uncertain terms that I had breached Section 31. I gave my reasons as to why I believed that this was not so, but he still maintained that I was in breach of it. I said that if he believed that, he should take steps to have me disciplined. In the event he did not do so. He was of course unaware before the broadcast of the fact that I had already cleared it with the Head of News. His view confirmed my belief that if my plan to broadcast the tapes had become more widely known, it would probably have been shot down, as management in general were very anxious not to breach the Act.

Following the broadcast it was also suggested to me at a meeting in the Department of Justice that I might be prosecuted under the Wireless Telegraphy Act for intercepting phone calls. I pointed out, of course, that it was not I, but the Gardaí, who had intercepted the calls. Whether the suggestion of prosecution was a serious one or whether the point was taken I don't know, but I was not prosecuted. The Garda Commissioner also appointed senior Gardaí to interview me in an attempt to find out where I got the tapes from but I refused to divulge my sources and I was not charged.

So I lived to tell the tale but I had sailed very close to the wind. Getting the tapes was a great exclusive. Getting them on air was a risky move. Some years earlier, Kevin O'Kelly had been sentenced to six months imprisonment for interviewing and broadcasting that interview with the then Chief-of-Staff of the IRA, Seán Mac Stíofáin. Nevertheless, in spite of Section 31, I managed to air the tapes. I didn't get much thanks for it, but I was happy that I managed to get information out to the public that otherwise would have been suppressed.

As a postscript, I should perhaps record the fact that following the Good Friday Agreement, the High Court in Dublin ruled initially that O'Hare was a qualified person for release under the agreement but it refused to order his release because of the seriousness of the offence. However, he was subsequently released early.

So perhaps the member of news management who said that I was in breach of Section 31 was right. However, I saw a window of opportunity and got away with it. And the result, as I have said, was that the public got a lot more information about a very brutal kidnapping than they would otherwise have got. In this and in other reports where there was a thin line on legal matters, I got great support from the then head of News, Wesley Boyd.

While Tom McCaughren was battling with whether or not the threat of prosecution under the Wireless Telegraphy Act would materialise, security forces had still the task remaining to track, find and take into custody the escaped kidnap gang members. Having taken a taxi from Limerick to Tipperary Town, the suspicions of an alert Garda were aroused and the two gang members apprehended. However, they made a run for it – one from the steps of the Garda Station, the other from actually inside it – both managing to temporarily escape. One was recaptured after a car chase and shots fired in Borrisoleigh, Co. Tipperary. The other man was arrested the following evening after a struggle four miles outside Cahir on the Tipperary road. As ever, however, the elusive Border Fox was still at large. On 10 November, the Government announced a £100,000 reward for information leading to the capture of Dessie O'Hare.

On 27 November 1987, at Balieff Crossroads – known locally as Minister's Cross – near Urlingford, Co. Kilkenny, there was silence after a sudden exchange of gunfire. After the ear-splitting clamour, the scene was suddenly one of stillness. The young Platoon Commander, himself having sustained a slight leg wound, had ordered 'cease fire'. However, the drama was not yet over because the danger was not yet fully passed. Nonetheless, the quiet of the descending calm was every bit as powerful and striking to the senses as the suddenness of what had just occurred. The checkpoint had become a showdown of the Border Fox's choosing, and he had lost out.

Just after 11 am that morning, Superintendent Tom Sloyan called into Stephens Barracks, Kilkenny, headquarters of 30th Infantry Battalion, and requested immediate military assistance for an ATCP operation. That particular week was no ordinary week as there was an ongoing nationwide operation in relation to the conduct of searches for Provisional IRA weapons caches, and most units had troops on immediate standby. The 30th Battalion had a Company formed and from this company a platoon was made available. It was standard practice in such circumstances to assign an officer as military liaison officer to the Garda officer-in-charge for the duration of the operation and this too was done.

It appeared that the Gardaí had information that Dessie O'Hare was travelling on the Freshford to Urlingford road in a car of a known make and colour and it was hoped to effect an arrest. A hasty road block was established in a dip in the road at Balieff Crossroads before 12.30 pm. Two Garda cars and an army Land Rover were parked lengthways across the road and soldiers and Gardaí took up positions behind them and to the sides. Approximately 90–100 metres forward of this two Gardaí established a checkpoint, standing in plain view on the roadway with a small army protection party hidden from view in the nearby ditches and fields. The purpose of the checkpoint was to identify the occupants of the car, ascertain if they had weapons and whether a hostage was part of the scenario, and if a clean arrest could be effected. Garda Inspector Pat Moriarty was uniformed and unarmed, Detective Sergeant PJ O'Rourke was in plain clothes and armed with a revolver.

Time passed and cars were stopped and the occupants checked and cleared. Inevitably, the authorities wondered if another blank had been drawn in the seemingly endless search for the Border Fox. Not so, as word was received that he was on his way towards the checkpoint. Inspector Pat Moriarty waved down the suspect vehicle and its two occupants. Dessie O'Hare was the driver and beside him was Martin Bryan, both were wearing seatbelts. Not instantly identified, efforts were made to establish who the occupants were, in the course of which there was movement inside the car and a weapon's presence determined; a real threat of danger or serious injury was now present. One of the army party protecting the Gardaí opened fire and the Border Fox gunned the engine, and with wheels spinning raced towards the roadblock. The car's tyres were ruptured by gunfire in response to O'Hare poking his hand out the driver's door window and firing indiscriminately. Fire was also opened into the body of the car. In all, Martin Bryan was hit six times and died and Dessie O'Hare was hit nearly as many times and survived. He aimed the car to hit the back of one of the Garda cars in the roadblock at speed, rammed into it and came to a stop. On the order 'cease fire' all fell silent.

Dessie O'Hare was still in the car and had a gun in his possession, so there was still a need for caution. Detective Sergeant O'Rourke went forward and placed his revolver against the back of Dessie O'Hare's head. Inspector Moriarty went alongside the car and opened the front passenger door. Martin Bryan's body, restricted by the seatbelt, collapsed only halfway out of the car. A priest was sent for to attend to him and an ambulance for the Border Fox. An inquest date was shortly settled on, and the checkpoint party accounted for their actions.

The mavericks, renegades and desperadoes of the paramilitary organisations were unpredictable, volatile and erratic. All violent, lawless and dangerous, it had been the experience of the security forces that when closing in on them they would only be taken by force, and when confronted their instinct was to open. To encounter them, as likely as not, was to be engaged in a firefight and you had better know what you were doing.

CHAPTER 13

Boatloads and Bunkers

Hand a professionally trained Irish soldier a weapon and the first thing he will do is carry out safety precautions. If his weapon jams and stops firing during range practice he will take immediate action and clear the weapon of the blockage; he'll remove the magazine from the weapon, pull back the cocking handle to the rear, tilt the weapon sideways and eject the damaged round. Without a magazine and no 'round up', the weapon is safe because the soldier has removed the source of danger.

The removal of the threat from elements that can cause harm and kill is essential in stabilising and addressing a situation. The Irish security forces during the Troubles were alert to removing the source of danger – the arms, ammunition and explosives – from the hands of the Provisional IRA and other groups. This was not an easy undertaking, because PIRA's operational capacity of covertly importing, storing and transporting such lethal means was well developed, and this highly organised supply chain facilitated their mounting of attacks, ambushes and assassinations. The capacity to capture arms caches in storage and seize these shipments before landing – or to intercept them in transit northwards to the 'war zone' – was always critical, because PIRA was constantly developing better and more sophisticated means of transporting and hiding their weapons. Each discovery of a weapons cache saved lives, and the failure to discover arms and explosive caches endangered them, because the use made of such weaponry was to murder and maim. Death and destruction followed these illegal arms importations so it was important to keep them out of Ireland, find where they were hidden, or waylay them when being transported. North and south, members of the British and Irish security forces were constantly challenged in this regard.

The securing of ever more modern and powerful arms was always necessary for the Provisional IRA to sustain and escalate their murderous activities. To conduct and continue their campaign of violence they needed to be better equipped. Tactical change followed technical change and game-changing armament was always being sought. The securing and stockpiling of a sophisticated arsenal of heavy weaponry, powerful Semtex explosive and surface-to-air missiles – to bring down helicopters – were long sought-after priorities of the Provisional IRA in order to help them to achieve their objective; forcing the British army out of Northern Ireland depended on having, deploying and getting best effect from the means available. As the situation evolved, the Provisional IRA believed that there were two major elements in bringing the British policy on Northern Ireland to its knees: bombings in Britain and the taking down of British military helicopters in Northern Ireland. At the same time, the paramilitaries sought to make Northern Ireland ungovernable by means of the 'Long War' – which meant conducting a sustained campaign of violence – and large quantities of arms, ammunition and explosives were needed to achieve this. These would almost certainly need to be brought in by sea, and they were. Operations mounted by the Irish security forces in countering these gunrunning activities were constant and were sometimes spectacularly successful.

In the early hours of 29 September 1984, the Irish Naval ships LÉ *Emer* and LÉ *Aisling* moved covertly into tactical position inside Irish territorial waters two miles from the Skellig Rocks off the south west coast of Co. Kerry. It was anticipated that the target vessel, upon discovery of the trap about to be sprung, would immediately realise a breakout attempt or efforts to outrun them would not be options. Nonetheless, it was likely they would resist arrest, maybe even engage in a firefight, and highly possible they would attempt to scuttle the ship and cargo. Prior information had been key, but now action was critical and the challenge presented to seize the cargo intact was crucial.

The naval ships observed strict black-out procedures and kept total radio silence as they moved in at full speed to cut off the target vessel, the trawler, *Marita Ann*. The LÉ *Emer* overhauled the *Marita Ann*, illuminating her with its searchlight, and called on the trawler to stop. Instead the trawler ignored the signals to halt and altered course. A ruse was employed by the Captain of the LÉ *Emer* who inquired of the *Marita Ann* if she had been engaged in salmon fishing. While this communication was ongoing, two high-speed Gemini craft from LÉ *Aisling*, with armed Gardaí and naval boarding personnel on board, approached the *Marita Ann* from the stern and mid-ship on the blind side of the vessel. The *Marita Ann* continued to attempt evasive manoeuvres but the LÉ *Emer*, tired of the cat-and-mouse game, fired four tracer rounds across the bow and forced the trawler crew to stop. The boarding party sprang into action and no resistance was encountered. The five-man crew surrendered and the boarding party found its cargo of seven tonnes of arms and ammunition. This seizure was to provide a significant setback for the Provisional IRA in the mid-1980s. The origin of the large quantity of illegal munitions was suspected to be a Boston-based Irish-American crime gang who had played a key role in procuring the weaponry, and the weapons denied to the Provisional IRA undoubtedly saved lives.

The *Marita Ann* seizure came eleven years after that of the MV *Claudia*, which occurred off the south-east coast. In the interim, several other attempted importations had been successfully intercepted. However, not all such efforts were detected and the Provisional IRA garnered a considerable arsenal of weaponry which they used to lethal effect. Neither did the seizures of the *Claudia* and *Marita Ann* dissuade the Provisional IRA from smuggling arms, ammunition and explosives into Ireland by sea. Three years later, on 30 October 1987, the MV *Eksund*, a Panamanian-registered coaster off the island of Batz, six miles north of Brest, was intercepted by the French customs service. On board there was a frighteningly large cargo – 150 tonnes of modern heavy weaponry – much sought-after by the Provisional IRA's active service units. The shipment included Soviet-made portable surface-to-air missile launchers, heavy machine guns, ammunition, Semtex explosive, anti-tank rockets, mortars and assault rifles. The haul had an estimated value of £15 million and it had a Libyan origin. Colonel Muammar Gaddafi, the Libyan head of state and sponsor of the MV *Claudia*, had taken a renewed interest in the Provisional IRA since the 1981 Hunger Strike. But he was also motivated by a desire to extract revenge on Britain for its part in the American bombing of Tripoli in 1986, when the United Kingdom had allowed US bomber aircraft based there to attack targets in Libya.

The *Eksund* seizure was a massive haul, which, if it had fallen into the hands of the IRA, would have had a destructive potential beyond anything seen during the Troubles to date. The Provisional IRA had come a long way from its old stockpiled 'Tommy guns' and Bren guns, now it possessed Kalashnikov AK-47 assault rifles, M60 machine guns, rocket-propelled grenade launchers (RPGs) and two surface-to-air missiles. From sticks of dynamite and gelignite, now PIRA were using military-grade explosives like Semtex and C4. Delight at the capture of the *Eksund* was tempered with the chilling knowledge that four similar, but much smaller, shipments had successfully made it through undetected and been distributed; 7-tonnes of munitions in August 1985, 10-tonnes in October 1985, 14-tonnes in July 1986 and 105-tonnes in October 1986 were landed at or near Clogga Strand, close to Arklow, Co. Wicklow, on the east coast. A total of 136-tonnes of modern weaponry were known to be in the hands of the Provisional IRA and it had the means to extend its 'Long War' for at least two more decades. Only this was not going to be enough to achieve its objective at its then current operational tempo. Something more was required because their campaign plan was not winning 'the war' for them.

The Provisional IRA had a plan, one already well advanced in its preparation and organisation and strikingly audacious at that. Just as the Vietcong's 'Tet Offensive' of January 1968 during the Vietnam War had weakened American resolve to continue fighting there, so the Provisional IRA hoped to emulate this effect in Northern Ireland. It planned a 'Tet' of its own in the shape of a sharp, short, but massive military offensive to weaken British resolve to stay in Northern Ireland. Militarily, the Provisional IRA were neither winning nor losing. Politically, the Anglo-Irish Agreement of 1985 was not to their liking and they had launched a significant bombing offensive in its wake in an attempt to destroy the political process, claiming to have used more explosives in 1985 than in any other year of their campaign up to then. Now they felt that perhaps the military route, the use of intense brutal force, could physically impose their will. They were not only going to replicate the effect of 27 August 1979, the day of the double bombing against the Paras at Warrenpoint and Lord Louis Mountbatten at Mullaghmore, but hugely and savagely surpass it; to outdo Warrenpoint for lethality by increasing the number of British army fatalities and excel it for shock effect. However, the seizure of the MV *Eksund* shipment, the discovery that four previous consignments had been successfully landed – and their intended use in the secretly planned 'PIRA Tet' having been exposed – PIRA's essential element for success, surprise, was lost. Their 'one last push' initiative was over.

If the sheer scale of the campaign was unprecedented, so to was the response of the Irish security services. 'Operation Mallard' was initiated to locate the whereabouts of the four previous weapons shipments. Mallard was a joint Defence Forces and Garda Síochána operation, which took place from 23 to 29 November 1987. The Defence Forces mission was to aid the Gardaí in the general area of the Garda Border Divisions in conducting searches for illegal arms, ammunition and explosives and in apprehending persons involved in trafficking them. On 19 November, OPORD 10/87 (Operation Order Number 10 of 1987) was signed by the Chief-of-Staff. There were few changes from the 'Decision and Concept' issued by the Director of Operations two days earlier as to how he saw Operation Mallard being conducted. His Draft Operation Order had been completed in consultation with Garda Síochána Headquarters and gave Commanders the opportunity to plan, though information passed on to subordinates was curtailed. Personnel of the 61st Irish Battalion and 16 Irish Component, UNIFIL Headquarters, just returned from UN Peacekeeping service in South Lebanon, were called back off leave. Money was allocated for the calling up of FCÁ personnel (part-time 2nd Line Reserve) on full-time security duty (Barrack Duties) in order to release permanent Defence Forces personnel for operational purposes. All leave was cancelled. The only notable alteration on the OPORD's signature by the Chief-of-Staff was the reduction from 140 to 80 of the number of Border Crossings at which joint Defence Forces/Garda checkpoints were to be established; a lack of available manpower and the indication that Northern Ireland security forces would show a presence on the Northern side of the other sixty crossings.

All current ATCP tasks continued during the period of Operation Mallard. Concentrated primarily in the border areas, the Border Battalions were reinforced from other units: the 27th Infantry Battalion (Dundalk and Castleblayney) got a Battalion Tactical Headquarters and one Company of three Platoons from 4th Infantry Battalion

(Cork); the 29th Infantry Battalion (Monaghan, Cavan, Cootehill) got a Battalion Tactical Headquarters and one Company of three Platoons from 3 Infantry Battalion (Curragh Camp), plus one Company from the Eastern Command (Dublin mostly); the 28th Infantry Battalion (Finner Camp, Lifford, Letterkenny and Rockhill) got a Battalion Tactical Headquarters and two Companies of two Platoons each from the 12th Infantry Battalion (Limerick and Clonmel). The 4th Infantry Brigade Headquarters got one Company of the two Platoons from 1st Infantry Battalion (Galway) plus one Company of two Platoons from 6th Infantry Battalion. Elements of the Army Ranger Wing were moved to Finner Camp in Co. Donegal. The Naval Service had a three patrol vessel involvement, one in Donegal Bay with the other two in Lough Swilly and Carlingford. The Air Corps located extra helicopters in Gormanstown, Co. Meath, and Finner Camp, Co. Donegal, while a third helicopter was held in Baldonnel for use by a joint Gardaí/Military Headquarters, which was located at Garda Headquarters in Phoenix Park. A Cessna fixed-wing plane was located in Finner Camp, Co. Donegal. Engineer Specialist Search Teams were located in Gormanstown and Finner, while two additional Explosive Ordnance Disposal (bomb disposal) teams were deployed in Longford and Monaghan Barracks.

Concrete results arose from the Operation, but initially not in the quantities hoped for. There were, however, gains in the short and medium terms and non-quantifiable results insofar as the amount of information collected by the Gardaí that would be of value in future operations. Nearly 60,000 premises were searched, there were over thirty arrests and small quantities of arms, ammunition and explosives were found. Bunkers, dug outs and firing ranges were also discovered. The weaponry from the Libyan shipment remained largely intact – though this situation was to change in early 1988 – but most importantly, Provisional IRA activities were hugely disrupted. Before 1987 was out, the Provisional IRA bomb explosion at the Enniskillen War Memorial in Co. Fermanagh on 8 November – resulting in eleven deaths and sixty people injured – was to cause massive and sustained outrage against the organisation.

In all, 1987 was a bad year for the Provisional IRA. A number of serious setbacks had befallen them, starting on 8 May 1987 when eight

PIRA volunteers were killed by the SAS, who were lying in wait for them as they attacked the North Armagh Loughgall village RUC Station with a bomb-laden mechanical digger, a *modus operandi* of PIRA's East Tyrone Brigade Active Service Unit. Then there was the seizure of the *Eksund* shipment on 30 October and the subsequent loss of the essential element of surprise for its planned 'Tet' offensive – and the IRA's abandonment of this undertaking – and finally on Remembrance Sunday 8 November and the Enniskillen War Memorial bombing, which was strongly condemned by all sides and undermined support for the IRA and Sinn Féin. In the south, the addition of the horrific kidnapping of John O'Grady added to the growing odium with which the Irish public increasingly held paramilitary groups. North of the border, the security forces were now aware that the Provisional IRA had plans to come at them with a renewed vigour and with an arsenal of modern weaponry and Semtex explosive.

Two large oil tanks dug into the sand dunes at Five Fingers Strand on the Malin Peninsula in North Donegal were used to conceal a cache of weapons. It was 27 January 1988 and the first known major discovery of armaments from the Libyan shipment. There were to be further finds and in all it was estimated that about 50 per cent of the total weaponry from Libya was recovered. Another large find occurred at Portmarnock, Co. Dublin, on 23 February and a smaller find at Ballivor, Co. Meath, was uncovered four days later, after which on 10 March there was another find at Patrickswell, Co. Limerick, six days later one at Finea, Co. Cavan, and back in Donegal at Ballymaleel on 18 March more ordnance was recovered. It became apparent that the 'PIRA Tet' offensive plan included the safe storage of the armament of the first four shipments, thereafter – and only thereafter – using the weaponry from the fifth consignment to effect the all-out assault. This was for security, ensuring no hint of the IRA having possession of such armaments would reveal itself prior to the surprise attacks. Only, of course, the fifth consignment, the largest, was intercepted at sea. The 'source of danger' stymied, the 'PIRA Tet' had been thwarted, though the danger had not passed – far from it. The IRA had Semtex, Russian DshK (Degtyarev) 12.7 mm heavy machine guns, detonators, assault rifles and a host of other lethal means to kill. Also, whatever the Provisional IRA needed that could not be imported, they manufactured.

Their ability to fabricate and fashion hand-made mortars, bombs and booby traps witnessed a frightening ingenuity, all of which demanded countermeasures on behalf of the security forces.

If the Provisional IRA's Quartermasters could not obtain what was required, then its Departments of Engineering and Research and Development would try to provide it. The IRA was the most advanced sophisticated bomb and IED (Improvised Explosive Device) maker in the world and their expertise extended into home-made mortar making as well. If PIRA could not source the weaponry then they made ingenious efforts to literally invent and make it, and they put in place networks to support both skill sets. Concrete bunkers were constructed beneath cowsheds and households, dug outs were hidden in forests and farmlands, and plastic barrels dug into hedgerows or embedded in slurry pits were among the many places weapon caches were secreted and stored until brought into use. Bomb-making and bomb-assembly factories were located in barns, derelict buildings, farm outhouses and dwelling houses, respectively, while component parts for home-made mortars were sometimes openly sent for manufacture as legitimate job lots to different commercial factories, collected and later expertly assembled in covert workshops. Advanced engineering operations were set up with a high level of workmanship, the prototypes being test fired, perfected and put into use. These would later be improved, upgraded and made more lethal. An entire series of home-made mortars and mortar bombs were manufactured; mortar tubes were welded onto metal frames and placed into Toyota HiAce vans or onto the back of trucks which were driven to and parked within range of their targets. One of the more infamous occurrences was on 7 February 1991, when PIRA launched a mortar bomb attack on 10 Downing Street in London as the British Cabinet, with John Major as Prime Minister, was in session discussing the first Gulf War.

The necessary networks, supply chains and both material and specialist support was in place to keep PIRA's bombing campaign nearly always one step ahead of the security forces. Be it with means of detonation, fuses, explosive materials or 'initiatives' – like putting timers and anti-handling devices on bombs, or planting a second device targeting the bomb disposal teams themselves – the expert Provisional IRA bombers took advantage of every technical advance they could to improve the effectiveness of their devices. On 12 October 1984, the Brighton bomb specifically targeting British PM Margaret Thatcher as she attended the Conservative Party Annual Conference was an occasion when PIRA employed a device with a long-term delay timer, planted some thirty days beforehand. Five people were killed, thirty-four were injured and the hotel was destroyed. Margaret Thatcher barely escaped. It was the marrying of the weapon storage and bomb factories and the possibility that they could be booby-trapped that was a further concern for security forces, as well as the instability of the devices themselves, having component parts made of materials the very nature of which were volatile and dangerous to handle.

The Libyan-supplied Semtex proved to be an enormous asset and was regarded to be of huge value to the Provisional IRA, so much so that they used it sparingly in order to make it last. It was an ideal booster for the home-made explosive mix (HME) they used for their three London 'city destroyers' (truck bombs) at the Baltic Exchange on 10 April 1992, the Stock Exchange at Bishopsgate on 24 April 1993 and Canary Wharf on 9 February 1996. These huge bombs were believed to have been mixed and fabricated in South Armagh and had a large shock effect. Their sheer size, timing and destructive power may well have influenced the British Government to seriously consider negotiations on Northern Ireland. To bring these bombs into play into the heart of London (and a later one in Manchester on 15 June 1996) involved explosive manufacture, logistic networks and Provisional IRA 'sleeper units'. All this and more combining to bring 'the source of danger' to where it could cause maximum impact, once again demonstrating PIRA's unpredictability.

The acquisition, sourcing, storage and supply of weapons and explosives meant that advanced war materials were still in the possession of the Provisional IRA and it was the job of the security forces to intercept, find and otherwise prevent their use. 'Operation Silo' was conducted continuously throughout the early 1990s and this unearthed a picture of the network involved, with large sealed underground bunkers being discovered across the republic. However, it became clear that this centred on Munster, with Limerick at the epicentre of the system of arms dumps. It emerged that there was a structured logic to how bomb making was organised and configured.

The Provisional IRA were very able adversaries and if the security forces did not afford them a grudging respect they were being unprofessional and underestimating the threat. The Irish Security forces had to step up to the challenge, modernise their equipment, procedures, training and operational capability if they were to have any hope of 'removing the source of danger'.

PART 5

BECOMING BETTER

CHAPTER 14

Capability Development

O n 11 September 1974 in Blacklion, Co. Cavan, a proxy bomb was driven into the centre of the village from the North and parked in the village's main square opposite the Garda Station, which had an army observation post attached to it. The driver hurriedly exited the car, alerting the Gardaí of the bomb in the car's boot. The Gardaí immediately set about warning the people of the village of the urgent and dangerous circumstances.

The drama started at 10 pm, when local farmer, Fred Elliott of Mullaghbawn, County Armagh, Northern Ireland, was stopped at gunpoint by a group of uniformed men on the Florencecourt Road. They loaded two milk churns into the boot of his Ford Cortina and having threatened him, ordered him to drive southwards across the border into Blacklion and park it outside the Army/Garda post in the centre of the village. The army Explosive Ordnance Disposal (EOD) team was called and its officer recalls:

I remember the incident very well because by the time I arrived, the Gardaí had the 150 or so occupants of the village evacuated within minutes. It was night time, so it was dark, and there were lights on in the houses but no one in the homes. The street, the entire village, was deserted; the houses, shops and business premises empty. I could hear their phones ringing unanswered. It was quite bizarre, surreal and dreamlike; only there was a very difficult and dangerous reality to it, also complicated further by the fact that there were a set of petrol pumps near the car with the bomb in it.

It was prudent to presume the bomb was on a timer, so it was best left to sit in situ for a while and anyway better attended to in daylight. So I left it until daybreak the following morning. The 'robot' had not yet entered service with EOD teams so we employed the 'rocket-line trick' – adapting the technique of firing a line at sea from one boat to another – and tailoring its use to the circumstances. We had to disrupt the device but at the same time maintain a safe distance from it. So I fired the rocket, with a rope attached to it, across the car from a distance of 100 yards to about the same distance beyond to a member of the EOD team. On this particular occasion, we had difficulty getting that man into position as there were no parallel side roads to safely get him securely located, so we used a helicopter to lift him there.

Once I had fired the rope via the rocket to him I attached a one-pound plastic explosive charge with a firing wire fixed to it. My aim was to align this explosive charge to blow the boot open, the force of the small controlled explosion simultaneously separating the bomb's detonating mechanism from the bomb's explosive content, thereby disrupting the bomb from exploding to full effect. That was not going to be easy to achieve, the results not entirely guaranteed and unpredictable. A further degree of difficulty of course being the close proximity of the petrol pumps. So a fire brigade and crew were put on standby just in case. A situation like this is where you, the EOD operator, become the State; you have all the resources and willpower to see the situation put to rights but while that may be, it seemed it was really down to the training, techniques and equipment you had. In those early days they seem primitive now but nonetheless were effective.

The small explosive charge attached to the rope was pulled and manoeuvred into position. In this case I aimed for the rear wheel of the car just after 11 am and set off the controlled explosion. It worked; the milk churns were blown clear of the car out from its boot, their contents spilling out onto the road without exploding. My fears were realised to a degree in relation to the danger to the petrol pumps insofar as the rubber along the hose began to catch fire, but this was quickly extinguished by the Fire Brigade coming into play. Some superficial damage was caused to surrounding buildings.

Hazardous, unpredictable and precarious, the incidents that occurred during the Troubles involving the necessary deployment of Irish army EOD teams were numerous, necessitating the permanent placement of teams at points along the border and throughout the Republic. Viable devices, hoaxes, false alarms, incendiaries, weapons finds, the discovery of bomb-making factories or bombs in transit – maybe booby trapped – were all part of the many and varied tasks they faced. There was a serious threat on or near the border, where deadly intent was supported by skilled bomb makers with a great understanding of what they were doing and of the need to constantly innovate, develop and update their tactics and techniques. The threat was there and a response was required.

The Ordnance Corps Base workshops at Clancy Barracks, Islandbridge, Dublin, were a large complex of specialist mechanical and electrical facilities necessary for the maintenance and repair of the weaponry and ammunition of a modern Defence Force. The staff were highly skilled technicians, both military and civilian (usually retired ex-Defence Forces technicians). It was also the location of the Defence Forces Ordnance School, where Officers and NCOs of the Corps received basic and refresher instruction. During 'the Emergency' (the Second World War) it became necessary to allocate the task of disposal of sea mines (still being swept onto our shores or caught in trawlers' nets many years later) and the occasional aerial bombs to the Corps. Training took place in the school and officers were issued with a personal specialist tool kit which they carried with them to the location of the bomb disposal. The advent of the Troubles saw the introduction of a new threat – the Improvised Explosive Device – necessitating the urgent acquisition of intelligence, retraining of personnel and the development of specialist disposal equipment such as portable X-ray machines. It also became necessary to reorganise the Bomb Disposal task to specialist teams consisting of an officer, NCO and driver; originally in a Land Rover vehicle but later, with the advent of robots, in a special van equipped with a rear door ramp and shelving. Communications and a security party was provided as required by the Command Formation Stand-To party. Teams were located at strategic locations and personnel rotated on a weekly basis.

In looking at the development of the Defence Forces Ordnance Corps capability, most people jump quickly to the introduction of the Reamda HOBO bomb disposal robot as being central to the capability of the Ordnance Corps to meet its tasking in the ATCP during the Troubles. Technically speaking, the HOBO was in fact a remotely operated vehicle

(ROV) whereas a robot is a machine capable of autonomously carrying out a complex series of actions. So really the core capability developed by the Ordnance Corps in bomb disposal was 'the Access and Render of Safe Procedures (RSPs)' in other words Bomb Disposal Doctrine. Because every IED incident (bomb disposal incident) is unique, the philosophy of the policy was and remains, not to lay down hard and fast rules to be followed. The real jewel in the Ordnance Corps crown was not the equipment that was developed; rather it was the doctrine and the training methods. That might sound simplistic, but in a situation where a bomb disposal team enters a scene where they are faced by an IED, or maybe IEDs, their focus may traditionally have been solely on the IED ('the bomb') itself. However, they needed to be able to go to a bomb's location and look around; read the ground and the environment, look for clues and try to see and appreciate the whole picture. Where are the routes in and out? Where are the likely firing points? Why has the IED been placed there? It is all about making the bomb disposal team think. Ultimately, they had to strive to acquire optional situational awareness and gain access to timely and pertinent intelligence in order to best develop a realistic threat evaluation, risk assessment and a viable 'render safe' procedure.

The need for an enhanced EOD capability emerged from those dark days known as the Troubles in Northern Ireland that few wish to recall, a need which escalated in the 1970s. There was a sense of fear as long-dormant resentments re-emerged, particularly in border counties, when the British army and RUC blocked and cratered the smaller roads to make all but the approved checkpoint roads impassable. In the early days, people were particularly worried as they did not know where matters were going to end. People were fearful that perhaps it was all heading towards civil war. As the tempo of military operations changed over time, from 'Civil Rights to ArmaLites', the growing menace of car bombs (vehicle-borne IEDs – VBIEDs) and other specific threats saw Irish Defence Force EOD teams have to deal with a variety of incidents. In Cloughfin, Co. Donegal, in mid-March 1973, a UVF car bomb exploded prematurely killing the driver and injuring fifteen in a pub crowded with St Patrick's Day revellers. Another car bomb, in Pettigo in late September 1973, injured two people, followed by a bomb blast in Swanlinbar, Co. Cavan, in late November.

It was not only potentially deadly loyalist UVF paramilitary attacks that required attention, but those being mounted in the south going northwards. In Carrigans, a huge PIRA bomb in a barrel in the yard of a shop was discovered as it was about to be driven to its target, a cross border British army post, which required the complete evacuation of the town before it could be defused. Another incident saw an EOD team from Finner Camp being tasked to address a call-out in Buncrana to a PIRA mortar bomb find, the variables and options to be considered and decided upon were multiple: was the cache old or in transit? Was it deliberately left by someone and booby trapped, were these home-made mortars a new version? Was there something significant or different about them? If not, then maybe their fusing system was new? In any event, they were inherently unstable and hence dangerous, and anything might set them off. After a very thorough examination by the EOD team, still cognisant of the dangers involved, they were wrapped in a 'ballistic blanket', removed and rendered safe, to be blown up later in a controlled explosion. Again in the Pettigo area, a suspect car had to be dealt with after the Provisional IRA used it in an attack on a British army patrol who returned fire on the car, hitting its radiator. Later the getaway car seized up and was abandoned on the southern side of the border and so had to be cleared by the EOD team.

There were many such EOD call-outs and they took many forms, each presenting their own challenge. It was on these and every occasion that the training emphasis on an all-round awareness and open-mindedness came into play. Another huge find of Provisional IRA explosives at Muff, Co. Donegal, where 4-tonnes of ANNI (a particular type of fertiliser-based explosive mix) was discovered on a trailer, required special attention because not only was it dangerous, but poisonous as well, necessitating the total evacuation of the town for days and the EOD team having to use breathing apparatus when defusing the bomb prior to its safe destruction.

The various degrees of difficulty were often raised because, strange as it might seem, while the EOD teams clearly saw what was in front of them, they were not always sure what they were looking at. Who would place a milk churn or beer keg bomb in the middle of an unapproved road, or in a field on the border, or in a place where it seemed counter-productive to disrupt the lives of those whose support the IRA relied upon? The truth was that on the ground Irish EOD operators were never to know who the perpetrator of an individual bomb threat really was, and more importantly what level of sophistication the bomb maker possessed – amateur or professional. All bomb disposal tasks were thus doubly dangerous and as IED construction evolved rapidly during the conflict, it became necessary to hold regular EOD conferences and refresher courses for operatives at the Irish Defence Forces ordnance school. Refresher courses were of two weeks duration, one week classroom instruction and the second at specially selected locations where students were required to undertake simulated EOD tasks under the direction of school instructors. Increasingly, requests were received from foreign armies and police to participate in Irish EOD training and this was agreed to by the Government. To date, highly successful and much sought-after courses have been developed by the Defence Forces which introduce and teach a concept of how to respond to threats in an IED-rich theatre of operations.

There was also progress and generational change in the arena of overall information handling. 'Not knowing what you don't know' is the Achilles heel of intelligence agencies. Their great vulnerability is not being aware, not having the information which can provide intelligence to the government concerning threats to the security of the State. The Directorate of Military Intelligence (G2), was responsible for the direction of efforts in this regard along with the Garda Síochána Special Detective Unit. For G2, the quality of knowledge was not necessary to be of legal evidential value. Their remit was to direct their efforts to collect essential information and process the particulars into accurate and timely analysis and assessment. It was a process to generate awareness and understanding, in a word, foreknowledge, the purpose of which was to reduce uncertainty. Military Intelligence in its purest form deals with information as to the threat, the 'enemy' and its dissemination as intelligence in an appropriate form and by suitable means to those who need it. Sources are what informs, analysis is what makes sense.

In the lead up to the outbreak of the Troubles there was no Provisional IRA, there was no enemy. There was uncertainty, though, which stemmed from the political status quo in Northern Ireland and was within the remit of politicians, an added complication, of course, being that Northern Ireland Protestant politicians saw the situation as having no remit whatsoever for southern politicians. What occurred was unimaginable and what was allowed to continue was unforgiveable. From the conflict emerged organisations, like the Provisional IRA that did not give up its secrets easily, nor was there any information on Loyalist paramilitaries. However, gaining intelligence was key to their defeat. Initially information was sparse; there was a mutual need for information by intelligence agencies, military and police, North and South, but there was mutual suspicion also. Of course this distrust ran to government levels as well. Nationally, the country was convulsed by the Troubles, while internationally the context of the Cold War prevailed.

The Provisional IRA internationalised their efforts by drawing on support from abroad; from the Basques, the Algerians, the Libyans, the PLO and, of course, the Americans, amongst others. All this extended the dimensions associated with the conflict in Northern Ireland and brought in necessary contacts with foreign security agencies. Meanwhile, there was a possibly different dimension developing in Northern Ireland, one which also had foreign origins. In efforts to defeat the Provisional IRA, the security forces applied 'low-intensity conflict' and the lessons learned by the British army when it put down insurrections in the post-War period in Aden, Kenya and Malaya. Utilising unorthodox and irregular methods of warfare, these counter-insurgency techniques concentrated on the adaptation of experiences of armies of fading colonial powers, the British, French (in Indo-China and Algeria) and other armies' innovations used to defeat urban and rural guerrilla insurgency. These strategies and tactics concerned the military involving itself in intelligence-gathering, infiltration of guerrilla gangs and imitation of their *modus operandi*. Those 'counter gangs' or 'pseudo gangs' launched false-flag operations, sowed confusion and discredit. Add the use of military psychological operations (Psy Ops) and information operations (Info Ops) to demoralise the enemy and integrate this military effort with flexible legal, media and political actions and you may have a basis to provide a favourable outcome.

This mix of measures could see some of the actions of these covert military units resembling those of the terror gangs, which of course was the point of it all in the execution of these so-called 'dirty wars'. The efforts of information-gathering by military services south of the border remained stringently within the bounds of orthodoxy and legal limits as well as expanding its structure and capacity to do so. Today, the Irish Military Special Operations Forces, the Army Ranger Wing (ARW), carries out physical tasks in support of Military Intelligence in Ireland and the Communications and Information Service Corps (CIS) provides technical and electronic support. During the Troubles, the need for exchange of information between the British and Irish saw this matter of co-operation formalised between governments and being part of the evolving agreements.

Strengthening, improving and expanding what capabilities were already there was one matter, recognising the need for others not already existing and putting them in place was another. One such was a specialist intervention capability, a highly trained, motivated, resilient and skilled counter-terrorist unit. Throughout the 1960s and 1970s, there was an explosion in international terrorism. To combat this developing threat, many nations established dedicated counter-terrorist units who specialised in conducting hostage rescue operations. With building instability in the North and a growing domestic threat, the Irish Government gave direction for the Defence Forces to establish such a unit. On the recommendation of the Chief-of-Staff, the unit was activated on 16 March 1980 and given the designation of the Army Ranger Wing (ARW). Initial focus centred on establishing a suitable recruitment and selection process along with procuring appropriate weapons and equipment. Eager to develop its specialist capabilities, the unit dispatched personnel to a number of foreign Special Forces and intervention units. Over the following years, the ARW developed its 'Green' conventional wartime special operations and 'Black' anti-terrorism capabilities, both skill sets mutually supporting each other with regard to skills and capabilities.

The significant investment in effort, finance and personnel provided by the Defence Forces resulted in the ARW developing land, sea and air capabilities which were on a par with their international counterparts; a combination of skills to match the challenge of a broad range of operational requirements. Mindful of the domestic security situation, the unit focus stretched to the international arena with regard to operational deployments: Somalia, East Timor, Liberia and Chad. A number of niche deployments since the recent rise in global terrorism has again shifted the focus to on-Ireland capability and the ARW remain prepared to meet any potential domestic threats.

Apart from preparing an elite military unit for highly specialised interventions, a keener, more honed intelligence capability and a cadre of EOD and counter-IED personnel are viewed as amongst the best and most highly trained in the world. With much of their expertise being developed during the Troubles of the 1970s and 1980s, and overseas in challenging mission areas, the ATCP 'soldiering situation' in the Republic required that the performance of internal security duties be regularised and regulated, particularly the daily threat of violence being faced by troops. An excellent and fully elaborate set of Current Operational Directive Guidance Documents and Standing Operating Procedures were drawn up for commanders to consult and adhere to. Practical and considered, they addressed critical issues such as when to open fire and its control, escalation of the use of force and other important issues, allowing military briefing officers to give clarity of thought and confidence to troops performing vital ATCP tasks. This codified range of instructions were compiled by their author, Colonel Michael Mullooly (Retd.), after much discussion in the Military College, at Defence Forces Headquarters Operations Section and crucially, with Peter Sutherland, the then Attorney-General.

Improved transport, upgraded communications and signals equipment, the introduction of Armoured Personnel Carriers (APCs) and Armoured Fighting Vehicles (AFVs), the initiation of Engineer Special Search Equipment, the availability of helicopters, the establishment of new permanent border units, these and other progressive measures meant that when 'truckloads of troops' were called for, the Defence Forces arrived in an ATCP mode with the capacity to deliver 'capabilities'. The army were living it, its soldiers understanding it. When deployed and moved into action on an operation, be it in Portlaoise Prison, along the border, or a Cordon and Search Operation, it was up to the Defence Forces to ensure it prevailed. The army of the 1980s was stretched, overextended and pulled in all directions; running old barracks, managing the overdue 'catch up' of its establishment and equipment, ATCP 'mission creep' manifested itself and, of course, fulfilling overseas service deployments. The commitment, courage and calibre of the soldiers were the real measure of the Defence Forces capability development. This patriotism of the soldiers, not paid commensurate to the responsibilities heaped on them and so not mercenary, should not be taken for granted.

CHAPTER 15

ATCP and Peacekeeping

Overseas Service in South Lebanon gave maturity to the Defence Forces generation of the late 1970s to the 1990s, and their service stood out from the shadow of the Congolese and Cypriot veterans before them. To be active overseas, on peacekeeping duties in South Lebanon, gave junior officers and NCOs the opportunity to learn and put in to practice the skills of leadership in an operational environment. Their confidence was built up in applying and seeing the effect of the operational procedures such as patrolling, manning checkpoints, observation posts, monitoring flashpoints and, most importantly, reporting incidents through the chain of command. This first-hand experiencing of all aspects of operating full time in the field gave them belief in themselves, their colleagues, the effect of teamwork on the collective whole, and in the application of the procedures of the organisation that is the military.

Receiving such exposure to this degree of practical involvement of one's profession, and to the knowledge and skills necessary and gained, was to undergo an encounter with self-assurance that was irreplaceable, all the more so for the first-timers. Many may well have come under fire, faced clashes and confrontations, or otherwise endured conflict and hostility, bringing into sharp focus the use of live ammunition when there was little alternative to defend one's life or that of one's comrades. This is an initiation unlike that in any other walk of life. Even if a soldier never came under fire, most were never quite the same on their return from the first tour of duty overseas and I do not believe they ever looked at their career and chosen path in quite the same way again. They were real after all; these contingencies that had played out in their minds. For many though, such were the realities of 'Life in the Leb'. The Defence Forces came under fire and responded with disciplined intent, because that was the job. And in this process, they found that the 'lines of command' proved solid and the training was worth it. Working in a multi-national environment, in a faraway country, immersed in a vastly different culture, was a mind-opening experience, and one of the more pressing lessons learned was that the Irish measured up well, even favourably, in comparison with the armies of the other nations they worked alongside.

In on-the-ground peacekeeping, the soldiers' role is a catalyst for peace rather than as an instrument of war, with the soldier armed but *not* threatening. He was trained to operate 'among the people' every day of the week and the Defence Forces' training, discipline and deportment, respect and courtesy – and operating in small clusters – in South Lebanon was all replicated at home. Transferred into the home internal security role, Aid to the Civil Power (ATCP) and Overseas Peacekeeping involvements for the Irish Defence Forces were symbiotic participations. The hard lessons learned in South Lebanon therefore had a duality of application both there and at home. Although the theatre of operations was entirely different, and the South Lebanon area of operations much more volatile and dangerous, the basic practices which were sound and proven in Ireland – even some of the home Current Operational Directive Guidance Documents – were tailor made for South Lebanon and exported well to what became regarded amongst the Defence Force members as 'the fifth province'. Importantly, though, the reverse was often true; operational involvement in South Lebanon, checkpoint situations, patrols and other convoy-like tasks could explode into nastiness at the drop of a hat and often did, which made the Defence Forces very wary when operating in similar situations at home, giving the lie to 'it'll never happen to us' syndrome.

The confidence accrued over multiple trips and active involvement in serious incidents had a hugely beneficial effect on the professional development of members of the Defence Forces. By definition, peacekeeping operations are established in areas of conflict where acts of violence and breaches of international and local agreements could be daily occurrences. Although it has been said that peacekeeping is not a suitable job for soldiers, it is only soldiers who can do the job. The Irish found that they had a particular suitability to it and are regarded internationally to be among the best peacekeepers in the world. The United Nations Interim Force in Lebanon (UNIFIL) Operations Headquarters staff was heavily populated by Irish officers and NCOs throughout and was generally a force for calm reactions to incidents.

In peacekeeping involvement pre-Lebanon – throughout the early part of the Troubles in the 1970s – young officers were aware of the concerns among their superiors that the Defence Forces might go down the route as prevailed in Northern Ireland, where the British army were increasingly involved. The opinion was that the Defence Forces should maintain a rigorous adherence to Military College doctrine of continuing to focus on conventional operations and apply their tried and tested principles to ATCP and to peacekeeping operations. Their concern was that the government would use the Defence Forces as a stop-gap 'gendarmerie' in support of a largely unarmed Garda force. They were disdainful of any instruction on the syllabus relating to 'police operations' and that essential procedures and practices would be eroded and improperly adopted to suit the ATCP requirements. There was a view among younger officers at the time that some of the older officers were perceived as being somewhat out of touch and out of their comfort zone, as few would have been operationally active during the IRA border campaign in the late 1950s. A number of *ad hoc* arrangements were applied and at times staff officers were satisfied to hide behind the mantra, 'that's what the Gardaí wanted' rather than insist that operations should follow proper procedure. A good example of this might be the search operations carried out in the Slieve Bloom mountain range during the search for the kidnapped Dr Tiede Herrema. The operation ended for the day when the Gardaí shift ended and everyone went home, instead of putting in an overnight cordon and resuming the search on the following day. Many officers felt that the Gardaí saw military assets as 'making up the numbers' when adequate Gardaí were not made available.

As the years rolled on, complacency set in and many in the Defence Forces were content to report: 'Strength of Military Party, Time Troops out of Barracks/Post, Time Troops returned, Nothing Special to Report.' In the period before the Current Operational Directive (COD) Guidance Documents were devised and the operational experiences from South Lebanon began to be imported, much of the procedures evolved by trial and some error. Sometimes, the military and pre-operational briefings were far removed from the realities on the ground and many soon learned to cope with a less than perfect co-ordination with the Civil Power in the shape of a poorly trained Gardaí and Prison Service. At that time both agencies, unlike the Defence Forces, did not have structured training courses and their respective chains of command were not set up to deal with twentieth-century terrorism and they found it difficult to adapt. Few organisations have the flexibility of the Defence Forces and their 'can do' approach.

The continuity of twenty-three years' service (1978–2001) in South Lebanon resulted in a hard-earned reputation in holding a very stretched thin blue line intact at an uncertain time. No less so at home, where peacekeeping experiences abroad helped the Defence Force develop a pragmatic response and face up to the serious threats from the IRA and Loyalist paramilitary groups. Operationally, a peacekeeping mission is a relatively reactive operation which tries to de-escalate conflicts by peaceful means. Certain important principles are central to successful peacekeeping, the non-use of force except in self-defence central amongst them. If peacekeeping was 'strange soldiering', the internal security ATCP role was somewhat stranger still. The everyday outwardly 'normal' routine belied the realities of a volatile situation. You had to become accustomed to the pace and tempo of events, mostly uneventful, matters calm, but yet not without potential for incident. This very unpredictability gave rise to a constant low, but nonetheless palpable, level of tension.

There was also a soldier's unease that in ATCP they were not deployed in the usual military mode. All duties, manning checkpoints and observation posts, patrolling, escorting, static guards, reporting, had all to be constantly performed – in all circumstances and in all weathers – with a consistent interpretation of standard operating procedures. ATCP duties were something of an irony for soldiers, although second nature and routine they were and remained unusual and irregular. The acceptance of the extraordinariness of the overseas journey undoubtedly made soldiers more susceptible and able to conform to – and perform better in – an ATCP role.

Conclusion
What If?

Throughout 1969 and the early 1970s, an uncertain Ireland could all too easily have become engulfed in an unwinnable all-Ireland civil war; it would only have been a pyrrhic victory, as in the aftermath of such a conflict any victory gained would have been at too great a cost to ever have been worthwhile. In terms of deaths and destruction, the country would have been ripped asunder. The unarmed Garda Síochána were not able to cope alone with the level of violence perpetrated and the Irish Defence Forces were deployed in their support, tasked by the Government to 'Aid the Civil Power'. The Defence Forces took the role very seriously and went about their duty in earnest. Initially, demands on the under-strength, under-equipped and unprepared security forces were great, only to exponentially increase as the crisis deepened.

At the outbreak of the Troubles, the Irish Government faced unprecedented turmoil and unimaginable unrest and confusion both internally and externally. If the forces of hot-headed militarism, sectarianism and intolerance had prevailed and allowed to triumph, it would have torn the nation apart. Now, at the remove of passing decades, it is difficult to fully grasp this grim reality, to appreciate the volatility of those times and to understand the dire, potentially explosive, uncertainty of the circumstances. The extraordinariness of the crisis was unparalleled and the likelihood of uncontrolled upheaval and strife was frighteningly close. There was a fortunate and early realisation by the majority in the Irish Government under Jack Lynch, that despite the recklessness of some individual members, only a peaceful reunification of the country with the consent of the Unionists could lift the centuries'-old curse of history that has beset the island. The Irish Government could have caved in to these elements that put the country at such risk, especially during the early 1970s. Instead they faced down the conspirators and the hard-liners. They, and succeeding Irish governments, took determined and resolute action to defend democracy and uphold the rule of law. It is not too much to suggest that, but for the Garda Síochána, and more so the Defence Forces, there might have been no state left.

When the Troubles broke out, the Defence Forces, despite being very badly neglected and always the 'Cinderella' of government thinking, proved over time to be professional and adaptable at getting around the problems; their commitment to the Oath, the people and the State was never in doubt. The Irish were and historically always have been good soldiers, and compare favourably with those of any nation on earth. Throughout the Troubles, the Defence Forces were loyal to the Constitution, the Government and the people.

The serious, complex and ever-changing challenge from paramilitary groups, the most sophisticated by far the Provisional IRA, meant that the crisis could have escalated at any stage – and sometimes did – and if unchecked could deteriorate into severe inter-communal strife to the all-out degree seen in the Balkans, Cyprus, Lebanon and elsewhere. If left unrestrained, the uncompromising extremism of sectarian 'tit-for-tat' killings could have brought the conflict towards the threshold of complete lawlessness and unimaginable disorder. 'Spill over' from the conflict in Northern Ireland was a constant concern for the Government, while, internally, the Provisional IRA were a source of severe stress to the stability of the country. This threat was addressed by the Irish security forces, and that the Defence Forces were able to perform in a quasi-police role is perhaps unique amongst armies, many having specifically organised, equipped and trained units designated for that purpose; the Gendarmerie nationale in France, the Arma dei Carabinieri in Italy and the Guardia Civil in Spain being examples of this. An unarmed police force was always favoured by the Irish public and the continuance of this practice helped ensure strong public support for them. However, the harsh fact was that the Provisional IRA was heavily armed and ultimately had to met and beaten with force.

The Defence Forces were the ultimate tangible means to ensure the Irish people and police were protected. The daily application of degrees of this official force was a necessary armed State response. This posture also involved the threat to use greater force, if necessary, with troops on constant standby in barracks throughout the country, ready to deploy immediately with one or two hours' notice to back up the Gardaí when necessary. Such call-outs were not uncommon and the Defence Forces were not found lacking in their resolution to act. Some argued for a greater concentration on the Defence Forces' internal security operations and for a more actively involved role, like that of the British army, especially along the border. The Defence Forces, many felt, were never fully 'let off the leash' to address the situation directly. If the Government had opted for a more visually vigorous offensive posture against the Provisional IRA, granting greater autonomy to the Defence Forces with more frequent patrolling and presence – without the Gardaí to disrupt, deter and detain suspected PIRA members – it would have helped dispel the sometimes floated notion or accusation that the Republic of Ireland was a safe haven for republican paramilitaries; of course, those making such claims knowing full well that it was not. However, the Aid to the Civil Power policy employed by the Government was very wise in the long run and the merits of a police-led campaign were vindicated. Its practice, applied purposefully on the ground by the Defence Forces, proved a highly relevant and appropriate approach to a very difficult security and political situation.

The sanctity of ATCP meant it was not really the Defence Forces' task to 'lead the fight'. Their mission was to develop and apply a capability to support the Gardaí within the limits of the logistical, operational and legal capacity provided by the Government. It is important to remember the Defence Forces did provide this onerous, difficult and essential role while concurrently continuing to train for its on-island conventional defence role and simultaneously executing overseas peacekeeping duties as well. This combination of concomitant roles, a massive commitment to the State, was provided through the vocational dedication of individual Defence Forces members, at a crucial time in the State's history over the thirty years of the Troubles. The ATCP mission generated a huge workload for the Defence Forces but also gave it a very real purpose, and the Defence Forces undertook its role in a very professional and committed manner. There was often frustration with the Garda style of conducting operations, but the Defence Forces adjusted to these expectations. Most within the Defence Forces, looking at the British army experiences in Northern Ireland, realised that soldiers were probably best kept away from direct contact with the civilian population. The Irish Defence Forces were drawn from the people and it was always important to continue to nurture and maintain that public support.

The constant conduct of 'framework operations', the day-to-day tasks performed by the Defence Forces in support of the State's institutions, saw them conduct numerous routine but important involvements, many unseen, unheralded and most neither sufficiently understood nor appreciated by the public at large. The competence of the Defence Forces was evident. The Emergency Powers Act allowed the Defence Forces deploy without Gardaí, though the official security policy only ever saw them in a support role to the Gardaí, which in itself saw them perform unswervingly in a huge incidence of security duties on cash, explosive and prisoner escorts, at mines during blasting, as guards on vital installations, with bomb-disposal capability and frequent deployments in Cordon and Search operations, riot (crowd) control and, of course, constant border operations.

The nationwide scaling up of standby platoons and companies during holiday periods, with the Defence Forces poised and ready to respond in strength at any time, meant that while everyone else was switching off to enjoy their holidays, the Defence Forces were gearing up for action and always available to respond to the slightest threat. While there was some level of remuneration, this was very low in comparison to that received by the Garda Síochána and Prison Service, and also cash-in-transit security company employees. Ironically, the Defence Forces, the State's very last line of defence – heavily relied upon by both the far better paid Garda Síochána and the Prison Service – were proportionately ill-rewarded for their service.

Neither were the Defence Forces ever equipped well enough for a possible deterioration in the internal security situation. The Panhard armoured personnel carrier was not well suited to the task it had to perform; a cheaper, lighter armoured vehicle was required for many internal security situations. Similarly, light armoured vehicles for escorts and checkpoints were also required, as were troop-carrying helicopters to convey troops in numbers responding rapidly to incidents in near or remote locations. The development of a realistic doctrine for unarmed riot control took far too long to develop, though the establishment of permanent border units brought great continuity and expertise to their operations. Overall, the Defence Forces can be very proud of the role they played; they were loyal but it was an unwavering faithfulness that was neither appropriately regarded nor rewarded.

Whether the Troubles will continue in other forms or to other degrees is a matter for the future, but undoubtedly the legacy of the Provisional IRA was to leave within the State the existence of dissident IRA groups and also to hasten the proliferation of weapons involved in gun crime in Ireland today.

The Provisional IRA could not carry on operating and prolonging their campaign of violence without risking the death and arrest of their remaining Active Service Units. They were heavily infiltrated by the security services, both electronically and with informers and agents. It was important that both the British and Irish governments had forces in place that were capable of intervening. Rule 8 of the Provisional IRA's 'Green Book' in principle prevented their members from 'taking on' members of the Garda Síochána and Defence Forces within the republic, a directive not always followed, which resulted in the deaths of uniformed members of the Irish security forces. From the Civil War (1922) through to their campaign during the 'Emergency' (1940–6) and into the border campaign (1956–62), the Irish State's response to the IRA's actions were always met with a harsh head-on response. While PIRA escalation of operations against the Irish State's security forces would have posed a very severe test, particularly in the early 1970s, there would have been no alternative but to eventually respond sternly. Although casualties would have occurred, the situation would have been brought on to a new level entirely, well beyond ATCP and more like an Emergency Situation, which would have been contested by the State and would have ended badly for the Provisional IRA.

The Defence Forces would have been forced to vigorously supress them while at the same time being careful not to be branded as in collusion with the British army. An active Provisional IRA campaign would have lost them huge support in the Republic amongst the ambivalent but the population would have had to choose sides and the vast majority of any support would been totally lost to them. The Irish public was appalled enough already. The response of the Garda Síochána and the Defence Forces would have seriously damaged the Provisional IRA; the Irish security forces would have won that battle. As it was, the PIRA campaign in the North, with all its military 'successes', had very real limits as to what it could ever achieve because the Provisional IRA lacked the means to persuade or coerce the Protestant loyalists. They

204 | *Soldiering Against Subversion*

had nothing to offer them and so could never hope to command the support of the majority of the population of Northern Ireland. Their 'Brits out' campaign was too limited in its scope, too narrow in its vision, too idealistically weak. It simply had nowhere to go, hence the 'ArmaLite in one hand and ballot box in the other' campaign begun in the early 1980s and the tactical use of violence employed towards a political end. Run to a standstill by security forces' successes both north and south of the border, the Provisional IRA looked for political gains through its political wing, Sinn Féin. Its military campaign was blocked and its 'armed struggle' essentially quelled, confined to an ever-decreasing geographical radius and a dwindling pool of active service units able to operate effectively.

The Defence Forces south of the border had done their job and done it well, making a huge contribution towards maintaining stability. The outcome was a real victory and a tangible success. Peace prevailed and an entire generation has grown up without witnessing violence.

There is much still believed about the Troubles that is untrue. In due course, history will record these events with detachment but until then it is important that the truth comes out. The first truth is the dispelling of the myth, even to those in the Republic of Ireland who lived through those turbulent times, that the Troubles were confined to Northern Ireland, when they had in fact a hugely significant impact down south also, and this will continue for some time. Second, the Irish Defence Forces had an enormous involvement in ensuring the stability of the State throughout those decades, when its sovereignty was placed under severe threat by the activities of the Provisional IRA. Third, this huge contribution by the Defence Forces was core to the State's continued existence according to the democratic will of the people. Fourth, a democracy has to be defended and to do so a force capable of intervening against threats to it must be maintained. There can be neither ambiguity nor ambivalence about this. Finally, today the invisibility of the Irish Defence Forces is almost taken for granted. This is a prominent reality within the Defence Forces, though it does a disservice to both the soldier and society because the interpretation of the military is an integral part of Irish citizenship in revealing aspects of the nation's identity.

The self-image of the military can reveal a lot about the culture within which it exists. Soldiers reflect the society from which they are drawn and military organisations are motivated by the standards of that society. Yet it is this state's soldiers – those who have served at home and abroad – who appreciate most acutely that peace and freedom have a price, are more fragile than first imagined, and must never be taken for granted. Can we safely assume then that the Good Friday Agreement will last? And if the answer to that is 'no', how prepared are we for the consequences? It is worth remembering that in Ireland, although an ancient country, the past is constantly present.

Epilogue

To move forward you have to look back. The systematic lack of parity of equality in Northern Ireland gave rise to a long-felt sense of grievance amongst the Catholic nationalist minority there. This prolonged wrong manifested in the civil rights movement, but the Provisional IRA also seized upon this opportunity and chose the path of violence over the peaceful path of politics. Initially, and for a while, there was a running ambiguity in the minds of the people in the balance between the support for the civil rights movement and that of militant republicanism. Bloody Sunday was decisive for many, and a historical moment was reached. A merciless, violent campaign of murder and bloodshed resulted, and atrocity followed atrocity in a vicious cycle of slaughter. The IRA was convinced that its aim would be achieved from the 'cutting edge of militarism' and not from vote-seeking or the pursuit of politics. 'Victory '72' became 'Victory '74', and they went from 'One Big Push' to 'the Long War'. This led only to more funerals, more grief, and a realisation that violence was *not* achieving what they wanted.

Then came the hunger strikes out of the H-Block protests, and when Bobby Sands was elected MP everything changed. They saw how politics *could* work for them and focused on it along with the 'tactical use of violence'. This 'ArmaLite in one hand and ballot box in the other' policy was how they moved forward, but not always with progress. As the Provisional IRA found their armed campaign alone had not – and could not – coerce the Unionists to be more reasonable nor remove British rule from Northern Ireland, they sought instead to build momentum for change through negotiation, and a part of that negotiation was 'One Last Push', maintaining the use of violence to encourage their presence in the peace process. Initially there were secret channels and conduits opened between the IRA and the government to explore the possibility of ending the violence without a British withdrawal. Such meetings were not without risk, as death and destruction continued with force being used as a political lever.

Would the 'peace process' ever succeed; could it put an end to the conflict and halt the violence? If it could not, what was the alternative? The spectre of a Balkans-like cataclysm was the haunting fear. Since the outbreak, and all throughout the Troubles, this great dread preyed on the minds of the population. Neither was the Republic immune, but the security forces – the Defence Forces in particular – defended Ireland, protected its people and secured the State. They contained the IRA in a complex political–military context, proving itself relevant, useful and adaptable.

Since the Peace Process' subsequent peaceful progression, the Good Friday Agreement has held and there has been a welcome absence of violence in the North. The historic visit of Britain's Queen Elizabeth II to Ireland in 2011 went well, evidencing a positive appetite for good will between both countries. The Defence Forces kept Ireland 'open for business' during the Troubles, and with its major contribution to the provision of a 'safe and secure environment', foreign direct investment was substantially maintained. Disruption to trading during individual incidents was kept to a minimum and the fulfilment of its internal security role proved also to be a positive economic factor for the country.

Politics and its primacy is a necessary part of the democratic process. In Ireland we have just emerged from an era of violence and the attempted subverting of the State's sovereignty. Defending our democracy was an under-resourced, overstretched, but steadfast Defence Forces. Today, in the post-Good Friday Agreement phase, the same Defence Forces are now largely overlooked and undervalued – but still steadfastly loyal. The politicians, it may be said, took a long time to achieve progress and are arguably still not achieving enough. In the North there is now an absence of violence, which is a major advance, and a generation has grown up without confrontation and conflict. But have the politicians done all that they could to expedite that progress instead of prioritising the advance of their individual parties? The worry is that it would not take much to invoke the ghosts of history for both recent and past tensions to be stoked, old wounds reopened and barely veiled bitterness to re-emerge.

There is a political responsibility toward progress, yet with progress thin and only on the surface, has the situation actually moved on, or are we heading in a direction we don't want to go? We must move forward while looking back, so that we do not repeat the mistakes of the past. This is equally true, in an increasingly unstable and uncertain world, of Ireland's security, defence and intelligence capacity.

Chronology of the Troubles in the Republic

Note: This Chronology highlights the main events only, with those in Northern Ireland included as context.

1968

5 October	A banned Civil Rights Association march in Derry leads to clashes between police and protesters, sparking widespread disorder and rioting across Northern Ireland. The officially recognised date of the start of the Troubles.

1969

5 August	UVF Bomb at RTÉ in Dublin.
12–14 August	Battle of the Bogside in Derry. Riots in Belfast.
14 August	'Operation Banner' begins (the British army arrives). Irish army (four infantry groups) sent to the border.
19 October	UVF man killed planting a bomb in Ballyshannon, Co. Donegal.
31 October	UVF bomb at Wolfe Tone memorial, Co. Kildare.
26 December	UVF bomb at Daniel O'Connell monument in Dublin.
28 December	UVF bomb outside Garda Central Detective Bureau in Dublin.

1970

26 March	UVF bomb at an ESB sub-station in Tallaght, Dublin.
3 April	Garda Richard Fallon killed in Dublin by Saor Éire during a bank robbery.
6 May	Two Government ministers sacked by the Taoiseach.
27–28 June	Battle of St Matthews, Short Strand, Ballymacarrett, Belfast.

2 July	UVF bomb damages the main Dublin–Belfast railway lines at Baldoyle.
3–5 July	Falls Road Curfew. Provisional IRA emerges and defends Catholic Nationalist areas.
13 October	Saor Éire member killed in premature explosion on railway line near McKee Barracks, Dublin.
23 October	Arms Trial in Dublin concludes. Four defendants found not guilty of arms smuggling.

1971

17 January	UVF bomb damages Daniel O'Connell's tomb in Glasnevin Cemetery.
8 February	UDA destroys the Wolfe Tone statue on St Stephen's Green, Dublin.
9 August	Internment without trial (Operation Demetrius) introduced, which was to continue until 5 December 1975. Upsurge of violence and number of deaths in the aftermath. Nationalists 'on the run' from Internment go south of the border, many to border counties.
September	Loyalists officially form the UDA.
28 October	British Army engaged in cratering and blocking unapproved border crossings. A stand-off at a cross border bridge at Munnelly on the Monaghan–Fermanagh border between British army and Irish Defence Forces.

1972

30 January	'Bloody Sunday' – 1st Parachute Regiment opens fire on Civil Rights Association march in Derry. Fourteen unarmed civilians are killed. PIRA holds unsuccessful talks in London with the Secretary of State for Northern Ireland and escalates its campaign resulting in 'Bloody Friday' when twenty-two explosions in ninety minutes erupt across Belfast.
22 February	Burning of the British Embassy in Dublin.

19 May	Riot in Mountjoy Prison, Dublin.
22 May	Special Criminal Court re-established.
3 June	Irish troops confronted by protestors at the Curragh.
8 June	Inspector Sam Donegan killed on the border.
21 July	'Bloody Friday'. PIRA explodes 22 bombs in Belfast.
31 July	More PIRA activists come south avoiding 'Operation Motorman'.
21 September	Riot outside Dundalk Garda Station.
10 October	AIB Grafton Street Dublin branch robbery. Two English brothers, Keith and Kenneth Littlejohn, are arrested.
28 October	Bomb in Connolly Station. Fire bombs left in bedrooms in four Dublin hotels.
26 November	Bomb left at the door of Film Centre Cinema, Dublin.
3 December	Two bombs explode in Dublin, killing two men. Amendment to the Special Powers Act passed by the Dáil.
28 December	Three bombs explode at Belturbet, Co. Cavan, Clones, Co. Monaghan and Pettigo, Co. Donegal. Two people are killed.

1973

20 January	Bomb explodes in Sackville Place, Dublin (one person is killed).
17 March	Car bomb explodes prematurely in Cloughfin, Co. Donegal (UVF driver killed).
28 March	PIRA arms shipment on MV *Claudia* intercepted off Helvic Harbour, Co. Waterford and five tonnes of weapons are seized.
1 September	The 27th and 28th Infantry Battalions are established in Aiken Barracks, Dundalk, and Finner Camp, Donegal, respectively.
10 October	Three PIRA prisoners escape from Mountjoy Prison by helicopter.
9 November	Prisoners are moved to Portlaoise Prison.

1974

12 March	Fine Gael Senator Billy Fox is shot dead by PIRA in Scotstown, Co. Monaghan.
2 April	PIRA hijack a helicopter at Gortahork, Co. Donegal, and force the pilot to fly over the RUC station in Strabane where they drop two milk churn bombs (which did not explode).
17 May	Three car bombs in Parnell, Talbot and South Leinster streets in Dublin explode within 90 seconds of each other killing 33 and injuring over 300 people. Another bomb explodes in Monaghan ninety minutes later. It was the single biggest atrocity in one day during the Troubles.
4 June	PIRA kidnap Lord and Lady Donoughmore.
8 June	Funeral of Michael Gaughan, who died on hunger strike in Parkhurst Prison, takes place in Co. Mayo.
18 August	Nineteen PIRA prisoners use explosives to escape from Portlaoise Prison.
10 December	PIRA hold a meeting with leading Protestant clergymen from Northern Ireland in Co. Clare (the Gardaí raid it).
29 December	Riot inside Portlaoise Prison. Defence Forces restore order.

1975

10 February–27 September	PIRA ceasefire.
17 March	Attempted break out from Portlaoise Prison fails – Defence Forces open fire (one person killed and two wounded by ricochets).
22 June	A man is stabbed to death; it is thought that he came across a UVF group attempting to plant a bomb on the railway line at Straffan, Co. Kildare, disturbing an attempted derailing of a train with 200 passengers on board.
31 August	The Miami Showband is ambushed and murdered by the UVF.

11 September	Garda Michael Reynolds is killed during a bank raid in Dublin.
3 October	Dr Tiede Herrema kidnapped by a PIRA gang. A massive manhunt follows leading to a seventeen-day siege in St Evin's Park, Monasterevin, Co. Kildare, which ended successfully after negotiations.
29 November	A bomb explodes at Dublin Airport; a man is killed.
19 December	A bomb explodes at Dundalk, Co. Louth. Two men are killed.

1976

February	A bomb explodes in the Shelbourne Hotel and eight incendiary devices ignite in shops in Dublin. No injuries.
7 March	A bomb explodes in Castleblayney, Co. Monaghan. One man is killed.
10 March	The Sallins Mail Train robbery – £200,000 is taken.
2 May	A civilian is murdered near Dundalk, Co. Louth. There are a number of killings in and around the Louth/Armagh border area.
6 May	Eight SAS troopers arrested at army/Garda checkpoint in what became known as the 'Flagstaff Incident'.
12 July	The funeral of Frank Stagg in Co. Mayo.
21 July	British Ambassador to Ireland and his Secretary killed by a bomb in Sandyford, Co. Dublin.
16 September	Emergency Powers Bill passed by Government and is referred by the President to the Supreme Court.
5 October	The 29th Infantry Battalion is established in Monaghan.
16 October	President signs Emergency Powers Bill into law. Garda Michael Clerkin is killed by PIRA booby trap bomb near Portlaoise.
17 October	At Columb Barracks, Mullingar, the Minister for Defence calls the President 'a thundering disgrace'. The President resigns after the Government takes no action.

1977

8 March	The eight members of the SAS arrested during the Flagstaff Incident (6 May 1976) are fined £100 each.
14 May	Captain Robert Nairac, Grenadier Guards attached to the SAS, is abducted, beaten and shot by PIRA. A search for his body is conducted along the Louth/ Armagh border area.
20 June	The 30th Infantry Battalion is established in Kilkenny.
5 October	Seamus Costello (IRSP) is shot dead in Dublin. An internal feud in the Irish National Liberation Army (INLA) subsequently plays out.

1978

28 January	Garda Special Task Force formed as part of the Special Branch.
May	PIRA Bank Robbery in Killygordon, Co. Donegal; one man fatally shot. Army/Garda searches uncover weapons and explosives.

1979

30 March	Under-car booby-trap bomb kills Airey Neave, MP in the House of Commons car park in London.
7 August	PIRA bank robbery in Tramore, Co. Waterford. One civilian fatally shot.
27 August	Eighteen British soldiers killed by PIRA double explosion at Warrenpoint. One civilian was killed and one wounded at Narrow Water, Co. Lough, in the immediate aftermath of the Warrenpoint explosions when British troops fire across the border, mistakenly believing they were being fired upon; in fact the casualties were innocent birdwatchers. Lord Louis Mountbatten and three other people blown up on a boat in Co. Sligo.
26 September	FCÁ (2nd line, part-time reserve) separated from PDF in Defence Force Formations.

1 November	PIRA arms shipment seized by security forces at Dublin docks.

1980

16 March	Army Ranger Wing established.
7 July	Detective Garda John Morley and Garda Henry Byrne killed after PIRA bank robbery at Ballaghaderreen, Co. Roscommon.
13 October	Detective Garda James Quaid shot dead following a double bank raid in Callan, Co. Kilkenny.

1981

11 June	Two H-Block Maze prisoners were elected as TDs during the General Election in the Republic. Kieran Doherty was elected in Cavan–Monaghan and died on 2 August. Paddy Agnew, who was not on hunger strike, was elected in Lough.
18 July	The H-Block Protest in Dublin turns violent as demonstrators are prevented from reaching the British Embassy in Ballsbridge.

1982

20 February	Garda Patrick Reynolds is fatally shot raiding a flat in Tallaght, Dublin after a bank raid in Askeaton, Co. Limerick, two days earlier.

1983

8 February	The racehorse Shergar is kidnapped by PIRA; a widespread search for the horse follows.
25 March	Chief Prison Officer Brian Stack is shot by PIRA. He dies eighteen months later.
7 August	A PIRA kidnap attempt of Galen Weston at Roundwood, Co. Wicklow, is foiled by the Gardaí who were lying in wait.
25 September	Thirty-eight PIRA prisoners escape from the Maze Prison. One prison officer died of a heart attack as a result of the escape and twenty others were injured.

24 November	Supermarket executive Don Tidey is kidnapped by PIRA outside his home in Rathfarnam, Dublin.
16 December	Private Patrick Kelly and Garda Recruit Gary Sheehan are killed by PIRA after Don Tidey is successfully freed at Ballinamore, Co. Leitrim.

1984

17 March	Dominic McGlinchey, INLA, captured during a shoot-out at Newmarket-on-Fergus, Co. Clare, after a nationwide hunt.
24 May	Stalker inquiry into alleged 'shoot-to-kill' policy set up.
10 August	Detective Garda Frank Hand killed at Drumree Post Office robbery.
29 September	PIRA arms shipment on the *Marita Ann* intercepted off the Skellig Rocks, Co. Kerry coast.
12 October	Grand Brighton Hotel bombing at Conservative Party conference. Five killed and thirty-four wounded. Prime Minister Margaret Thatcher narrowly escapes.

1985

28 February	PIRA mortar attack on Newry RUC Barracks.
27 June	Garda Sergeant Patrick Morrissey killed at Ardee following a robbery.
15 November	Anglo-Irish Agreement signed by both governments (Margaret Thatcher and Garret FitzGerald).

1986

7 August	An incursion by loyalists into Clontibret, Co. Monaghan is dispersed by Gardaí. The 'Clontibret Invasion' occurred in the context of loyalist opposition to the Anglo-Irish Agreement, fearful that it is a stepping stone towards a United Ireland.
October	PIRA Army Convention abolishes 'Abstention' policy.

1987

8 May	Eight PIRA ASU members killed in an attack on an RUC station at Loughall.
13 October	Dentist John O'Grady kidnapped in South County Dublin by the INLA.
30 October	MV *Eksund* intercepted by French Customs off Brest; it was carrying a massive 150 tonnes of arms, ammunitions and explosives for the PIRA.
5 November	Dentist John O'Grady freed by Gardaí.
27 November	Dessie O'Hare, the 'Border Fox' arrested by security forces after a shoot-out at Balief Crossroads, Urlingford, Co. Kilkenny.
8 November	A PIRA bomb explodes on Remembrance Day at the Enniskillen War Memorial, causing a huge wave of revulsion.
23–9 November	'Operation Mallard' is conducted throughout the border counties searching for arms, ammunition and explosives successfully landed by the four arms shipments prior to the interception of the *Eksund*.

1988

6 March	Three unarmed PIRA members on a bombing mission to Gibraltar are shot dead by the SAS.
16 March	Ulster Loyalist Michael Stone attacks the triple funeral at Milltown Cemetery and three people are killed.
19 March	At the funeral of one of the three Milltown Cemetary victims, two off-duty plain-clothes British Army Corporals in an unmarked car happen upon the cortège and are savagely set upon and killed by the mourners, thinking they are being attacked.
27 January	Arms find at Five Fingers Strand, Malin Head, Co. Donegal.
23 February	Arms find at Portmarnock, Co. Dublin.
27 February	Arms find at Ballivor, Co. Meath.

218 | *Chronology of the Troubles in the Republic*

10 March	Arms find at Patrickswell, Co. Limerick.
16 March	Arms find at Finea, Co. Cavan.
18 March	Arms find at Ballymaleel, Co. Donegal.

1989

12 February	Pat Finucane, a Belfast solicitor, is shot dead.
15 June	Sinn Féin fair badly in the Irish General Election (1.2 per cent of votes and no seats).
23 November	The Taoiseach reaffirms the Anglo-Irish Agreement.

1990

24 October	PIRA use a proxy bomb; five soldiers killed at a checkpoint.

1991

7 February	PIRA Mortar Bomb on 10 Downing Street.

1992

10 April	The Baltic London Exchange area is bombed; an enormous explosion causes spectacular damage and a huge repair bill.
August	PIRA sniper campaign begins in South Armagh.

1993

February–March	Warrington Bombings in England. Two children are killed in the second bombing on 20 March, Jonathan Ball (3) and Tim Parry (12).
24 April	A massive bomb is exploded at Bishopsgate, London.
23 October	In Northern Ireland a bomb explodes in a building on the Shankill Road.

1994

19 January	Broadcasting Ban (Section 31) lifted in the Republic.
9–13 March	PIRA carry out a series of mortar attacks on Heathrow Airport.

1995

16 March	Gerry Adams attended a reception hosted by US President Bill Clinton at the White House.

1996

9 February	London Docklands (Canary Wharf) bombing.
7 June	Detective Garda Jerry McCabe killed during a Post Office van robbery in Adare, Co. Limerick.
15 June	Corporation Street, Manchester bombing.
11 July	Conflict erupts in Drumcree with the blocking of an Orange Order March through the Nationalist Garvaghy area of Portadown.

1997

12 February	Last British soldier killed by PIRA sniper in Northern Ireland.
26 June	Sinn Féin wins its first seats in Dáil Éireann.
19 July	PIRA resumes its ceasefire.

1998

10 April	The Good Friday agreement (Belfast or Stormont Agreement) signed.
22 May	Two referendums held on the ratification of the Good Friday agreement; over 70 per cent in Northern Ireland and 90 per cent in the Republic are in favour.
5 July	Drumcree Standoff commenced when the Parades Commission decided to ban the march from Garvaghy Road. Over the next ten days there were loyalist protests and violence across Northern Ireland in response to the ban, including the murders of Jason (8), Mark (9) and Richard Quinn (10) who were burnt to death on 12 July when their home was petrol bombed by loyalists

15 August	The Omagh Bombing, carried out by the Real IRA, a PIRA splinter group who opposed the ceasefire and Good Friday agreement killed twenty-nine people (including a woman pregnant with twins) and injured 220. The bombing caused international outrage and was the death knell of paramilitary action in Northern Ireland.
22 August	The INLA declares a ceasefire.
16 October	John Hume and David Trimble jointly awarded the Nobel Peace Prize.

Acknowledgements

Throughout its history, the Defence Forces has only ever seen development and expansion in response to external stimuli and threats. In between such times, it has been allowed to become run down and has not thrived. In a sense, it is a healthy reflection of our democracy in Ireland today that the Defence Forces is mentioned so little and perceived to be so unimportant to the State.

The worth of the Defence Forces has often been more costed than valued. Highly valued by me, however, was the advice and assistance I received for this book from the following:

Mr Des O'Malley; Lieutenant Generals (Retd.) Jim Sreenan, Pat Nash and Sean McCann; Brigadier Generals (Retd.) Seamus O'Giollain and Colm Campbell; Brigadier General Joe Mulligan; Colonels (Retd.) Harry Crowley (RIP), Terry O'Neill, Brian Dowling, Lenny Mullins, Leo Brownen, Bill Eager, Tony Murphy, Mick Mulooley, Dick Heaslip, George Kertin, Tony O'Hanlon; Lieutenant Colonels (Retd.) Sean Scanlon, Diarmuid O'Donoghue, Mick Murphy, Dermot Igoe, Noel Byrne, Ted Shine, Tom Heskin, Mike Clements; Commandants (Retd.) Paddy Boyle, Wally Young, Brendan Rowan, Eamonn Kiely, Eoghan Allen, Barry Studdard, Peter Daly, Ray Stewart, Joe Fallon; Captains (Retd.) Greg Kelly, Mick McGinley, Noel Carey, Jim Rea, Maurice McQuillan, David Gunning, Martin Murphy; Company Quartermaster Sergeant (Retd.) Tom Brace; Acting Company Sergeant FCÁ (Retd.) Barry Bowman; Garda Superintendent (Retd.) PJ McGowen, Garda Sergeant (Retd.) Kevin Sweeney PhD; RTÉ Security correspondents (retd.) Tom McCaughren and Joe O'Brien; Kevin Myers; author Don Mullen; ex PIRA activist Kieran Conway.

A special word of thanks to Deirdre Maxwell for her unstinting clerical support. Illustrations make clear the subject through a visual snapshot of the chronological events and those who feature in them. For these photographs I wish to thank Sergeant Wayne Fitzgerald, Editor of An Consantóir, the Defence Forces magazine. Thanks to Captain Dan Ayiotis and Lisa Dolan of the Military Archives, Dublin, for use of their images, to Gerry and all the staff in Cork City Library, and to Dan Linehan and the photographic staff at the *Irish Examiner*. To those at Irish Academic Press/Merrion Press for their faith in the story and resilience in bringing it to a reality, Conor Graham, Fiona Dunne and Myles McCionnaith, I thank you all sincerely. For their continued forbearance, patience and understanding, I sincerely thank my children Eva, Lynn, Mary-Claire and Hugo. It is for their generation that I write.

The views expressed in this book are the author's alone and not those of the Irish Defence Forces.

Operation Armageddon

There is a saying in the military that 'a plan rarely survives past its first contact with the enemy' and another saying that, 'plans are nothing, but planning is everything.' So it was prudent that contingency planning was directed to be conducted in late August 1969, to prepare for the possible, but unpredictable, plight of vulnerable Catholic communities in the event of the further rapid deterioration of the crisis situation in Northern Ireland. Cabinet discussions on the unfolding crisis had previously led to a number of actions being agreed, measures which included the setting up of 'Field Hospitals' (First-Aid stations), refugee centres (emergency accommodation), putting troops on the border, and appointing two Government ministers with responsibility to oversee the preparation of the army for a worsening of the situation (the Minister for Defence and the Minister for Finance). Plans then were drafted at the start of the Troubles, envisaged neither as an invasion nor an intervention, but a humanitarian incursion; an extraction *in extremis*, an evacuation in the emergency eventuality of a nightmarish doomsday situation.

On 27 September 1969, the Defence Forces 'Interim Report of the Planning Board on Northern Ireland Operations' presented an outline of a possible concept of operations. Its significance lay in its stated acceptance that the Defence Forces had 'no capability' to engage successfully in conventional offensive military operations against the security forces in Northern Ireland and that any operations undertaken in Northern Ireland would be 'militarily unsound'. The plan, to 'secure the safety of the minority population' envisaged the dual use of firstly unconventional guerrilla-type operations in the North-East corner (against Belfast Docks, Aldergrove Airport, the BBC studios and other key installations) in order to draw away the attention of the British army from the border, and secondly, with that unfolding, a more conventional series of two company strength size incursions to execute the safe evacuation of beleaguered Catholic communities in close proximity to the border.

A number of months later, with the British army faltering and the Provisional IRA emerging, concerns over the changing circumstances led to further thoughts about a complete breakdown of law and order within a severely destabilised Northern Ireland. This gave rise to considerations of contingency and circumstances where the Irish Taoiseach, Jack Lynch, ordered the army to 'train and prepare', in a purely humanitarian response should such an extreme situation – 'Armageddon' – occur; to execute, if necessary, the extraction of those under attack by Protestant mobs and those wounded and frightened. This became known as the 'February Directive'. There were those who may have represented this plan differently than how it was discussed within the Government. The majority present were aware that the Irish army going across the border could not have held out any hope whatsoever of ending partition, and the context within which the Directive was framed was purely and solely in circumstances of the catastrophic collapse of order in Northern Ireland; and then only to protect Catholic nationalist communities in close proximity to the border from mass loyalist mob attacks by evacuation through safe exit routes. In the event, the plan was dropped in October 1969, but only after the necessary planning made this evident.

Bibliography

Anderson, Don, *14 May Days: The Inside Story of the Loyalist Strike of 1974* (Dublin: Gill & MacMillan, 1994).

Bowyer, Bell J., *In Dubious Battle: The Dublin and Monaghan Bombings 1972–1974* (Dublin: Poolbeg Press Ltd, 1996).

Browne, Johnson, *Into the Dark 30 Years in the RUC* (Dublin: Gill & MacMillan, 2006).

Clark, A. F. J., *Contact* (London: Martin Secker & Warburg Ltd, 1983).

Conway, Kiernan, *Southside Provisional* (Dublin: Orpen Press, 2014).

Coogan, Tim Pat, *The Troubles* (London: Hutchinson, 1995).

Courtney, John, *It Was Murder* (Dublin: Blackwater Press, 1996).

Edwards, Aaron, *The Northern Irish Troubles, Operation Banner 1969–2007* (Osprey: 2011).

Edwards, Aaron, *UVF: Behind the Mask* (Dublin: Merrion Press, 2017).

English, Richard, *Armed Struggle: A History of the IRA* (London: MacMillan, 2003).

Feeney, Brian, *A Short History of the Troubles* (Dublin: The O'Brian Press, 2004).

Harnden, Toby, *Bandit Country: The IRA & South Armagh* (London: Hodder & Stoughton, 1999).

Horgan, John, *Divided We Stand, The Strategy and Psychology of Irelands Dissident Terrorists* (Oxford University Press, 2013).

Ingram, Martin and Harkin, Greg, *Steak Knife, Britain's Secret Agents in Ireland* (Dublin: The O'Brian Press, 2004).

Kevin, Kelly, *The Longest War: Northern Ireland and the IRA* (Brandon Dingle, Co. Kerry, 1982).

Keogh, Dermot, *Jack Lynch, A Biography* (Dublin: Gill & MacMillan, 2008).

Matchett, William, *Secret Victory: The Intelligence War that Beat the IRA* (Lisburn: Hickey Ltd, 2016).

Maloney, Ed, *A Secret History of The IRA* (New York: W.W. Norton Ltd & Company Inc., 2002).

Mooney, John and O'Toole, Michael, *Black Operations, The Secret War Against the Real IRA* (Maverick House Ashbourne, Co. Meath, 2003).

Mullen, Don, *Eyewitness Bloody Sunday: The Truth* (Dublin: Wolfgang Press, 1997).

Mullen, Don, *The Dublin and Monaghan Bombings* (Dublin: Wolfgang Press, 2000).

Mulroe, Patrick, *Bombs, Bullets and the Border* (Dublin: Irish Academic Press, 2017).

Murray, Raymond, *The SAS in Ireland* (Dublin: The Mercier Press, 1990).

O'Brian, Brendan, *The Long War: IRA and Sinn Féin* (Dublin: The O'Brian Press, 1993).

O'Brian, Brendan, *Pocket History of The IRA from 1916 Onwards* (Dublin: The O'Brian Press, 1997).

O'Brian, Justin, *The Arms Trial* (Dublin: Gill & MacMillan Ltd, 2000).

O'Callaghan, Sean, *The Informer* (London: Bantam Press, 1998).

O'Malley, Desmond, *Conduct Unbecoming: A Memoir* (Dublin: Gill & MacMillan, 2014).

O'Sullivan, P. Michael, *Patriot Graves: Resistance in Ireland* (Chicago: Follett Publishing Company, 1972).

Oppenheimer, A.R, *IRA, the Bombs and the Bullets: A History of Deadly Ingenuity* (Dublin: Irish Academic Press, 2016).

Patrick, Derrick Lieut-Col, *Fetch Felix: The Fight Against the Ulster Bombers, 1976–1977* (London: Hamish Hamilton, 1981).

Peck, John, *Dublin from Downing Street* (Dublin: Gill & MacMillan, 1978).

Rees, Merlyn, *Northern Ireland: A Personal Perspective* (London: Methuen London Ltd, 1985).

Ryder, Chris, *A Special Kind of Courage: 321 EOD Squadron – Battling the Bombers* (London: Methuen Publishing Ltd, 2005).

Taylor, Peter, *Provos: The IRA and Sinn Féin* (London: Bloomsbury Publishing Ltd, 1997).

Taylor, Peter, *Brits: The War Against The IRA* (London: Bloomsbury Publishing Ltd, 2001).

Tiernan, Joe, *The Dublin and Monaghan Bombings* (Eaton Publications, 2006).

Walsh, Liz, *The Final Beat: Gardai Killed In The Line Of Duty* (Dublin: Gill & MacMillan, 2001).

Wharton, Ken, *Wasted Years, Wasted Lives, Volume 1: The British Army in Northern Ireland 1997-77* (England, West Midlands: Helion & Company Ltd, 2013).

White, Robert W., *Out of the Ashes: An Oral History of The Provisional Irish Republican Movement* (Dublin: Merrion Press, 2016).

Van Der Bijl, Nick, *Operation Banner: The British Army in Northern Ireland 1969-2007* (South Yorkshire: Pen & Sword Books Ltd, 2009).

Index